MAN BITES
MURDOCH

MAN BITES MURDOCH

FOUR DECADES IN PRINT, SIX DAYS IN COURT

BRUCE GUTHRIE

MELBOURNE
UNIVERSITY
PRESS

MELBOURNE UNIVERSITY PRESS
An imprint of Melbourne University Publishing Limited
187 Grattan Street, Carlton, Victoria 3053, Australia
mup-info@unimelb.edu.au
www.mup.com.au

First published 2010
Text © Bruce Guthrie, 2010
Design and typography © Melbourne University Publishing Limited, 2010

Text design by Phil Campbell
Typeset by TypeSkill
Printed by Griffin Press, South Australia

National Library of Australia Cataloguing-in-Publication data:

Guthrie, Bruce.

Man bites Murdoch: four decades in print, six days in court / Bruce Guthrie.

9780522858167 (hbk.)

Includes index.

Guthrie, Bruce.
Guthrie, Bruce—Trials, litigation, etc.
News Limited—Trials, litigation, etc.
Newspaper editors—Australia—Biography.
Journalists—Australia—Biography.

070.41092

For Janne, Susannah, Scott and Ruby

'When a dog bites a man, that is not news, because it happens so often. But if a man bites a dog, that is news.'

New York *Sun* editor John B Bogart and others

'I am not what I am.'

William Shakespeare, *Othello*, Act I, Scene 1

Contents

Contents

Acknowledgements

This book would not have happened without the encouragement and enthusiasm of MUP CEO, Louise Adler. Got issues of self-doubt? Talk to her; she'll fix that.

Man Bites Murdoch started as a very different enterprise. Just weeks after my unexpected sacking from the *Herald Sun* in November 2008, Louise approached me to consider writing a book about the troubled state of the Australian newspaper industry or, at least, an aspect of it.

This followed her discussions with another former editor of *The Age*, MUP chairman, Alan Kohler. I am indebted to both of them for coaxing me out of my post-dismissal trauma to get working on the project.

Along the way, the book changed complexion, aided by the extraordinary events that culminated in a six-day trial in the Victorian Supreme Court in April–May 2010. Suddenly I was writing a very personal story about the industry that had sustained me for almost four decades and a court case that threatened to define me.

I have others to thank at MUP too: executive publisher Foong Ling Kong was a terrific sounding-board throughout. Thanks also to Jacqui Gray, Terri King, Cinzia Cavallaro and Ross Wallis. Freelance editor Susan Keogh made some crucial last-minute saves and suggestions. I am particularly indebted to Susan for removing the curse of the dangling modifier, which had haunted me for most of my career.

I will also forever be indebted to the legal team who not only prosecuted the case against News so skilfully, but also assisted me in the writing of the book, particularly the final chapters devoted to the trial. Chief here were Tony Macken, principal of A.J. Macken & Co, and senior counsel Norman O'Bryan. Tony's son Dominic was also a constant source of strength, knowledge and wisdom throughout the case and the writing. Who would have thought an Essendon supporter could become so fond of three ardent Collingwood fans?

There are a great many journalists and editors to thank too, although some have asked to remain anonymous. Inevitably a book such as this focuses on the detractors and foes I encountered along the way. But there have been many more benefactors and allies— how else would I have attained some of the most senior positions in Australian journalism? I am indebted to them all, particularly those who helped with their insights and memories. As former VFL coach Tommy Hafey might have said when pressed for names: 'They know who they are.'

That said, I would like to publicly thank my long-time friend and colleague Eric Beecher for his early advice and encouragement; author Les Carlyon and another former *Herald* colleague Bruce Baskett for their recollections and insights into the Murdoch takeover of HWT; my good friend Gabrielle Trainor for her wise counsel throughout; author and editor Roger Franklin, who helped with some of the more descriptive passages in the book; former Syme managing director, Greg Taylor, for clarifying aspects of the banks' move on Fairfax; the aptly named Larry Writer for his help on the *Who Weekly* chapter; and the extravagantly monikered Cutler Durkee III who, along with fellow *People* magazine staffer Rob Howe, assisted with the chapters on my time in New York.

Katie Flack and other staff of the newspaper reading room at the State Library of Victoria also deserve thanks. I spent many hours there poring over microfilm, refreshing my memory about specific newspaper editions and stories. It was an invaluable resource, shoring up the diary notes, documents, transcripts and recollections that are the basis of the book.

I also referred to Max Hastings' autobiography, *Editor* (Macmillan, 2002), to bolster my memory of a conversation with him over the origins of the Tourang syndicate's bid for Fairfax, and to William Shawcross' 1992 biography of the News proprietor

(*Murdoch*, published in Australia by Random House) when recalling a gathering of News executives at Aspen, Colorado, in 1987.

I want to acknowledge the support of my late mother, who passed away just six months before we triumphed over News, and the assistance of my brother Ross on life in Broadmeadows and my sister Janice on the Footscray years. Dr Loris Figgins was extremely patient in answering my queries about my two years in the Austin Hospital. She was a lifesaver in more ways than one.

Finally, I wish to thank my wife, Janne Apelgren, and our children, Susannah and Scott, not only for their forebearance over the past 22 months, but their unconditional love and support. My son deserves special mention for coming up with the title of the book; never has a drive to Saturday morning sport been so productive. They are the real heroes of this book, particularly Janne, who has supported me throughout all my endeavours and remained steadfast in the face of some appalling intimidation as the court case loomed. She gave me the strength to stand tall.

Bruce Guthrie, Melbourne, August 2010

I

Spiked

1

Rupert comes to town

The executive offices of the Herald & Weekly Times, publishers of Australia's biggest selling daily newspaper, are lined with gold. Or, at least, they appear to be. In some ways this is apt: the Victorian-based HWT makes more than $100 million profit in a good year, with Melbourne's *Herald Sun* contributing the great bulk of it. And there have been many good years.

Huge doors, as wide as they are tall and painted a glistening gold, greet you on the thirteenth floor of the HWT Tower, the company's home on Melbourne's Southbank. It's not the sort of decor you expect from the people's paper, bought by more than 500 000 a day and read by almost three times that many across Victoria. The *Herald Sun* is an Australian publishing phenomenon that dwarfs Sydney's *Daily Telegraph*, Brisbane's *Courier-Mail*, Adelaide's *Advertiser* or any other local daily you care to name. If it was published in the United States, it would outsell all but a handful of American papers, despite drawing on a population of only just over 5 million.

It's not just the golden doors that strike you about its executive row either. Compared to the crowded hubbub immediately below on the main editorial floor of the *Herald Sun*, the executive offices are sparsely populated and eerily quiet. You might occasionally hear a raised voice at the Thursday morning management meeting in the main conference room or from a lunch—no alcohol allowed—thrown for members of the business or political elite in the dining room. For the most part though, things happen here in a whisper and at a dignified pace.

The eastern and northern sides of the executive floor are home to HWT's most powerful players, the managing director and the chair of HWT respectively. Between their offices is another, right on the north-east corner of the thirteenth floor. It is the best office in the whole place but, save for the occasional squatting executive waiting on a more permanent home, it is vacant for most of the year, in a constant state of readiness in case The Great Man should drop in. It is Rupert Murdoch's office and it so happens that on this day, 27 October 2008, he is in town. Consequently, everyone is on edge.

Managing director Peter Blunden, who imagines himself the most influential man in Melbourne and so enjoys the panoramic views over *his* city, across to the MCG and beyond, has come to work especially early this day. So has Rupert's sister, Janet Calvert-Jones, HWT chair.

The volatile and pugnacious Blunden was my immediate predecessor as editor-in-chief of the *Herald Sun* and then became my boss at the end of my first year as editor-in-chief. He couldn't really decide whether he liked the job or not. Daily newspaper editors tend to think in 24-hour blocks and there's always a chance to fix today's mistakes tomorrow; managing directors are supposed to think strategically, not Blunden's strong point.

As the world financial crisis gripped, robbing the *Herald Sun* and the *Sunday Herald Sun* of crucial circulation and advertising revenue, the increasingly rotund and vexed Blunden had been heard to say more than once: 'This fucking job is doing my head in.' Worse, he would often append some derisory comment about the latest directives from News' head office, such as: 'You won't believe what those cunts in Sydney have done today.' These outbursts were one part pressure valve, one part bonding ritual. But they did nothing to engender confidence, a little like watching a pilot don a parachute at take-off.

Janet Calvert-Jones, one of three daughters to Sir Keith and Dame Elisabeth Murdoch, had been chair since her only brother bought the company more than 20 years earlier. In 1988 she had spent a morning at my side when, as a young deputy editor, I saw off that day's first edition of *The Herald*, the once venerable, now defunct afternoon broadsheet. Seeing as she was going to run the place, Rupert had thought it would be good for his sister to get a taste of a newspaper backbench, the name given to the news collective who each day process the stories and pages that make up the front of the paper.

I had left *The Herald* 12 months later in early 1989, but returned in February 2007 as editor-in-chief of the *Herald Sun*, the paper born when Rupert eventually tired of his losses on the afternoon broadsheet and merged it with its morning tabloid stablemate, *The Sun News-Pictorial*, in 1990.

Taking the job was a huge personal gamble. I had left Melbourne in early 1998 after a not entirely happy time editing *The Age* at the other end of town. We had been very successful editorially but Victorian Premier Jeff Kennett was rampant back then and had made life very difficult for me professionally. When I left the paper after losing out on a powerplay at Spencer Street, my wife Janne and I decided to move with our small children to New York, where I had taken a position.

In time we had found our way to Sydney and had been very happy. My children, now teenagers, had pretty much grown up there and saw it very much as *their* hometown. When I came home one night in November 2006 and announced I had been offered the editorship of Australia's biggest selling newspaper in Melbourne,

I met outright opposition. But after about six weeks of deliberations the four of us took a collective breath and committed to moving to Melbourne.

Despite Blunden's reputation as a gifted tabloid editor, I had actually inherited several problems at the *Herald Sun*: it was losing circulation and readership, and its website was growing more slowly than most. By 2008, I had slowed the paper's sales decline, significantly boosted readership and jump-started our website. And my family had settled in Melbourne. To complete the shift we had decided to buy a house and sell our Sydney home. It seemed pretty clear I would be at the paper for at least five years and that meant the children would finish school in Melbourne.

Midway through the *Herald Sun*'s morning news conference on 27 October, I had been summoned to the thirteenth floor for a meeting with Rupert Murdoch. These meetings between proprietor and editor were legendary, often humbling and sometimes career-ending. If he was unhappy with my performance on the *Herald Sun*, this is where I would find out—I would get a bollocking, as it was known in the organisation.

There were other certainties that came with a Rupert visit, the most predictable being job shuffling—someone would be given a new 'challenge', pushed aside for an up-and-comer for reasons that weren't always clear. Sometimes there would be wholesale changes, depending on Rupert's mood and the state of profits and sales, but it was extremely rare for someone to be left without a job. Despite his reputation for ruthlessness, that wasn't Rupert's style. He would simply find a new role for the hapless executive somewhere within the company's enormous worldwide operations.

The other certainty at News Limited papers was bespoke pages. As is normal practice, we had carefully crafted that morning's paper with the proprietor in mind. When an editor first learns that Rupert is on his way, he'll call together senior executives and start planning the Rupert papers—the editions to be published while he's in the neighbourhood—sometimes weeks out. There'll need to be lots of happy snaps and stories about subjects close to his heart. He's particularly fond of animal pictures. This is how the empire thinks most of the time. In five years at News, I had learned that the most senior executives don't do anything without first asking themselves: 'What will Rupert think about this?' He's an all-pervasive presence, even when he's not in town. I was pretty confident we had nailed the Murdoch formula that morning. Still, there was no telling.

Walking up the internal staircase from the twelfth floor to the thirteenth-floor conference room, I found myself thinking back 20 years to a similar meeting with Murdoch on Royal Melbourne Show Day, September 1988, when HWT occupied its purpose-built office on the corner of Flinders and Exhibition streets. These days it's the site of a high-rise office and apartment building and one of Melbourne's most lauded restaurants, the two-hatted Press Club; only the HWT façade survives.

Back in 1988 I was deputy editor of *The Herald* under editor-in-chief Eric Beecher, who would later go on to find great success as a publisher in his own right. We had been running the paper for Rupert for almost 18 months and, although it had garnered widespread praise for the improvements we had ushered in, profits and circulation were still struggling. One of the other things you quickly learn at News is that audience is more important than journalism, and ours was shrinking. Certainly the numbers were well short of Rupert's expectations, which were unusually high given *The Herald* had been the paper his father, Sir Keith, had built up when he ran HWT 50 years earlier.

Traditionally a sluggish news day, Show Day 1988 was anything but. It fell slap-bang in the middle of the Seoul Olympics, meaning we had plenty of news to fill the paper. Beecher and I knew Rupert would want to see us after the first edition, so we set about producing it side by side on the backbench surrounded by sub-editors and production executives while we waited for our summons.

About 15 minutes before we were due to go to press, news came through that Australian pentathlete Alex Watson had failed a urine drug test and had been told by Australian officials to pack his bags and leave the village. This was a massive story and we pulled out all stops to get it in the first edition, remaking page one so we at least got it on as the picture story. We would give it the full splash treatment in later editions. Having successfully redrawn the page and reworked the copy, HWT general manager, Roger Wood, appeared at our sides.

'Are you ready?' Wood asked, with a certain foreboding.

We headed for the HWT boardroom where about half-a-dozen men were waiting for us, all seated on one side of the board table. Among them was HWT managing director, John D'arcy, no fan of Beecher's at the best of times. Everyone nodded hello but no-one spoke. There was one chair vacant on their side of the table.

On the other side were two chairs to which Beecher and I were directed. For several minutes we all sat there silent; I felt like whistling, just to break the tension. After several excruciating minutes, Murdoch finally arrived. Moments later a freshly minted first edition was brought to him.

He began by apologising for bringing us all in on a public holiday. Then what can only be described as a forensic dismembering of the paper began.

'Why did you do this?' he asked of Beecher, motioning to a page-one headline. Then, without giving Eric time to answer, he skipped to the page-one Watson story: 'You've underplayed this. This is a big story.'

'It broke late, Mr Murdoch,' I said. 'We did well to get it in. It will be bigger next edition.' He looked unconvinced.

Then the page turning started. 'Oh no, don't do this ever again,' he said, as he spied a story that ran the full length of a single column, from the top of the page to the bottom, a pet Murdoch hate. And on and on it went. We had, said Murdoch, created a paper that was intellectual, when he wanted only intelligent, and literary, when he only wanted well written. It was a poor man's *Sydney Morning Herald*, the paper Beecher had left to work for Murdoch. Ouch.

After about 20 minutes, our bollocking was complete. Murdoch never raised his voice and was unfailingly polite. But he had flattened us. Beecher and I shuffled out of the boardroom and into Eric's office. It was obvious what had just happened—we were now officially 'on the drip'. Unless there was some divine intervention and sales, revenues and profits started heading north, we would be looking for jobs within six months. Sure enough, we were gone by the following March.

So here I was, 20 years later, being summoned anew by The Great Man. I deliberately travelled light, carrying only a notebook and a pen. I had made a brief note to myself to mention certain key points if the opportunity arose: we had just been named daily newspaper of the year by the Pacific Area Newspaper Publishers' Association (PANPA); we had successfully launched five new daily sections; we were growing our internet site at an extraordinary rate; and we would soon announce another readership increase. Yes, circulation was down, but that was true of pretty well every paper in the world. Why, even our Sunday edition was down almost 20 000 copies year on year, unheard of for a product that was still relatively new and growing.

When I arrived at the conference room, I was surprised to find it wouldn't be a one-on-one. Relieved too; Murdoch is not a screamer and would be even less given to histrionics with an audience in the room. Blunden was there, that day's edition close by, as was advertising director, Fiona Mellor. Surprisingly, the *Sunday Herald Sun* editor, the corrosively ambitious Simon Pristel, had been invited. He had come armed with piles of Sunday papers, dummies of new sections, page proofs, notes, you name it; I thought it a strategic mistake because it gave Rupert too much ammunition.

Murdoch arrived last, and in a discursive mood. The first thing I noticed was that his tailoring had improved since I had last seen him. I'd swear he had been styled. Everything appeared to match and blend, except perhaps his hair, which had a curious orange-reddish hue.

He spoke in generalities about the state of the business, and expressed a kind of calm resignation about the circulation challenges facing News titles around the world. Most of his mastheads were down by between 2 and 8 per cent, he said. I took heart from this because it meant our fall was at the lower end of the scale.

Eventually Murdoch picked up a copy of the day's paper. I tensed.

'Well, Bruce,' Murdoch said. 'The whole town would have been talking about your page one today. It was very good; just what we need.'

Page one that day featured a whopping great mulloway that a professional fisherman had caught on our behalf in the Yarra as part of a series we had done on the health of the river, and our page-one lead reported that bullying and violence were growing in state schools. Both had been hand-picked—education was a favourite subject of Murdoch's and the fish story restated our preferred role of being a paper that cared about its city.

'Thank you, Rupert,' I said humbly. 'We're trying every day to give the readers stories they won't be able to get anywhere else. It seems to be working. The worst thing that can happen to a daily newspaper is that it becomes a discretionary spend.'

'Yes, yes,' agreed Murdoch. 'People have to feel they must buy it every day.'

Then he turned to Pristel's paper, grabbing a fistful of pages. The previous day's edition had featured a story on a teenage Australian singer's sordid fling with British singer-songwriter James Blunt and Murdoch was quick to zero in on it, questioning its place in a family newspaper. As Pristel stammered his defence—essentially that it had come down from *The Sunday Telegraph* in Sydney and he had simply picked it up—Murdoch turned his attention to Eddie McGuire, Pristel's star opinion columnist.

'Is this fellow good enough to be your only opinion page commentator?' asked the proprietor.

Finally, he turned to sales of the *Sunday Herald Sun*, which were plateauing at around 600 000, fewer than 20 years after the paper had launched in August 1989.

'It should be selling a million by now,' said Murdoch matter-of-factly.

As the meeting wound down I felt uplifted. After all, I now appeared to have Rupert's imprimatur, and that left me pretty much untouchable. How was I to know that sometime that week, perhaps on the very day that he had applauded my performance, Murdoch would sign off on my dismissal, plunging me into a professional crisis? I hadn't factored in his ruthlessness but it should have been clear from our final exchange.

'How is *The Age* faring these days?' asked Murdoch.

The general consensus in the room was that we were in a very strong position. This hadn't been the case when I took the job. In fact, there had been a genuine fear within HWT in 2007 that Fairfax would reduce the format of *The Age*, perhaps taking it tabloid, sparking a war that could cost us valuable circulation. We had taken the threat so seriously that Blunden's predecessor as managing director, Julian Clarke, had established a special group that included me and several other senior executives who together war-gamed the possibility on a regular basis.

I had decided, with the support of the team and Clarke, that it wouldn't hurt to make the *Herald Sun* a more intelligent tabloid, in case *The Age* did try to take us on. In time the threat had waned, partly because Fairfax management had been spooked by the cost of such a move. We felt stronger than ever, prompting the observation that Melbourne could be a one-newspaper town in five years.

Murdoch, lately portrayed as the protector of print, squared his jaw and looked determinedly at us.

'That,' he said through gritted teeth, 'has to be our goal.'

2

And the winner is . . .

There is a picture of Rupert Murdoch taken around 10 p.m. on 31 October 2008, four days after we had our meeting in Melbourne. In the photo, I'm standing beside him, clutching what looks to be a relay baton; in fact, it is one of the company's internal awards, one of a score or so handed out each year at News' night of nights in Australia. I had just accepted the gong for Website of the Year, awarded to the *Herald Sun*. Murdoch and I are smiling broadly.

But here's the thing: if you actually pulled back from the photo of us, you would find lots of other people in the picture—all the winners from that night. Fate meant that for one shining moment, I stood side by side with Rupert Murdoch. I even remember shaking his hand.

News CEO John Hartigan must have been mortified by this, because I hadn't been expected on stage. Organisers had determined the prize should be accepted by someone else, but he became ill and had to return to his hotel, so I stepped in at the last minute. I even got to make a short speech.

'Great night, Rupert,' I said, as we all slowly headed off the stage.

'Thank you, it was, wasn't it . . .' he said, his voice trailing off as he struggled to remember my name.

I suppose I could have given him a clue: I'm the bloke you just cut adrift. For it had to have happened by then. At some point between Monday's convivial session and Friday night's onstage celebrations, my fate was sealed. But I didn't know that then. The axe was still 10 days away.

Looking back, I realise there were little niggling things that should have set the alarm bells ringing, not that I could have done a damn thing about any of it.

First was the lunch in the HWT dining room, straight after my session with Rupert on the Monday. He was in Australia primarily to deliver the annual Boyer lectures, and had brought along the man who had written them for him, former George W. Bush speechwriter, Bill McGurn. They were the guests of honour at the lunch, and about a dozen of us, including the *Herald Sun*'s marquee columnists, Terry McCrann and Andrew Bolt, were on hand to fete the pair.

As lunches go, it was a pretty tame affair. As is usual at such gatherings, Murdoch is afforded such respect that the atmosphere winds up being quite stilted. The most significant moment for me occurred before the lunch got underway.

During my 22 months in the job, Janet Calvert-Jones had been a largely benign presence; we had never had a single one-on-one meeting. That said, she had made it known recently she was unhappy with our reporting on her good friend Christine Nixon, the Victorian police commissioner, caught junketing with Qantas—or, at least, I had been led to believe she was unhappy.

Mrs Calvert-Jones had the endearing habit of giving me a peck on the cheek whenever I met her, usually at a thirteenth-floor lunch or external function. But at the Monday lunch with her brother she didn't move from her spot as I arrived in the dining room to join the pre-meal drinks. So I advanced on her and planted a kiss on her cheek. I have to admit, looking back, she didn't seem entirely comfortable with this. She may have even shrunk back; certainly there was no warmth in her greeting that day.

As the lunch got underway, I was sufficiently troubled by her reaction to reflect on the Nixon coverage. It was fresh in all our minds as we had splashed with it just four days earlier, on 23 October 2008. The paper's Los Angeles correspondent Peta Hellard had interviewed the chief commissioner outside the Los Angeles hotel at which Nixon was staying with her husband during a three-day visit paid for by Qantas. The airline had invited the couple on the inaugural flight of their new A380 plane and the story had broken on morning radio. Hellard asked Nixon if she thought it appropriate for the state's most senior law enforcement officer to be taking free trips. Nixon's vigorous defence of the trip became the basis of our page-one report.

After publication, which included a picture of Nixon and her husband outside their LA hotel under the headline *Beverly Hills Cop*—I had cheekily used the same pink type and font as the Eddie Murphy movie poster—there was widespread debate about her decision to accept the free travel. Around 12.45 p.m. on the day of publication, Blunden called by my office. We were due to lunch that day with a couple of senior executives from the Seven network. As I went to leave my office, he motioned me back in.

'Janet's upset about our coverage of Christine Nixon this morning,' Blunden said. It was the only time during my editorship that any concerns she may have had about my performance or the paper's editorial positions had been brought to my attention, hence I regarded it as enormously significant.

Blunden said she felt we had gone too hard on Nixon and her husband, who were entitled to take the trip.

'They're mates,' said Blunden.

'Who are?' I asked.

'Christine and Janet,' he said. 'Don't know where it comes from.'

I told him I thought our coverage had been first-rate. We had to demand the highest standards from our public office holders. Blunden said he wasn't sure Nixon had done anything wrong.

We would be carrying an editorial on the subject the next day. I had already briefed the writer, I explained.

I was brought out of my lunchtime reverie when Murdoch unexpectedly made an observation about Nixon: 'I gather the police commissioner has been in trouble.'

Bolt mentioned her ongoing attempts to 'feminise' the force, but no-one mentioned the LA junket. So I did.

'She got into strife for taking a free trip with Qantas that she probably shouldn't have taken,' I said, adding: 'But basically she's done an okay job over a long time. The good judges reckon she'll give it away in April when her contract is up'—which she subsequently did.

My comments were as much a peace offering to Calvert-Jones, who sat at her brother's side, as anything else. Murdoch merely nodded and moved on. I was troubled that he had obviously been briefed on the story and quickly concluded it must have come up in discussions with his sister or in briefings by Blunden.

Four days later it came up again when, en route to Sydney for the News awards, Blunden raised it anew. We had sat side by side on the flight up—he was to spend the day with his fellow managing directors while I was to spend the day with my fellow editors before we all gathered at the awards ceremony—but it wasn't until we were in the Sydney terminal that he again brought up Nixon.

'Not sure we did the right thing with Christine Nixon,' said Blunden, apropos of nothing. I thought it very curious that it would suddenly be on the agenda again, especially as the vast majority of internet comments, letter writers and talkback callers believed Nixon

16

should not have taken the trip. Certainly it hadn't been mentioned during our flight up from Melbourne. Why would he raise it again?

As I repeated my view that we had done nothing wrong, my instincts told me it had come up again because either it had been the focus of much attention in conversations with Rupert, or would be at that day's confab of MDs, when the performance of editors would no doubt be discussed.

Whatever the explanation, Blunden's reference to Nixon at Sydney Airport was especially perverse because in between the Monday lunch with Murdoch and the Friday discussion with Blunden, Nixon had made a public statement that she had decided to pay for her fare.

The Friday sessions came and went followed by the awards night. I had had a brief conversation with Blunden at the bar about our website win but he had been in a hurry to get away from me. Not that I was bothered by that. Frankly, I wasn't in the mood for the late-night boozing that typically follows such News events. News CEO John Hartigan is known within the company as a man who enjoys a celebration and it's regarded as good for your image if you're seen to be a 'good bloke who enjoys a drink'. I couldn't be bothered with any of it, and headed back to my hotel room around 11 p.m.

Days later I was in the Myer marquee at the Melbourne Cup. HWT always takes its own tent in the Birdcage at Flemington, principally because Blunden is a racing nut and has convinced himself and the HWT board that it's good for business. In 2008 it was just a few steps away from the Myer set-up. As Myer is a major advertiser, it's expected that key HWT executives will at least be seen there; Janne and I made sure we were ticked off at the door and then planned a brief walk-through. In a matter of moments we bumped into Michael Wilkins, editorial manager at News' Sydney headquarters in Holt Street, Surry Hills, and his wife.

Wilkins, tall and bald, bears more than a passing resemblance to rocker turned politician Peter Garrett. So much so that after one company cocktail party in Canberra, loyal News apparatchik Malcolm Colless remarked to John Hartigan that 'Peter Garrett's not such a bad bloke you know'.

'Oh really,' said Hartigan. 'What do you base that on?'

'I chatted to him for about half an hour at the cocktail party,' said Colless. 'He's all right.'

Replied Hartigan: 'That wasn't Peter Garrett, you fuckwit, that was Michael Wilkins. He's one of ours!'

Rupert had flown out of the country 48 hours before the Cup and, as usual, around News the death watch had started. It was accepted that within weeks of Rupert's departure, the job shuffle would begin. Who would get promoted, who would get demoted? It always happened; it was just a question of when and who.

After exchanging pleasantries and introductions, Wilkins got straight to the point.

'Heard any rumours from Rupert's visit?' he asked.

'No, not a thing,' I replied.

'The only one I've heard,' said Wilkins, 'is that Phil Gardner's got some big new gig.'

'Really?' I said. I wasn't feigning ignorance; I simply hadn't heard anything.

Gardner was a tall South African who had been Sports editor of the *Herald Sun* before being appointed editor of Adelaide's *Sunday Mail*. He had battled serious illness during his stint in the role there, which most viewed as competent if uninspired. He had overseen a succession of circulation drops. I liked him, if only because he would regularly send herograms telling me what a great job I was doing at the *Herald Sun*. At one point he had sent me a couple of South Australian reds after admitting he had stolen the design of my new opinion pages for his paper.

When the Cup came around, Janne and I headed for the Emirates marquee, always the best place in the Birdcage to watch the race. Blunden and Anna Brodie, his wife, were there. She had been his secretary before becoming the paper's fashion editor.

Again, Blunden seemed uninterested in deep conversation, although we watched the race almost shoulder to shoulder. He seemed courteous, if detached. Anna never came near us.

At one point, Janne and I swapped stories with Sarah and Steve Vizard. The former television funnyman was only three years into his 10-year ban from managing companies for insider trading but his reputation was already being rehabilitated. Then I spied Christine Nixon and her husband heading in our direction.

'Look who's coming our way,' I said to Janne. 'This could be interesting.'

Vizard asked what the problem was and I quickly updated him—Nixon was likely to be frosty because of our recent coverage of her Qantas jaunt.

But she was eager to know what we had backed, and how we had fared on the day. Her husband, a newspaper junkie who read widely and closely, was also unfailingly polite. Then, after about three minutes of pleasantries, they were gone.

'Well, she was friendly,' I said to the group.

Whispered Janne: 'Too friendly.'

Once the race was run I jumped into a waiting car to take me back to our Southbank editorial office. The Cup edition is always a huge seller for the *Herald Sun* and this year would be no different. Bart Cummings had won his twelfth Cup, this time by a nose with Viewed. On page one we married the nail-biting photo finish with a post-race picture of Cummings hoisting the Cup. The edition walked off newsstands the next day.

Later that week we did a great job of documenting the transport chaos that marred Oaks Day as thousands of racegoers were left stranded in the heat by Melbourne's notoriously unreliable rail network. At our Friday morning news conference I suggested we push Connex, the operator of Melbourne's trains, for some sort of compensation.

'What about we ask them to make the trains free on Saturday?' I suggested to the chief of staff. This would be the last day of the Spring Carnival at Flemington, called Family Day. It seemed an obvious public relations play for Connex, whose profile was forever taking a battering because of the unreliable train network.

Remarkably, when we put the idea to them, they rejected it. I couldn't believe their stupidity.

Around 4 p.m. that day, Victorian Premier John Brumby rang me. This was unusual. Even though I had a good relationship with him, we usually only talked at functions and might lunch once or twice a year. This suited me fine. I've always held that the closest an editor should be to any politician should, at best, be a nodding acquaintance. So the Friday afternoon phone call came as a surprise. Brumby was ringing to give me a heads up on a government initiative that he would unveil the following week. I listened politely, then told him I thought Connex—and his government—had missed an opportunity to improve relations with rail commuters.

'How so?' asked the premier.

I told him of our idea for free Saturday train travel and that it had been rejected by Connex.

'Let me make a call on that,' said Brumby. 'I reckon we might be able to fix that.'

I told the news desk we might yet have our page one. Sure enough, within 30 minutes Brumby called to tell me to stand by my phone because the Connex boss would be ringing me with some good news for our readers. Five minutes later the company's executive chairman, Jonathan Metcalfe, was on the line.

'We've decided to make train travel free for all rail travellers to Flemington tomorrow,' said Metcalfe. 'I gather this was your idea, Bruce, and, upon reflection, it's a good one.'

I put him onto a reporter immediately and we were able to tell readers the next morning—and on our website from midnight that night—that the *Herald Sun* had won free train travel for all Family Day racegoers. It was the sort of win mass-market tabloids crave. We had produced great papers all Cup week and had won an important concession for the city.

When I went back into the office after the weekend, I was ebullient. I had spent about an hour in there on the Sunday working with key editors on our coverage of the execution of the Bali bombers and Monday's paper was striking. It capped off a remarkable two-week run of accomplishments.

Of course, it couldn't last.

3

The dismissal

A couple of hours later, around midday, I was again summoned to the thirteenth floor. This time I was to see News Limited CEO and chairman, John Hartigan. Once tellingly described as 'terminally charming' and something of a champion of mine in recent years, I had nothing to fear from Harto, as his staff and executives prefer to call him. Or so I thought.

It was Hartigan who had given me the *Herald Sun* job on a late November day two years earlier in Holt Street with the words, 'An opportunity has come up.'

I had been editor of *The Weekend Australian Magazine* for three years by then, and had launched a successful monthly magazine, *Wish*, for *The Australian*. I was very happy in my dual role.

Bizarrely, our bond was built on a pair of cowboy boots Hartigan had bought during a Los Angeles stopover 20 years before. Having lived in the city for some time, I was able to steer the rising News exec to a reliable western-wear store that stocked such things. He wears them to this day and always lets me know. He had them on at the fiftieth birthday celebration of our mutual friend, broadcaster and author Wendy Harmer, on Sydney's northern beaches a couple of years back and pointed them out just before he marvelled at the breasts of Peter Garrett's wife, Ingrid. 'Have you seen the tits on Garrett's missus?' he exclaimed to Janne and me. My wife was taken aback; it was the first time she had met Hartigan.

On this Monday morning, Hartigan had taken up residence in Janet Calvert-Jones' office, right next door to her brother's, vacant again after he had made his way back to New York. As usual, Hartigan was a sight to behold. In his early sixties, he looked at least five and possibly 10 years younger. The shirt was cut tight, the suit pants were tailor-made, and the shoes had a sheen that almost matched the glint of the door. Hartigan works very hard at maintaining a sleek silhouette, almost too hard. Is it vanity or a determination to match the longevity of his great mentor, Rupert Murdoch? I never could decide.

I had no idea why I was there. As I walked up the internal staircase I ran through the possibilities: a pay rise—no, just got one of those; a bonus—nope, got one of them too; perhaps belated personal congratulations for the Newspaper of the Year and Website of the Year wins.

Or maybe he was going to offer me the editorship of *The Australian*. It was well known within News Limited circles that editor-in-chief Chris Mitchell's marriage was under stress and that he might put family ahead of duty and step off the treadmill of daily editing. One or two mischief-makers had suggested in recent weeks I was a logical replacement because of my previous experience editing broadsheets, *The Age* and *The Sunday Age*. I was terrified by the prospect—how the hell would I tell my family we were going back to Sydney when there were boxes still unpacked from the move down two years earlier?

Within seconds though it was obvious: this wasn't about remuneration or congratulation and it certainly wasn't about promotion.

'It's good to see you, John,' I said, as I took the seat the CEO gestured towards. 'I didn't know you were in town.'

'I had to come to town to have a conversation neither of us is going to enjoy,' he said.

Much of journalism is about taking the room temperature, knowing when to press and when to withdraw. With that one utterance, the temperature in Calvert-Jones' office plummeted to sub-zero.

'Is there a problem?' I asked in a voice that had suddenly grown thin.

'Yes,' said Hartigan, his own voice a little thin too. 'We are going to make a change.'

'To what?'

'Editor-in-chief.'

With that, the floor dropped away. There are some conversations you feel viscerally: a spouse tells you she's leaving or a doctor delivers a grim diagnosis. I was so shocked by what Hartigan was saying that I was physically jolted. Worse, I was sacked after doing some of the best work of my life and the bloke doing it couldn't really tell me why.

'Well,' said Hartigan in response to my obvious question. 'I can't have a situation at the *Herald Sun*, one of our most important papers, where the managing director and the editor-in-chief are not getting on.'

Hartigan was on shaky ground here. Months earlier Chris Mitchell had confided to me that he had offered his resignation to Hartigan because he couldn't get on with Rupert's son-in-law, Alasdair Macleod, then managing director of News' Sydney arm, Nationwide News, publishers of *The Australian*, *The Daily Telegraph* and *The Sunday Telegraph*. It was time to reveal that I knew this.

'Chris Mitchell tried to resign over Alasdair Macleod a few months back,' I said, a little provocatively. 'Are you going to sack him too?'

'No,' Hartigan said, and I thought I could detect a glimmer of guilt in his eye.

I had made my point but it wasn't going to do me one ounce of good. Blunden and I were not close, but we were not at war either. At least, I didn't think we were. In newspapers, the relationship between those responsible for the content and those responsible for the profits is always problematic, often tense. Clearly Hartigan had been led to believe we were at each other's throats.

'That is simply not true,' I told him and while Hartigan began to soften—he looked completely nonplussed, as if he had just realised he had been conned—it was obvious nothing could be done.

'I can't turn this back now, there are too many things in place,' he said, adding, 'I am very sorry ...We are prepared to be generous because we have given you a real shit sandwich.'

Then it hit me: Hartigan's heart wasn't in this. He had been instructed to do this by ... whom? It could be only one man: Rupert Murdoch. No-one else would have the power to direct the chairman and CEO to do something he didn't really want to do. Clearly the edict had been issued during Murdoch's visit and Hartigan was now doing the dirty work.

As I was led next door to examine 'the numbers', I was freefalling. Hartigan's 'generous' offer turned out to be what I was owed on my contract—and what the law required them to pay—plus another 20 weeks for notice and redundancy. The second component was a long way short of what the contract suggested.

Hartigan said, 'You might want to get a lawyer to look over this.'

Then he left me with News' human resources manager, Keith Brodie, another long-time supporter of mine who had been waiting in the adjacent boardroom. Pictures of Rupert and his father, Sir Keith, gazed down upon us from the western wall. Brodie also appeared nonplussed by the unfolding events. 'I don't know what this is about, Bruce, but I'm desperately sorry it's happened.' It was an astonishing admission by the company's head of human resources.

I grabbed the phone in the boardroom and rang Janne, who was working on the eleventh floor; she had recently come on board as editor of the paper's new food section. Minutes later we sat on a bench in the Queen Victoria Gardens opposite the National Gallery of Victoria, discussing our unravelling life.

One of the paper's writers wandered into our midst and immediately realised something was amiss. We must have looked like a couple planning a break-up, an affair or a crime.

'It's okay,' I said. 'We're married.'

Back in my office, I rang a defamation lawyer.

'Do you know any employment lawyers?' I asked, sounding desperate or defeated. Probably both.

'The best employment bloke in town is Tony Macken, up in Queen Street,' said my defamation friend. I gave Macken a call immediately, explaining that I had just been sacked as the editor of Australia's biggest selling daily newspaper.

'Why don't you come up straight away?' said Macken, exuding great calm and confidence. At that moment I needed every bit of both. 'I'll put the kettle on the hob.'

Within the hour I was sitting in his office. I was not to know it at that point, but over the next 17 months Macken, a devout Catholic with the kindly face of a priest, was to become one of the most important people in my life. The principal of a firm where everyone appeared to be related to him in some way, Macken sounded a little like Ryan Bingham, the George Clooney character in Jason Reitman's *Up in the Air*, when he told me I would eventually emerge stronger and happier. Unlike Bingham though, he meant it.

After I sketched out the details of the sacking, he was spoiling for a fight.

'They had no right to do this to you,' said Macken. I was warming to the prospect of taking on Rupert and News Limited, but could I really do it?

I've had other big jobs end badly, even talked to a lawyer or two at those times, but I've always stayed well clear of the courts.

'I'll sleep on it,' I told Macken.

★ ★ ★

Even though no official announcement had been made, the word was out back at Southbank. People filed into my office wondering if the rumours were true. The afternoon news conference flashed by. Around 5 p.m., I walked onto the editorial floor to check page one and immediately wished I hadn't. All eyes follow the editor whenever he appears on the floor, but suddenly they were burning in. I retreated to my office and called up copy, pages, editorials. Anything.

Soon the official announcement was made: Phil Gardner, the no-nonsense South African Michael Wilkins had tipped for a 'big new job' was announced as the new editor-in-chief and he would get an assistant too. Being replaced with two people might normally be seen as a compliment, but the second man turned out to be the *Sunday Herald Sun's* Simon Pristel, who was given the title of editor, a position I had never filled. It was not a compliment; I had never been a fan of Pristel as an editor, even though Beecher and I had given him his cadetship almost 20 years earlier.

Throughout all this I took only one call, from Andrew Rule of *The Age*.

'I can't talk,' I told him, but couldn't resist a crack: 'It's the curse of the Newspaper of the Year award,' I said to a chuckling Rule. Andrew Jaspan, who had led *The Age* to the same award in 2007, had been sacked himself only months before. The gong hadn't saved him either. My off-the-cuff remark made it into *The Age* the next morning.

Then, around 7 p.m., just when I thought the day couldn't surprise me any more, my phone rang again. The caller ID indicated it was managing director Peter Blunden. This was as unexpected as a corpse sitting up at a funeral. Was he ringing to gloat? I briefly considered not picking up, but my journalist's curiosity got the better of me.

Blunden disarmed me totally with this: 'Bruce, I am sick to my stomach about what has happened today.'

'Why mate?' I asked. 'Harto says it's what you want.'

'I am not driving this,' said Blunden. 'This is not me.'

'Harto says we are at war,' I said.

'That is not true,' said Blunden. 'I have told him that. I told Harto we have a good working relationship. I told him we watched the Cup together.'

About a minute into our conversation I realised Blunden was labouring pretty heavily. A hypertensive asthma-sufferer, would he expire on me mid-sentence? During his first year in the job as deputy managing director, when he was wearing L-plates, I'd had to make a mercy dash to Sydney carrying his blood-pressure tablets. His personal assistant had warned me: 'It's imperative he get them tonight—he cannot not take them.' Eleven years of editing a daily newspaper will do that to you. Certainly, as our conversation continued, his breathing became more shallow and more rapid. I'd hate to think how *he* would handle being sacked.

'Let me close the door,' I said to him. When I returned to my desk, I asked him simply: 'Mate, what is this about?'

'It's complicated and it's confidential,' Blunden said. Then, out of nowhere came the statement that would prompt guessing games in newsrooms across the country when it was revealed in my writ.

'I can't go into it too deeply,' he said. 'But essentially a third party got involved. That person said something to someone who said something to someone else and it went from there.'

So I had been brought down by a game of Chinese whispers. Was it Janet Calvert-Jones? No-one else would have the influence over Murdoch to make this happen. Or was Blunden making the whole thing up to cover his tracks?

I headed for home and my mobile rang. Eric Beecher, whose own time at HWT had ended badly two decades ago, was incredulous at what had happened. That made two of us.

'When are they going to stop treating people like pieces of meat?' he said.

My family greeted me at the front door and threw their arms around me. We resolved a couple of things: we would stay in Melbourne, at least until Susannah finished Year 12, and we would complete the purchase of the house we had put a deposit on just eight weeks earlier, even though Lehman Brothers had collapsed and our Sydney home was plummeting in value. Jobless, I was not a good candidate for a mortgage. Surely News would help us with all that; after all, we were only buying in Melbourne in anticipation of a few more years in the job.

Determined to put on a brave face, I presented for work the next morning in the usual way. It would be my last day in the job. Rule's story had appeared and in it he speculated that I had lost my position because of rancour between Blunden and me. But Blunden was having none of it, directly contradicting CEO Hartigan for the second time in 24 hours in an email he sent me on Tuesday afternoon.

It read:

As I said last night, I sincerely regret that it ends this way. Despite the reports this morning, there is no way that any personal tension (real or perceived) is responsible for this.

I've made that clear to John Hartigan and anyone who asks.

I won't dignify Andrew Rule's rubbish this morning with comment.

Of course I do not harbour any ill-feeling whatsoever towards you. On the contrary, I wish you every happiness and success in the future.

When the company decides to move in another direction, it simply happens. I imagine it will happen to me one day, too.

As for leaving, I'm happy for you to say all the farewells you like and vacate the office today with your head held high.

There is no need for you to be here after then, or work for that matter. Best of luck, and let me know if there's anything I can do.

The same day, buoyed by Hartigan's expressed spirit of generosity, I put a compromise to News Limited consigliere, Ian Philip. I had committed to buying a house in order to do my job for News, and, with the current state of the economy, faced the possibility of not selling our Sydney house. Could News help out with the transaction fees, or the stamp duty, or even the agents' fees for the Sydney house? If they could pick up the tab, I'd sign and be on my way.

There are moments in time when just a misplaced word or phrase can tip events, steel resolve, galvanise the reluctant into action. Wars, or at least skirmishes, have no doubt started because of such ill-considered utterances. This would be one of them.

Philip considered my settlement plan, then said flatly: 'Bruce, we are not in the business of underwriting your real estate investments.'

He was not to know it but I was sitting in Macken's office as I made the call. So was Janne. We were both on our lunch break. Macken insisted from the earliest that she be there, realising the importance of her informing and supporting all decisions. I told her what Philip said.

Macken arrived and for the first time I showed him my contract. News had acted immorally, but illegally?

Macken said, 'If you take them on, you'll almost certainly win.'

It was at precisely that moment, on Tuesday, 11 November 2008, with Philip's words ringing in my ears, that I decided there was nothing else for it: I would sue the world's most powerful media proprietor because of his bastardry and that of his lieutenants.

4

'Hi, I'm Rupert Murdoch . . .'

Tallow Beach stretches several kilometres south from the light-house at Byron Bay, the most easterly point on the Australian mainland. It has none of the serenity of Byron's famed Main Beach and is nowhere near as pretty; the water is often choppy and erratic, making it dangerous to most. But it has a wild beauty about it, particularly as the weather sweeps in.

On Monday, 8 December 2008, Janne and I woke early, gathered up a couple of deckchairs and positioned them on the ridge above Tallow and, as a lone surfer battled unpredictable waves, watched the sun come up. We knew this was going to be one of the most important days in our life together and we wanted to mark it somehow.

It had been almost a month since my dismissal and these few days at one of Australia's most picturesque spots were our first break from the constant questioning that followed us wherever we went. Our lawyer had urged us to get out of town, given what was about to unfold. We had dreaded a media pack at our front gate, so had grabbed some cheap airfares, rented a house off the internet and headed for northern New South Wales.

Certainly we had the time to do it. Our children were now on school holidays and Janne and I were both unemployed. She had decided her continued employment at the *Herald Sun* would be untenable—not to mention decidedly uncomfortable. Meanwhile, our purchase of a house in Melbourne was quickly turning pear-shaped. We no longer had the option of servicing a mortgage that might have allowed us to hold on to our Sydney property until the collapsing market rallied. Each opening for inspection brought worse news from the real estate agent, who had gone from confidently predicting an easy sale to expressing genuine fears about being able to move it at all.

As the days ticked down to the settlement on our new Hawthorn home, the strain began to show. Throughout most of the ordeal we had stayed solid as a family but with our savings dwindling, tempers frayed.

'Why did we buy the bloody house in the first place?' I had spat at Janne.

'Why did we take the bloody job?' she had shot back. She had a point.

There were many reasons to be concerned about the future but on this morning we were feeling strangely empowered. For this was the morning we were going to sue Rupert Murdoch and his men.

The anger that had convinced us to issue a writ had quickly turned to resolve. This is not to say there weren't moments of self-doubt, even outright panic. After all, this wasn't just City Hall we were taking on; it was a giant media empire.

For those moments I composed a mantra that helped get me through. It said simply: 'The sacking denied my performance, my contract, any principles of natural justice and the enormous commitment and sacrifices made by myself and my family.'

It arose, in part, from a conversation I had had with my 16-year-old daughter, Susannah, one afternoon when I was driving her home from school just days after the sacking.

Two years earlier she had appealed to me not to take the *Herald Sun* job—her life was in Sydney, she'd said, and she would lose the friends she had made over almost a decade growing up there. I had eventually convinced her that the shift would be well within her capabilities and that the family benefits that would flow from such a position—financial security, exposure to new experiences, the chance to renew old Melbourne friendships—made it an acceptable risk. Besides, the world she would live and work in would increasingly require such shifts and changes.

My son Scott had been a little easier to convince but I still had to make this pledge to my family when we finally headed for Melbourne in January 2007: after one year we would have a family vote and, if that vote was to return to Sydney, then that's what we would do. When the vote was finally taken, it was three to one to stay—only Scott wanted to return to Sydney.

I've no doubt such scenes have played out in homes across Australia many times and will do so even more into the future as economic and job security become more problematic. Still, my daughter's eventual decision to support the move was courageous for a teenager anxious about where she fitted in.

As it turned out, she was made captain of her adopted school within 18 months of arriving and became dux a year later—but it could have been very different. On the drive home that night in November, she crystallised what had been nagging me for some time. 'It's not just you they've sacked, Dad,' she said. 'They've sacked all of us.'

I began to stew: how could Rupert Murdoch have sat there 10 days before my dismissal and complimented me on my performance, then signed off on my removal? Worse, how could he have shaken my hand at the awards night four days later? As I reflected on these things, I sometimes found my fists clenched in rage.

Soon the spin started. Mark Day, a regular columnist in *The Australian*, and a close friend of Hartigan's, wrote that I had lost my job because I had moved the paper away from its newsbreaking core values. This was garbage but it was clear the revisionism had begun.

Then a particularly scabrous piece appeared on a gossip blog. Dripping with malice, it talked of our impending financial difficulties with unvarnished glee. It described Janne as an heiress and even named Susannah's school. I had never met the author and certainly never been contacted by him. While most of it was nonsense, there were one or two facts relating to my remuneration package that could only have come from very high up in HWT.

As November moved on I spent hours with lawyers, crafting the statement of claim that we were going to lodge. It was unusual in that it set out some pretty detailed particulars—my transcript of the Hartigan and Blunden conversations on 10 November that directly contradicted each other—to support our claim.

In the end it had been a relatively easy decision to pursue litigation. Certainly Tony Macken was up for the fight. In his sixties, the father of six had spent his entire legal career practising employment law and had even written a book on the subject; *Macken's Employment Law* was something of a bible in legal circles. After several days of meetings with Janne and me in his Queen Street offices, he considered our position and said this: 'Ultimately it's your decision, but I have never seen anything closer to a lay-down misère in my career.' It didn't decide the issue, but it gave us great confidence.

As the lone surfer battled the unpredictable waves at Tallow Beach, I asked Janne nervously: 'We've done the right thing, haven't we?'

'Absolutely,' she replied.

'Absolutely,' I repeated.

Three hours later there was no turning back. Around 9.30 a.m., the statement of claim was formally lodged at Victoria's Supreme Court Registry.

I was now officially on a collision course with Rupert Murdoch, the world's most powerful media player and probably one of the most powerful men on the planet.

★ ★ ★

How had it come to this?

I wasn't entirely sure; certainly the prospect didn't occur to me the first time I met Rupert Murdoch. It was the 1980s and I was enjoying one of the first peaks of my journalism career, running the Los Angeles bureau of HWT, while Murdoch was ascending seemingly every peak in his sight. Having already embarked on building a fourth US television network—industry observers laughed when he first floated the idea—he was then completing the purchase of HWT back home.

I was having the time of my life as a foreign correspondent, covering world title fights, the Academy Awards, major breaking news stories like the *Challenger* space shuttle disaster and travelling all over the country to report on everything from Mexican illegals pouring across the American border to long-delayed funeral services outside Montana for troopers lost at Custer's battle of Little Big Horn. Then there were the celebrities: a young Mel Gibson on the set of his first *Lethal Weapon* movie; a stunning Jane Fonda reinventing herself yet again; a surprised and embarrassed Paul Hogan in a clinch with his *Crocodile Dundee* co-star Linda Kozlowski; potty-mouthed author Harold Robbins at his sprawling LA mansion. It was going to take something special to shift me out of there.

It began with a mid-afternoon telephone call on 3 December 1986 from Steve Price in Melbourne, the chief of staff of *The Herald*, now a radio shock-jock.

'Are you sitting down?' Price asked mysteriously.

'Er, yes,' I said, thinking I was either being recalled to Melbourne or he was getting married. Again.

'You won't believe who's just walked in here and gone straight into the boardroom with a big fat cheque.' Pause. 'Rupert Murdoch and he's got Ken Cowley [Rupert's CEO of the Australian businesses] with him.'

'Huh, what's this about?' I asked, dumbfounded.

'He's trying to buy us, and they reckon he'll own us by the end of the day. Stay tuned.'

This wasn't Murdoch's first tilt at HWT. He had launched an unsuccessful assault in 1979. His new bid was again being portrayed as a man trying to reclaim his birthright—Murdoch's father, Sir Keith, had built the company into a national media group as both managing director and chairman. At its height HWT not only owned newspapers across the country but also television (HSV-7) and radio (3DB). Rupert had even done a short cadetship at *The Herald* after finishing his studies at Geelong Grammar.

I remember calling our Washington correspondent, Geoff Barker, who had come from *The Age* to take up the post, and breaking the news to him of Murdoch's audacious takeover bid. The usually voluble Barker could only manage two words: 'Oh, shit.'

Fewer than six hours later Price called me back. 'Mate, we're now all working for Rupert.'

Rightly or wrongly, Murdoch already enjoyed a reputation as a hard-driving employer, not particularly troubled by the constraints of good journalism. Fairfax and HWT journalists tended to regard News journalists with a certain disdain. Now they would be running the show. Oh shit.

Over the next eight weeks Murdoch had to see off or accommodate a number of competitors keen for a seat at the HWT table. Most notable was Robert Holmes à Court, who launched a counter-bid only to drop out after he and Murdoch cut a deal that left the Perth-based millionaire with HSV-7 in Melbourne and West Australian Newspapers. It meant that by late January 1987 Murdoch had fulfilled what many saw as his destiny: he now owned the company his father had enriched as managing director and chairman until his retirement through ill health in 1949. Despite the key role Sir Keith had played in building up HWT, he felt he had never been properly rewarded for his efforts.

I watched all this from Los Angeles with a certain detachment, putting aside my apprehension that one man now controlled so many newspapers. Looking back, I see it as one of the first great body-blows against the Australian newspaper industry. The HWT purchase concentrated far too many papers in the hands of a single proprietor with disastrous effects on competition and, by extension, innovation. Worse, the only other serious competitor to News Limited, Fairfax, operated in an entirely different market segment. Pretty soon the two settled into a cosy duopoly.

Murdoch had been permitted to extend his reach because of the infamous policy switch by Prime Minister Bob Hawke and Treasurer Paul Keating in 1986 that allowed moguls to be what Keating called either 'princes of print or queens of the screen' but not both. Murdoch would have to offload his television interests but he would control about half of Australia's newspapers. A generation later, he controls about two-thirds of them.

Quite apart from the potential effect such concentration could have on public discourse, I had a more pressing concern: now I would also be servicing morning and afternoon papers in Sydney and they were more like London red-tops, the term given to the UK's racier tabloids, than the mid-market *Sun News-Pictorial* in Melbourne. I had never filed for anything quite like *The Daily Telegraph* or *The Daily Mirror*, Sydney's morning and afternoon tabloids, although Brisbane's afternoon tabloid, the now-defunct *Telegraph*, occasionally came close. I recalled the murder in a Montana bar of the parents of *Dallas* star Patrick Duffy in 1986. I filed the story after speaking to local cops on the telephone. It made a brief in *The Herald*, but led *The Telegraph* in Brisbane. Perhaps I wouldn't struggle to get a run in the Sydney papers. After all, the LA bureau probably provided more reader-friendly copy for those papers than, say, Washington. And the new proprietor owned a movie studio in Los Angeles. So, I told myself, at least my job was safe.

Because of the great distances between them and home base, foreign correspondents can spend an inordinate amount of time on the phone trying to keep up with office gossip and moves. It is rare to have a short conversation with a correspondent who, more than anything, wants assurance that their work is satisfactory and that they are not going to be hauled back ahead of time. Most conspire to get postings extended and wages and conditions improved.

With a takeover in full swing, the telephone traffic between Melbourne and all bureaus must have threatened to bring down international communications. Certainly I was rarely off the phone as the dominoes began to fall back in Australia.

The first casualties of the Murdoch takeover were HWT chairman John Dahlsen—who made way for Rupert's sister, Janet Calvert-Jones, the first woman on the board—and then HWT editor-in-chief Les Carlyon and *Herald* editor Neil Mitchell. Both had toiled mightily in their roles during very difficult times. In the end they both resigned, ultimately developing new careers—Carlyon as an author and Mitchell as a radio show host.

I had absolutely no doubt that their spirited campaigns against policies of the Hawke government, particularly their opposition to a proposed assets test on pensions, had contributed to the barely disguised hatred of HWT by the Prime Minister and his Treasurer. It almost certainly contributed to the government's dramatic media policy switch, Murdoch's subsequent takeover, and their inevitable departure from the company.

I would particularly miss Carlyon's early morning calls into Los Angeles. They would often come around 9 a.m. local time and I would suddenly realise it must be 3 or 4 a.m. in Melbourne. The insomniac Carlyon and I would talk at length about newspapers generally, *The Herald* or *The Sun* specifically, and writing.

Carlyon was a great believer in writers finding their voice, developing their own distinctive style. He was impatient with the traditional inverted pyramid approach to news—with the most salient facts in the introduction and the less important material at the bottom—and encouraged his journalists to construct stories so that they had a beginning, a middle and an end. He was years ahead of his time in that sense: as newspapers struggle to differentiate themselves from the internet, they surely have to be better written, photographed, designed and edited than ever before. Carlyon and Mitchell—and Carlyon's predecessor Harry Gordon— pushed for that a generation ago, but Murdoch wasn't interested back then. He isn't now.

While Carlyon and Mitchell respected and encouraged good writing, they also valued good reporting. I've worked for editors who prize one over the other, but it's rare to find those who value both. I've tried to be that sort of editor. Simply put, if you only value reporting, you can end up with a drab, lifeless publication that places stories and recites facts in diminishing order; if you only value writing, you put form ahead of content, ignoring the single greatest purpose of journalism—to shed light in dark places.

With Mitchell and Carlyon gone, the guessing games started about who would succeed them. Suddenly and unexpectedly, I was drawn into the takeover orbit.

One of the curious elements of the Los Angeles job in the mid-1980s was the relatively clunky nature of communications between the bureau and head office back in Melbourne. While we had normal phone links, our computer set-up was primitive for a communications company—I had to file off a laptop in takes of about 10 paragraphs and we had no telex facilities at all. That meant every morning I had to call our New York bureau chief, Bruce Baskett, to learn of the latest story requests and how the previous day's filings had fared. Each day the foreign editor would dispatch a brief summary of the run we had received, typically: 'Eastwood for

Carmel Mayor, page 3 *Sun*, page 5 *Courier-Mail* and Hobart *Mercury*.' Often these brief run-downs could make or break your day.

There was more than a trace of irony in having to call Baskett each morning. I had risen through the reporting ranks of *The Herald* in a most traditional way—from copy boy to cadet, D-grade general reporter, then all sorts of specialist rounds or beats. Baskett had been my chief of staff during my stints at the industrial round and then the state politics round and here I was still calling him on the other side of the world when we were now living and working on opposite sides of the United States. I deferred to him on most matters; he was a first-rate newspaperman, sometimes misjudged because of his no-nonsense demeanour.

In late January 1987 he took me into his confidence: 'I've been asked to fly back and have a talk to Rupert.' Ironically, Baskett had developed a relationship with Murdoch during the period the takeover was in the balance. As New York bureau chief it fell to him to call Murdoch whenever he was in town to find out the latest developments. He also had to front him at Kennedy Airport, usually on a Friday night when Murdoch would use the Concorde to fly from London to New York.

John D'arcy, a big, burly Queenslander who had retained his position as HWT managing director despite the takeover, was an unabashed fan of Baskett and was recommending to Murdoch that he replace Mitchell.

'Just remember that if you get the job,' I told Baskett, 'I want nothing more than to serve out my three years here, maybe longer.'

'Done,' he said.

I could see no downside to any of this and looked forward to at least another two years in Los Angeles. Even better, I would now have a direct line to the new boss. As I had learned long ago, it really doesn't matter what the organisational charts indicate; the most powerful people in any business are those who can get to the boss directly and immediately.

But while Baskett was en route to Melbourne from Los Angeles, the landscape changed again. Another name started to surface as a candidate: *Sydney Morning Herald* editor Eric Beecher. The prospect both intrigued and troubled me; in 1985 Beecher, regarded by the industry as an editing wunderkind, had tried to get me to the *SMH*, but I had rejected him.

I cautiously raised the prospect with Baskett when he arrived in Melbourne. Had he heard the rumours? To my horror, he hadn't. I was cast in the role of Cassandra: the drums were beating pretty loudly, I told him; he might want to check it out.

In a matter of hours, two very surprising things happened: in a major coup for Rupert, Beecher was announced as both editor-in-chief of HWT and editor of *The Herald*, replacing both Carlyon *and* Mitchell. And then Beecher rang me. Would I return to become an assistant editor of the paper?

The next day's call to Baskett was particularly uncomfortable. He'd had his conversation with Murdoch who wanted his impressions of Flinders Street staff. There was no talk of the editorship for it had already gone to Beecher. Despite that, Murdoch wanted Baskett back in Melbourne. I came clean to Baskett; better he find out from me that Beecher wanted me back, than hear it from someone else and think I had been duplicitous. He took the news well, even offering his best wishes.

Then I said, 'But I'm not going to go back, Bruce.'

I didn't say this lightly. I had only been in Los Angeles 15 months and was less than halfway through the posting. So much of your first year in any new country is devoted to the tedium of establishing yourself: bank accounts, drivers' licences, health insurance. It was only now that we were beginning to understand the rhythms and ways of the United States. My best work was definitely ahead of me.

After a decent interval of a couple of days I rang Beecher to give him my decision. He wasn't happy but he didn't pull rank;

after all, he could have simply ordered me back. In the decades since I have learned that he does not accept 'no' for an answer—he immediately set about trying to get me to change my mind.

'Why don't you offer the job to Steve Harris?' I suggested, almost as a diversionary tactic.

Beecher said he would think about it and promptly went after Harris, an assistant editor of *The Age*. After a protracted negotiating session, Harris decided to stay at Spencer Street. All I had done was help get him a pay rise.

In no time Beecher was back on the phone to me. 'Look, I'm assembling a first-rate team here and I want you to be part of it,' he said.

It wasn't empty rhetoric. Murdoch had clearly opened up the purse strings for Beecher, promising more news pages, new sections, and signing off on the hiring of, among others, Terry McCrann, Peter Smark and Ben Hills, three of the biggest names in Australian journalism.

Still I said 'no'. After my third refusal Beecher played his trump card. 'Rupert wants to have lunch with you,' he said matter-of-factly. 'Can you give him a call?'

A week later, on a beautiful early spring afternoon, I drove up to the gate of Fox Studios on Pico Boulevard in Century City and informed the guard I was lunching with Mr Murdoch. It was to be the single most important appointment of my career.

In those days the Fox executive offices had a distinct nautical feel to them, modelled on the sets for the original *Titanic* film, produced in 1953 by Twentieth Century Fox. There were portholes, polished wood walls and brass rails everywhere.

I was ushered into Murdoch's executive suite, which had all that and more. I sat in an outer office and waited patiently. I had arrived slightly early—I'm nothing if not punctual—and although a trifle anxious, was very much looking forward to meeting The

Great Man. He kept me waiting, his secretary explaining that he was in a meeting with Barry Diller, the head of the studio, and other key executives. Five minutes became 10, then 20 and eventually 30. Our lunch was for 1 p.m., but it was now 1.40 p.m. Perhaps he was going to stand me up.

Then, the outer door burst open and in he walked, grinning from ear to ear. 'Hi, I'm Rupert Murdoch,' he said, proferring his hand. 'You must be Bruce.'

'Yes, Mr Murdoch,' I said, standing to attention.

'I've just got to make a couple of phone calls and then we'll get something to eat. Come in, come in,' he said as he bustled his way into his inner office, which looked very much like a ship captain's lair. I'm sure he wasn't deliberately trying to impress me, but the two phone calls he placed had that effect.

'Can you get Marvin Davis on the line for me,' he said to his secretary.

Davis was a Texas oilman and then one of America's richest men. He and Murdoch owned Twentieth Century Plaza, a shopping centre and hotel development a short distance from the studios.

'Is that you Marvin?' Murdoch said, as I gazed around the office. He went on: 'I can get $320 million today for the Plaza. I think we should sell. Are you in or are you out? You're in? Great. I'll get the papers drawn up.'

Hmmm. He had just made $160 million and it had taken all of 30 seconds. Any resistance to going back to Melbourne would be futile.

'Just got to make one more call,' he said to me. Then to his secretary again: 'Can you get Howard on the line for me.' I took this to be Howard Rubenstein, the legendary New York public relations man who had effectively become Murdoch's spokesman as he built his empire in the United States. Like Davis, he was very quickly on the line. People tend to drop everything when Murdoch calls.

'Hi Howard, it's Rupert here. Listen, what do you know about Michael Dukakis? Ah, ah, well he's going to announce tomorrow that he's running for the presidency and he wants our backing,' said Murdoch.

Once again he was way ahead of the game. The governor of Massachusetts, Dukakis did indeed announce his candidacy the next day and eventually won the Democratic nomination only to be soundly defeated in 1988 by George Bush. He had obviously come looking for Murdoch's endorsement, but Rupert wasn't so sure.

'Check him out,' Murdoch said, adding: 'Give the people at the *Herald* a call.' He had bought the *Boston Herald* in 1982, saving it from almost certain extinction. No doubt they would be fully versed in Dukakis. With that he cradled the phone, beamed again, and said: 'Right, let's go to lunch.'

When we finally got to the Fox commissary shortly before 2 p.m., it was packed. All eyes went to the studio boss, then to me. I could almost hear diners asking each other: 'Who the hell is that with Rupert?'

I chose an innocuous first question. 'Are there any big movies on the way?'

Murdoch had had a good run lately, with Paul Hogan's *Crocodile Dundee* being particularly successful for Fox, but he wasn't brimming with confidence.

'Well, we had high hopes for a new comedy by that *Blazing Saddles* bloke but I've just seen it and it's garbage,' he said.

This was a slightly uncomfortable conversation for reasons that became immediately obvious.

'I can't think of his name,' said Murdoch, 'but he's wasted $12 million of our money.'

'You mean Mel Brooks, don't you?' I said helpfully.

'That's him, that's him,' said Murdoch. 'This latest thing is called *Spaceballs* or something and it's crap.'

44

'Mr Murdoch,' I said. 'Mel Brooks is sitting at the next table and he's looking in your direction right now.'

'Oh Christ, is he?' With that Murdoch swivelled in his seat, saw Brooks nodding and smiling from just a metre or so away, and returned the goodwill.

'Do you think he heard me?' the studio boss asked.

'I don't think so,' I said, not entirely convincingly.

We quickly moved through a range of topics: David Letterman would be a great host for a forthcoming tonight show he planned for his Fox network but he was proving difficult to lure away from NBC (he never succeeded); Ronald Reagan was doing a first-rate job as president and almost certainly Bush would be his successor; Hawke would win another term as Prime Minister back in Australia.

Then, finally, the conversation turned to *The Herald*.

'I want it to be a great paper again,' he said. 'It hasn't been for a long time, but I believe it's possible.'

Beecher had done a terrific job editing *The Sydney Morning Herald*, he said, and if anyone could turn around the afternoon broadsheet, it would be him.

'Eric tells me he needs people like you so I urge you to take up the offer. It's going to be a very exciting time,' Murdoch said.

Throughout all this, a steady stream of people made their way to the table. Murdoch shook hands, made small talk, waved every now and then, almost in benediction. Somewhere between the main course and dessert I decided I had to be part of this attempt to resuscitate the paper that had given me my start.

As we said our goodbyes, Murdoch urged me to have a skiing holiday before I bade farewell to the United States.

'There's nothing like the powder at Aspen,' he said. 'You should fit in a visit before you go home.'

Wishful thinking. Beecher was delighted that I was finally accepting his offer, but impatient for me to return. I gave up the notion of a holiday but was determined to cover at least one final

Academy Awards ceremony. *Crocodile Dundee* creators Paul Hogan, Ken Shadie and John Cornell had been nominated for best screenplay and I was keen to see how they fared.

Hogan co-hosted the ceremony on 30 March 1987 and although he lost out in the Oscars race he pretty much stole the show when he vowed from the stage: 'If they read out someone else's name instead of mine, it's not going to be pretty. I'll probably spill blood.' (In the end the screenplay Oscar went to Woody Allen for *Hannah and Her Sisters*.)

And then we were gone. I still vividly remember closing the door on our Los Angeles home with a heavy heart—a wonderful chapter of our lives had closed abruptly and prematurely. Ironically, Bruce Baskett and his family were on the same flight, both of us heading home to largely uncertain futures. (He would become day editor of *The Sun*.)

By accepting Beecher's offer I had exchanged the reporter's life for an editor's desk. Three weeks after my lunch with Murdoch— and 15 years after I first walked in there—I was back at Flinders Street as a senior player.

I was now a Murdoch man.

II

Widford Street to Spencer Street

5

Broady boys

What, exactly, is a Murdoch man?

The proprietor gave his greatest insight when he told *Esquire* magazine in 2008: 'There may be more brilliant people wandering outside sometimes, [but] you have to favor the people that are prepared and ready to give themselves to you.'

Within the News empire, talent is one thing but absolute dedication to Murdoch's world view and various causes is another. And it's far more important than talent. The most highly regarded people at News are little more than Murdoch robots, programmed to consider him first and the issue second. Journalism—and all those other 'isms' the people at Fairfax and the ABC routinely fulminate over—run a very distant second. While there are many fine journalists and editors at News, there is only one visionary and it's the proprietor; elsewhere in management there are plenty of schemers, plotters and acolytes. The people Rupert prizes most are the ones who might struggle to rise in other organisations. Even better if they know it. He cares little about university degrees, excuses workplace indiscretions and will even forgive egregious journalistic errors. Deep down he knows that the culprits will be even more indebted to him: they are his forever.

Given I was from the wrong side of the tracks, my pedigree was perfect for the Murdoch empire. Broadmeadows boys almost never harboured lofty ambitions; if they did, they kept them to themselves. There was too much failure and hard-grafting in our midst to think about anything but survival; achievement and aspiration were the preserve of others.

The suburb was something of a social experiment for the conservative Bolte state government, which, in the 1950s, thought it a good idea to dump tens of thousands of working men and women—Labor voters—on Melbourne's fringe without any infrastructure or facilities to speak of.

The theory was okay. The government would attract manufacturers like Ford, communications company Ericsson and biscuit maker Nabisco out there and then put cheap labour in dormitory housing as factory fodder. Problem was, that's about as far as the plan went; no-one thought to include the resources that normally go with such plans—a hospital maybe, perhaps a community centre or a library.

Even the government eventually admitted they had stuffed it up. On his last day in the job as head of the premier's department, Major General Ken Green was asked by journalist Frank McGuire what was the greatest failure of the Bolte administration. 'One word,' he replied. 'Broadmeadows.'

The suburb was supposed to be the Guthrie family's deliverance but, like the experiment itself, it fell short. It was a hard-scrabble kind of place. Another Broady boy, Frank's brother Eddie McGuire, who grew up about 100 metres from me and carved out a stellar career in television, joked that if the public housing tenants paid their rent on time, the police turned up 15 minutes later wondering where they had got the money.

Certainly there was a different moral code in Broadmeadows. I remember my father proudly bringing home the Christmas ham one year and hanging it in the laundry at our Widford Street house. By morning it was gone, stolen to feed another family that Christmas Day.

But if Broadmeadows was tough, our beginnings were even harsher.

When my parents met at a postwar dance in northern Queensland, my father was a meatworker trying to raise two daughters on his own after the death of his first wife from cancer, and my mother was a registered nurse, raised in Cairns but working in Rockhampton. Eager to escape the ghosts of that first marriage and to give his new wife some breathing room, Bob applied for and got a job as a foreman at Angliss' meatworks in Ballarat Road, Footscray. Back then it must have felt like a moonshot, but my mother Ruby had made the trip before, to train as a nurse at Bethesda, the Salvation Army hospital in the inner suburb of Richmond.

They newlyweds arrived in Melbourne without my half-sisters, deciding to send for them when they found permanent accommodation. After boarding or renting at several addresses, they were eventually offered accommodation on-site at the meatworks, in one of three tiny weatherboard cottages that directly abutted the saleyards and abattoir where Dad worked. In time the girls joined their father and stepmother in Melbourne and my older brother and I were born.

Ballarat Road was a long way from the pages of *Home Beautiful*. The kitchen had no sink, the laundry just a concrete trough and copper (but no lighting) and a large pool of fetid water sat permanently under the floorboards of the house. And, as soon as you stepped outside, you were hit with the overwhelming stench of the holding pens. There was an almost permanent parade of cattle and sheep heading for the slaughterhouse. Mostly they arrived during the day, but some loads would be delivered at night. My sister Janice recalls farewelling her boyfriend after a night out, surrounded by lowing cattle or bleating sheep.

My mother always knew my father was coming home not by his footsteps but by his cough. Then I developed it and so did Janice. In time we were all diagnosed with tuberculosis—Dad was sent to a sanatorium, my sister to another, while I was admitted to the Austin Hospital, in those days devoted to the treatment of chronic or incurable illness. I was barely two years old.

The TB had made its way into my spine so I spent all my time in bed on a frame, face down during the day, face up at night, in a ward allocated to children suffering from the disease. I was saved from paraplegia or worse by a young medical officer in the hospital's orthopaedic unit, Dr Loris Figgins. She had chanced upon a treatment in 1952 while caring for a four-year-old at Frankston Hospital. Dr Figgins gave the boy, who was suffering from TB and hip disease, a blood transfusion to treat a bout of anaemia. Almost immediately his condition improved and within six weeks signs of active infection vanished. Dr Figgins realised she was on to something, even if she wasn't entirely sure why. Perhaps it was the antibodies in the transfused blood? In any event, she tried the treatment on others with great success and brought it with her when she took up her post at the Austin. Thank God she did. I had regular blood transfusions and almost daily shots of streptomycin and have the scars to prove it. My mother, spread thin trying to visit an ailing husband, stepdaughter and son in three different locations—and using only inefficient public transport to do it—while caring for another son and stepdaughter at home, could visit only once a week. My father occasionally visited on Sundays. In the end I survived with only reduced lung capacity.

My mother sang the praises of Loris Figgins for the rest of her life. When I was old enough to understand how she had saved me, I wanted desperately to track her down to give her my thanks. But my mother patiently explained that the doctor had left Australia to study in the United States where she had developed leukaemia and died. She hadn't; my mother was sadly mistaken. Dr Figgins had left Australia for Britain in the 1960s, returning three years later. Despite her great success at the Austin and a 1962 book detailing it, she never returned to the treatment of TB, instead spending the rest of her career working with victims of road and industrial trauma. After my mother's death in 2009, I tracked down Loris, a widow now living on her own in Melbourne's south. Proud of her achievements at the Austin, she regretted that no-one had ever taken her groundbreaking work and developed it further.

More than 50 years after my discharge from the hospital, Dr Figgins was able to fill in some of the many gaps in my understanding of my time at the Austin. I spent two years there, but have no memory of any of it. I was eventually discharged on the eve of my fourth birthday after finally beating the disease and getting back on my feet again. During my time in hospital doctors had urged my parents to move out of the heavily polluted western suburbs to one of the bright, shiny new ones to Melbourne's north. And so we became one of the first families on the new Broadmeadows public housing estate, run by the state government's Housing Commission.

Having spent half my life in hospital, it was probably no surprise that, when my mother brought me home, my first question was: 'Which ward is mine, Mummy?' My mother couldn't tell that story without crying.

★ ★ ★

Our house was in Widford Street, right near the Jacana Avenue roundabout and about 100 metres from the Olsen Place shopping centre.

There was always an undercurrent of menace in Broadmeadows back then, a measure of the frustration felt by so many getting by on so little, but two early incidents affected me deeply. One afternoon in the mid-1960s, during a school holiday break, a bored teenage boy climbed into the roof cavity of his family's Widford

Street home carrying a .22 rifle. He probably meant no harm as he took potshots at some of the signs that dotted the otherwise bleak and blank landscape.

He soon took aim at the Shell sign that loomed large over the service station that sat at the junction of the two streets. We could see it from our front- and backyard. The teenager hoped to shatter the sign but instead the bullet bounced off and struck a 10-year-old girl, killing her. The death made it on to the nightly news and reverberated throughout the community and our school, forcing us all to confront our mortality at an age when you shouldn't be concerned about such things.

I walked under that sign a dozen times a day, running errands for my mother or visiting friends in the neighbourhood. It could so easily have been me or my brother, Ross. It could have been any of us. To this day I can still see my classmate presenting to us in a loud and confident voice at a morning show-and-tell session. Weeks later she was dead. These sorts of events didn't seem to happen in other suburbs. It was another hardship that went with the territory, or so it seemed.

We had also become used to motorists, usually drunk, ploughing their cars into the roundabout outside our home. Given her training, my mother would be one of the first on the scene at these accidents. She would offer whatever assistance she could before either the driver restarted the battered vehicle and headed off into the night, or an ambulance arrived to cart them off to hospital. Not all were so lucky.

'The driver needs a blanket,' said my mother, ashen faced but moving with great purpose towards the bedroom I shared with my brother.

She had run into the street on a cold winter's night at the sound of the familiar thud. Moments later, and clutching the cream blanket off my bed, she returned to the scene and carefully draped it over the body that lay on the roadside, watched over, it seemed, by

54

the entire population of the northern suburbs. Then, after authorities had taken down details and removed the dead driver and debris, the blanket was popped into the wash and eventually returned to my bed. I slept uneasily under it for weeks.

The Housing Commission homes were a long way from the pages of *Home Beautiful* too. Painted grey or white, they were little more than concrete boxes, with three bedrooms, loungeroom, kitchen and bathroom. The saving grace was the backyard—huge and for a kid keen on cricket and football, mercifully free of any real flora. Games would go on long after dark, unhindered by trees or shrubs.

We had neighbours on one side who weren't disposed to children. A childless couple, they complained to my mother about my incessant cricket practice—an unerring accuracy meant I struck the rubbish-bin wicket pretty consistently—and our matches, and one night erected a sign that warned: 'All balls will be confiscated.' Over the fence had always been six and out but now it became a threat to life, limb and reproductive powers too.

My mother paid the fortnightly rent in person in cash at the Commission office, about a kilometre and a half from our home. The office was appallingly drab, like the homes the Commission provided, and the staff uniformly glum, even sour.

My most bitter memory is of the annual 'inspection' by a Commission official who would chide my mother if we had dared paint a wall or, worse, scuffed or marked it. They never seemed to notice the appalling mildew that gathered on the walls every winter. My mother's appeals to have it removed went unheeded. In the end it became part of the decor.

Throughout these inspections she would listen respectfully, fidgeting with the apron she always seemed to be wearing. She lived in fear of us being turfed out by one of these men, who seemed to enjoy their small measure of power. As a boy, I stood at her side filled with concern and later, anger, but always holding my tongue until they were gone. I suspect this fed my tendency later in life to speak up, often to my cost.

In winter, the concrete housing would be damp and cold and in summer it would be stifling. On really hot summer nights, the only relief in bed would be to actually roll up against the cool concrete until it became too uncomfortable to hold the position any longer; in winter my brother and I would huddle around the tiny gas heater that was supposed to miraculously warm the whole house. You had to be almost on top of it to get any benefit at all.

The suburb's infrastructure was pretty well nonexistent. For a time my father was secretary of the Broadmeadows Progress Association, which, back then, was a cruel oxymoron. Dad had a wonderful sense of humour and a vast reservoir of jokes, but there was a sadness about him. Many nights he would sit alone at our kitchen with a bottle of beer, no doubt reflecting on the losses in his life. There was another contradiction about him too: we barely had two coins to rub together, but he hated the Labor Party. These days he would be known as a working-class Tory. I suspect his time as a foreman in the meat game, every day coming up against the notoriously militant meatworkers union, explained it all.

There were no parks to speak of, and we didn't get a local swimming pool or library until much, much later, despite the efforts of Dad and the PA. Somehow though, we filled our days happily.

My mother had abandoned her nursing career to raise her sons but she regularly suggested a return to the workforce. Dad, who had become a salesman in the transport industry, would have none of it. He was determined to be the sole breadwinner. When my mother turned 50 and I was in my early teens, she broke the shackles, returning to full-time nursing until she was 65.

Despite all the privations that went with life in the northern suburbs, when I asked my mother on her deathbed what was the happiest time in her life, she replied: 'Raising you and Rossy in Broadmeadows.'

Just about everyone around us was pretty much in the same situation—one low-income earner, almost always the father, a mother toiling away to make slim resources stretch ever further, and two, three and sometimes more children attending the local primary school and living on the estate.

There were kids everywhere. We spent our summers playing cricket and our winters playing footy. I dreamt of one day being recruited by Essendon and followed their weekly exploits with obsessive interest. I even sent 'get well' cards to injured favourite players, including my hero Jack Clarke, who captained the team to a VFL premiership in 1962.

I attended Broadmeadows East State School and, although I was an above-average student, I really lived for the Friday afternoon sport. One of my proudest moments was being asked by the school football coach to play for the senior team when I was only in Grade 4. It was against Glenroy and I only got one kick, which I passed backwards to the skipper because he looked like he would kill me if I didn't. I wound up captaining the team myself a couple of years later and we won the premiership. The banner should still be hanging at the school somewhere, but they bulldozed it a couple of years back. I captained the cricket team too. These weren't positions that I sought; they were conferred by teachers and teammates.

Looking back, it probably gave me an early sense of leadership. I figured out that the worst that happens to you in these situations is failure. I've also learned that it's often a better teacher than success. Better to be engaged than disengaged.

After Broadmeadows East State, I went to Broadmeadows High School. It sounds like a natural transition, but it wasn't. My mother and father badly wanted to send me to a private school—Essendon Grammar, or maybe, given we were good Methodists, Wesley. This was like suggesting I go to the moon for a few years. I put up such a fight—wouldn't sit scholarship exams, wouldn't fill out entrance forms—that they eventually gave up. More than anything, I couldn't imagine leaving my friends. But I believe it was a mistake to be so obstinate. I suspect my education would have been better elsewhere. Perhaps the experience informed my attitude to our move 40 years later and why the family's acceptance of it resonated with me so much.

Broadmeadows High was, like the rest of the suburb, critically under-resourced but the headmaster was an extraordinary man named George Perry who was determined to build it into something special. Every lunchtime he would have us out in the front paddock picking up rocks and boulders in the hope that it would one day become an oval. We would all fan out in one long line, pick up a stone or two, and then deliver them to a pile at a pre-determined spot. I wasn't sure what the private school kids were doing during their lunchtimes, but I'm pretty sure they weren't clearing fields. George used to tell us at assembly that if we raised three dollars, the government would give us one dollar. One for three? It sounded like a good deal, but looking back it bordered on shameless. I haven't been back to Broadmeadows High since the day I left in 1971, but I hope somewhere there's a plaque in honour of George Perry.

My education at Broadmeadows was solid. In the crucial final two years, I had a couple of teachers who encouraged me to write. Ironically, an earlier English teacher had told my mother at a parent–teacher night that 'Bruce has problems expressing himself'.

Years later I bumped into him and I reminded him of this. He asked what I was doing with myself. I told him with a straight face: 'I'm editor of *The Age*.' He had the good grace to be embarrassed.

With my teachers telling me I could write I guess it was inevitable that I would start thinking about journalism as a career. It seemed to offer excitement, diversity, glamour, perhaps even travel. Broadmeadows sat at the end of the electrified rail network, but the main freight and interstate passenger line continued on to Sydney. Most nights, either nestling against the cool cement wall or huddling under a mountain of blankets to keep out the bitter chill, I would go to sleep hearing the wail of a train heading north to faraway places. I thought it was the most exotic sound in the world. Part of me wanted to be on that train; part of me still does.

6

Read all about it

One midwinter's night in 1964 my father, always a sucker for door-to-door salesmen and the occasional messenger of God— to the horror of my no-nonsense, Salvation Army-raised mother who would simply say 'not today thank you' and slam the door— ushered into our home a young man who would change not only our day-to-day reading habits, but the direction of my life.

This unlikely messiah had appeared unannounced and was going from house to house trying to sell newspaper subscriptions. He struck the motherlode when he knocked on our door and had it answered by my father. Dressed well in suit and collar and tie, his patter was just as neat: he was trying to put himself through university and he pocketed a percentage of every subscription sold. In no time he had talked his way into our loungeroom and onto our couch. (Jehovah's Witnesses and Mormons managed this pretty regularly too, forcing my exasperated mother into the kitchen for hours on end bemoaning Dad's pliability. My father wasn't terribly religious but, as a salesman, understood rejection better than most.)

Within 20 minutes, Dad, who loved words and language and often sketched out short stories that would never be published, had signed up for not one but two long-running, daily subscriptions: to

The Herald, which regularly found its way into our house anyway because of street-corner *Herald* boys, and *The Sun*, its morning paper stablemate, with which we were much less familiar.

My mother probably objected, worried we wouldn't have the money to cover these commitments, but Dad would have brooked no dissent. And so, at the age of 10, newspapers suddenly became my window on the world, morning and night.

The Herald, perhaps because of its broadsheet format, always struck me as a more serious newspaper. It loved a good police-rounds story, but had first-rate political and foreign coverage too. Its sport reporting was peerless, with the legendary footy writer Alf Brown's massively detailed match previews compulsory reading on Friday nights. Because Brown would start writing early in the week, he would obtain team selections from the coaches before they went public with any of them. They trusted him implicitly.

The Sun was a breezier product, full of heart-warming human interest stories, but still with a hard news edge. It had the up-and-coming Laurie Oakes in Canberra, Douglas Wilkie interpreting world events and the greatest columnist of his generation, Keith Dunstan. (Decades later I would bring both Oakes and Dunstan back to the *Herald Sun*.) Most of all, it had pictures, and it knew how to use them, which is why its full name was *The Sun News-Pictorial*.

While *The Herald* had been published in Victoria in one form or another since 1840, *The Sun* had only been launched in 1922 and was acquired by HWT three years later. It had all the energy and exuberance that went with its relative youth and tabloid format and soon became the company's most profitable title. Frankly, *The Age* was never discussed in our house, much less read. It was seen as earnest, even dull. Certainly it didn't speak to the people of Broadmeadows.

What I loved about HWT's two Melbourne dailies was their accessibility, energy, humanity and intelligence. One of my key editing rules is 'Noah is a better story than flood control'. Most stories are better told through the people at the centre of them, than by dwelling on the minutiae of the issue they're driving or the events that may have ensnared them—or, at least, they are the best entry point for most readers. *The Herald* and *The Sun*, at their peak, understood that. I didn't know it as a teenager but it was what made the papers such compelling reading day after day. It was an alchemy I would apply decades later at a host of publications.

The idea of a career in journalism crept up on me. There was no epiphany; I simply tried to match what I liked to do—read, even devour newspapers—with what I was good at—English, and not much else.

My first foray was with the *Broadmeadows Observer*, the local give-away that appeared in our letterbox midweek. At football training one night, the club president had asked for a volunteer to write up the weekly match reports for the paper. Urged on by a couple of teammates, I put my hand up hesitantly and, being the only one who did, got the job. I suppose it was an early taste of that late 1990s mantra: the world is run by those who show up. I was 15.

Throughout the season I would write out four or five paragraphs in longhand and drop them under the door of the *Observer* on a Sunday night. The benefits were many: I got some understanding of newspaper practices, experienced the joy of publication (and the occasional horror of editing), and made the best players' list pretty much every week, regardless of my performance.

In my final year at Broadmeadows High School, encouraged by my parents and a couple of teachers, I applied for a cadetship at HWT. I didn't bother contacting *The Age* or the ABC or any of the other organisations that took on school-leavers. My world view was limited. In modern parlance, I was clueless, with none of the networks or knowledge that might have helped me get a start. Save for a distinction in English expression, my final-year performance was less than stellar. My letter to HWT detailing my results and their letter rejecting me appeared to cross in the mail.

Dejected, I took a job in the public service, sorting and delivering mail. While I enjoyed the meagre income, the independence and the socialness of working in an office, it was definitely not what I had in mind for a long-term future. The tertiary place I had been offered started to weigh on my mind, but no member of my family had ever attended university. Besides, it would be costly.

My parents, sensing my dismay and fearful that, like so many of my schoolmates and friends, I would disappear into drudgery, urged me to take up the place at LaTrobe University, which had opened just five years previously at Bundoora, in Melbourne's north-east. Somehow they would find the money. So, barely one month into my mail-sorting career, I bid farewell to the public service and headed for the campus.

It was a time of student radicalism, and The Who's 'Won't Get Fooled Again' blared across campus all day, every day. I didn't know it at the time but one of my fellow Humanities students at LaTrobe was Steve Perkin, son of *The Age*'s editor Graham Perkin. Steve was building his network at various papers by alerting them to the more eye-catching goings-on on campus, including student strikes and building occupations.

I wandered pretty aimlessly through my first months at university, eventually deciding it would be a better idea to defer and start again the following January. In truth, I was dispirited and dejected, with little idea of what road I might choose. Journalism seemed lost, at least until I could graduate with some sort of degree and try again at Flinders Street.

Then, not for the last time, chance intervened.

Douglas Lockwood was a distinguished journalist at *The Herald* who had made his name principally with his reporting out of Darwin for the paper. I had even studied his book, *I, The Aboriginal*, at Broadmeadows High.

So when he rang one August afternoon in 1972 I was at once flattered and a little intimidated.

'Are you still interested in working at *The Herald*, son?' he asked matter-of-factly.

'Yes,' I replied, I hoped with enthusiasm.

'Well, if you can get yourself in here tomorrow for an interview we might have a job for you.'

'Tomorrow, actually I'm supposed to go to—'

'Oh, forget it then.'

'No, no,' I jumped in. 'I can definitely be there tomorrow. What time?'

'Ten a.m. and don't be late.'

This was nothing short of divine intervention. But Christ, look at me! Hair halfway down my back, no time for a haircut, and no decent suit in my wardrobe.

The next day I fronted in my Sunday best, which actually wasn't very good at all.

'You're in luck,' Lockwood said. 'One of our copy boys has left to become a greengrocer, so there's a vacancy in our sub-editors' room.'

Copy boy. Hmmm. It wasn't a cadetship: in fact, it involved every menial task on the paper—which is probably why a career in fruit and vegetables seemed more appealing—but it was a start.

'We don't promise anything, but if you make a good fist of it, you could be offered a cadetship down the track,' said Lockwood. 'Are you interested?'

'Yes sir.'

'Right, if you get your hair cut and get yourself a suit, you can start on Monday,' he said. 'And remember, reporters don't take days off and they're never late.'

'I understand, Mr Lockwood. What time would you like me to start?'

'Five a.m.'

Gulp.

7

'Jump, boy, jump'

My first full day as a copy boy at *The Herald* in August 1972 began with a 4.30 a.m. cab ride from home. Every day of my six months as a copy boy at the paper began with a pre-dawn cab ride from home. A free one. This was almost too much for a Broadmeadows lad to contemplate. I think I would have done the job just for the thrill of the free taxi.

Because I started so early and there was no public transport to be had, the paper provided the ride—and a cab docket to go with it—every morning. In the first weeks I would book the cab each night before going to bed, but quickly I gave the job to the same driver every day. It was like having a chauffeur.

We would swap stories as we drove through the last of the night to *The Herald*'s Flinders Street building where I would report for work to John Hall, the paper's foreign-page sub-editor. I was there early to sort through the foreign cables and to separate them into four stacks: news, finance, sport and off-beat, the sort of items that could be used to break up an otherwise heavy page or be used in a column of one- or two-paragraph 'briefs'.

Around edition time—and there were four a day—*The Herald* newsroom would be a cacophony of trilling phones, pounding typewriter keys and voices shouting 'copy' in the reporters' room, or 'shute' in the sub-editors' room. But at this hour the only sound was the chatter of the telex and the occasional ping of the bell if the Associated Press wanted to alert you to something it thought was a major news event. It was like setting up backstage at an arena spectacular before the crowds arrived.

The editorial divisions of *The Herald* and *The Sun* shared the third floor of the squat HWT building that sat on the corner of Flinders and Exhibition streets. The company had a diverse share register and no real majority shareholder. In that sense, it was truly independent. It also had significant holdings in newspaper groups across the country. Both papers were pitched at conservative audiences. Today only the shell of the building survives; Rupert Murdoch sold the site in the mid-1990s when his global empire almost toppled under crippling debt. A high-rise tower climbs from behind the façade of the building where I spent more than 15 years of my working life.

Murdoch shouldn't have sold. Today, the old building would be perfect as a modern integrated newsroom, combining old and new media. As it is, the company's adopted home on Southbank spreads the *Herald Sun*'s editorial section over three floors, a nightmare for any editor wanting to stay in touch with staff.

The editorial floor of the Flinders Street building was tiled in black and white, and was dominated by a huge reporters' room, shared by the two papers. Staff sat at grey steel desks that were fixed to the floor and worked at typewriters that should have been—you could lose a good one in the blink of an eye to a reporter on deadline. It was the same with chairs.

The floor had several enclaves, each bordered by waist-high partitions and a small swinging door or gate. They fenced off *The Sun* chief of staff and his assistants at one end, and *The Herald* chief of staff and his cohorts at the other. We called them the playpens. Star columnists Keith Dunstan ('A Place in the Sun') and John Larkin ('In Black & White') had their own playpens too.

The sub-editors' rooms for *The Herald* and *The Sun* abutted the far ends of the reporters' room. They consisted of long, communal tables arranged in a horseshoe with subs sitting either side, pretty much eyeballing each other.

Along the Flinders Street side of the main reporters' area ran so-called 'mahogany row', where the most senior HWT executives, including former mailboy turned managing director, Sir Keith Macpherson, were housed. There were no high and wide golden doors in those days, although there was a polished brass plate or two. *The Herald* 'Women's' also branched off this corridor. Headed up by star writer Claudia Wright, it provided most of the paper's feature material.

When you got about two-thirds of the way along mahogany row you could either continue on to the executive toilets or head through swinging double doors to the reporters' room. If, a few steps on, you took a left turn, another corridor ran all the way to Sport and Pictorial. A rabbit warren of offices branched off this, housing everyone from the editor and his leader writers to another star columnist, On the Spot's John Hamilton.

Around 6 a.m., the first of the sub-editors would arrive. *The Herald*—and *The Sun*—prided themselves on their subbing skill in those days. These men, and the occasional woman, worked under incredible pressure, often bringing together on deadline a breaking story from multiple strands.

They were usually graduates from the reporters' room, having proven themselves in the field and under pressure. Sub-editors were highly regarded at the two papers and often better paid than their reporting colleagues. But there was little or no glamour attached to the job and, certainly, no prospect of a day spent interviewing dazzling celebrities or witnessing great events. It was a case of head down and bum up for seven or eight pretty intense hours. That said, most of the senior editorial executives of the era came from the sub-editing ranks.

One by one they would file in, many hung-over from a late night drinking. I would ply them with instant coffee that I had started preparing as soon as I saw them in the distance, having committed their orders to memory. Around 6.45 a.m., the editor, Cec Wallace, would arrive and would have an immediate, galvanising effect on them. As he walked down the corridor lining the reporters' room, word went around that the boss was in the building. Backs straightened and heads rose. Wallace, a former sports editor who seemed to forever have a cigarette in his mouth and a face flushed as red as its ember, would nod to the chief of staff and then pause in the subs' room, usually to tell a joke. Subs, who moments earlier had looked in need of life support, roared with laughter at the editor's humour, then collapsed again as he headed to his office and out of earshot. Every editor I've worked with since tends to have the same effect on their staff; I suspect it goes with the position.

The bulk of *The Herald*'s staff would be in by 7 a.m. The paper had moved start times forward by 30 minutes when David Syme, publishers of *The Age*, launched an afternoon competitor on 30 September 1969. Called *Newsday*, the tabloid lasted just seven months, barely laying a glove on the broadsheet. *The Herald* emerged stronger than ever and at its peak was a wonder to behold.

Reporters typed their stories on slips of butcher's paper—or filed to a phone-room girl if they were in the field—then a copy boy ran the story into the neighbouring subs' room, hence the cry of 'copy'. Each slip of the story had about six carbon copies behind it, to be distributed to various parts of the building including radio station 3DB, which HWT owned in those days, and interstate bureaus. The copies were stapled together and it was the job of the copy boy—or girl—to separate the original and run it to the subs, and then separate the carbons for distribution.

Legend had it that one copy boy's career came to grief when, on deadline, he was hailed by a reporter, told to tear up the copy—in other words, separate out the various copies and run them to their various destinations—and promptly did so, leaving it in shreds.

The initial assessment of the story in the subs' room would be made by the copy 'taster'. His job was to look for obvious gaps in content or lapses in style and syntax, then either take the matter up with the chief of staff or the reporter—these conversations could be quite willing at times—or, if he was happy, move it further along the production line. When a sub-editor was finished with the story he would yell 'shute' and I would run, collect the copy, and send it in a canister up a hydraulic shute to the typesetters upstairs.

There were usually two or three other copy boys in the subs' room. We were known collectively as, well, 'the boys'. But only one of the group had journalistic ambitions and was usually rotated each year. The others were content with life as messengers in what we believed was the greatest afternoon newspaper in the world.

Around 10.30 each morning the printing presses in the bowels of Flinders Street would start up, the building would give a slight shudder, and the paper would be on its way. By 11 a.m. the first edition was on the street, a daily marvel. It was frantic, occasionally chaotic and wonderfully exciting.

Although *The Herald* demanded a lot from its staff, I found it a very welcoming place. Most people were kind and extremely generous with their advice. Soon I had a small cheer squad willing me on to a cadetship. As Douglas Lockwood had said at my initial interview, there would be no guarantee. But I figured if I worked extremely hard, came to terms with the extraordinary rhythms of the place, and won the confidence of the sub-editors, particularly the most senior of them, I stood a good chance.

But soon, I ran into a roadblock— a very significant one.

Geoff Clancy was a legendary police roundsman, much decorated for his work in the field, including multiple Walkley Awards for excellence in journalism. His exploits on the road included nabbing a murderer and delivering him to police for arrest and being roughed up by Frank Sinatra's henchmen after he was caught peering through a keyhole at Melbourne's Festival Hall as Ol' Blue Eyes had his way with a prominent Australian songstress.

Then, as newspaper organisations still do to this day, someone had the bright idea of trying to turn a great reporter into an executive. Suddenly Clancy, a short, pugnacious man with the demeanour of a hard-bitten cop, stopped doing what he did best—chasing down stories that sold large numbers of newspapers—and took a desk job, albeit an important one.

As chief of staff he was responsible for marshalling and deploying the entire reporting staff of *The Herald*. It was probably the most stressful position on the paper. It was the chief of staff's job to prepare a list of potential stories—the news list—for presentation at a 7.15 a.m. conference where their relative merits would be discussed and priorities established. The list would form the backbone of the first and later editions.

Given that responsibility Clancy was an early starter too, working phones, cajoling roundsmen and women—the specialist writers with their own beats—to come up with page leads and better. A good chief of staff anticipates the next move in a story that might have developed overnight. He makes sure the day's diary is checked and rechecked and ensures all potential news angles and set pieces are covered. Apart from the editor, there was no more significant person at the paper in those days. It was not a particularly good career move to get offside with Clancy fewer than 10 weeks into my journalistic career.

One day, around 6 a.m., the early start reporter yelled at me across the sub-editors' room telling me to get the chief of staff some milk for his coffee. It wasn't a request, it was an order, delivered with all the charm of a prison officer.

I simply turned to John Hall and asked: 'Is that okay, John?' He thought about it a second or two and replied: 'I suppose, but don't be too long.'

Clancy wasn't happy.

'Hey,' he said. 'Come here.'

As I walked to his desk I noticed a long line of medications, many of which he popped into his mouth as he dressed me down.

'I run this place, mate,' said Clancy. 'So, the next time I ask you to do something, you don't turn around and ask someone else if it's all right: you jump, boy, jump. Get it son?'

'Yes, Mr Clancy.'

'If that happens again, you're out.'

Over the next few months I did a lot of jumping, particularly when Clancy barked orders. And, despite my pessimism, it paid off. In December I was called in by Cec Wallace and told I was going to be given a cadetship.

It was cause for great celebration but Clancy wasn't done with me yet.

In January the new cadet intake assembled. It was a large group, numbering close to 20. It included Steve Perkin, whose father Graham was editing *The Age* at the time. He and the editor of *The Sun*, Harry Gordon, had come to a unique agreement over the hiring of their boys who both wanted to follow their fathers into journalism—they sent them to opposite ends of town: Steve did a cadetship at *The Herald*, while Harry's son Michael did his cadetship at *The Age*. The plan worked—both Steve and Michael not only remain in the profession, but after many twists and turns are back at the papers where they began. Sadly, Graham Perkin didn't get to see the success enjoyed by his son or his daughter, Corrie, a senior writer at a string of prominent broadsheets. He passed away suddenly in October 1975.

Winning a cadetship meant I now moved from the subeditors' room to the main reporters' room, taking my place at whatever desk I could find. Naturally the degree of difficulty rose spectacularly—so did the level of hostility. While I was sitting at a desk deep in the reporters' room on my first day in January 1973, a bearded *Sun* reporter appeared at my side. It was around 1 p.m. and his shift was just beginning. This changeover was always awkward because there were never enough desks to go around and some senior staff resented newbies moving in on their territory.

'Who are you?' the beard barked at me.

Clearly he was not my friend but I decided to be charming and courteous anyway, giving my name and the fact that I had started a cadetship that very day.

'Good,' came the reply. 'Now, fuck off.'

As a cadet, you spent three and a half days in the office and the remainder of your five-day week at RMIT working on your journalism degree. That was the theory. Stories had a way of getting in the way of your studies. Besides, we much preferred life at the paper to being stuck in a classroom. This meant I didn't often make it to RMIT. Word soon reached Geoff Clancy, who once again threatened my ongoing employment.

Now, it has to be said he had every right to do this. In fact, if you had graphed that year's intake and the likelihood of each person's success, I would have certainly finished in a lower percentile. We were an interesting bunch, ranging from callow school-leavers and university dropouts like me to well-credentialled graduates. Our group included a blonde bombshell who turned up to shorthand class one sultry summer's day wearing just a bikini and who soon found herself on the front page of the scandal sheet *Truth* after being assigned to interview Mick Jagger, only to allegedly end up in his bed.

Eventually Clancy's patience ran out and he banished me to captions, the traditional graveyard of cadets. Not for me the daily challenge of general reporting assignments that could take me far and wide; instead, I laboured over the two- and three-line captions that went with *The Herald*'s photographs. Initially despondent, I soon came to see the upside. The discipline of explaining a picture in, say, 30 words taught me great economy when writing, while

I got to work with some of the great shooters of the day and better understand what makes a great news picture. I learned to break it down to two simple qualities: energy and emotion.

Under the rules of the Australian Journalists' Association, cadets could not be assigned to any department for longer than 12 months. The provision was designed to ensure exposure to as many facets of the business as possible during the three-year training period. In the end, Clancy left me in pictorial for exactly 12 months.

Finally, a typewritten note signed by the chief of staff appeared in my pigeonhole one Friday morning. It informed me that my stint in captions was over and that I was to report to the general reporters' room at 7 a.m. on Monday.

'Right', I thought, 'I have to make the most of this.' I had to prove to my nemesis that he was wrong about me, that I could become the journalist he needed and that I wanted to be. I bought a new suit over the weekend, had a haircut and rose very early on the Monday.

As I stood beneath the shower at Widford Street, I said to myself: 'I'll show him.'

Suddenly there was a knock at the bathroom door. It was my mother, about to head out to her nursing job.

'Bruce,' she shouted through the door to make herself heard above the shower. 'Do you know a Geoff Clancy at *The Herald*?'

Bloody hell, I thought, surely he's not ringing me at home already. 'Yes,' I replied. 'He's my boss and he hates me. Why?'

Mum said: 'He died last night. It's just come over the radio.'

With that my career trajectory changed forever.

8

Death in the afternoon

Thirteen years later, in March 1987, I was back at Flinders Street, having forsaken California and all its sun-kissed attractions for an editorial floor that hadn't really altered since I had first walked in the place. The ownership had changed but would Rupert Murdoch make that much difference? He was certainly going to try.

The reality of what I had done struck me around 4.20 a.m. on my first day back. That was the time I had to get up each morning to meet the schedule Beecher had established as we set about trying to resuscitate *The Herald* for our new boss. It was an awfully long way from sunny Manhattan Beach and painfully close to my beginnings at the paper. I still wake many mornings around the same time.

The tall, bespectacled Beecher had been clever with his executive appointments. He had taken the two most senior positions himself, giving him direct control of *The Herald* and ultimate authority over *The Sun*, not that he necessarily needed it. The morning tabloid was booming under the relatively new editorship of a former *Herald* deputy editor, Colin Duck. There was now no designated deputy or number two on *The 'Beecher' Herald*, as it came to be known, at least not initially.

The four assistant editors Eric had appointed were each responsible for key elements of the paper: I was given Features; Steve Price was responsible for News; Sydney import Shelley Gare, a gifted and uncompromising editor, oversaw the paper's sections; while long-serving *Herald* sub-editor Jim O'Brien was put in charge of production.

Beecher had a simple explanation for this approach: if everyone did his or her job well, in theory he would have little to fret about. In a sense, he would merely conduct his orchestra. But there was another reason for the carve-up—creative tension. Though it was never stated or discussed, each of us suspected that somewhere in the not-too-distant future one would be anointed deputy editor of the paper. This would put that person in line to succeed Beecher when, as expected, he would go on to work for Rupert in London or New York. Enormously gifted, while a young reporter at *The Age*, Beecher had benefited from what many called the 'Ranald Macdonald scholarship', sent by the managing director of David Syme to further his education at some of the great newspapers of the world. Beecher saw his future at one of these and so did we. If he could make a success of *The Herald*, no doubt he would be rewarded with either *The Times* or *The Sunday Times* in London, given Murdoch's ownership of them.

The prospect of succeeding Beecher at *The Herald* appalled me as much as it intrigued. Fresh off the road, I was far from convinced that a life behind an editor's desk held any real appeal. The modern editor is expected to be both a manager of business relationships—with advertisers, sponsors and partners—and also a creative manager of content. An editor is always wearing two hats, and one of them has a propeller on it. Given a choice, most editors would prefer to spend the bulk of their time on the creative side but increasingly they are being asked to manage their papers rather than create them. I once attended an editors' conference in the United States that had an entire session devoted to this growing quandary. It was called: 'I Didn't Have Time for Editing Today'.

It was entirely apt. On a typical day now, an editor can be expected to not only chair a morning and afternoon news conference and an editorial conference, but perhaps attend a marketing brainstorm, an advertising whip-round, a meeting of the senior management team, numerous phone hook-ups with lawyers, a one-on-one with a visiting politician, endless budget planning meetings and deal with many and varied complainants. It's led to an explosion in titles on the editorial floor—managing editors, executive editors, assistant editors, editors-in-chief. There will be more titles as editors struggle to juggle the enormous job of managing hundreds of people and tens of millions of dollars in editorial budgets, while at the same time being expected to deliver a first-rate product every morning.

It's a scary moment when, exhausted, you walk out of the newspaper office at 10 p.m., after another 12–14-hour day, and you realise you've read barely a quarter of the next day's paper. Not only that, you've forgotten to read the gossip column—always a defamation minefield—and the latest offering by your star columnist, who always sails close to the wind. That means another session on the terminal at home. You'll be lucky to get to bed before 1 a.m.

And all this plays out against a background of total responsibility for every word in the paper and on the internet site. At worst, this can see you sent to jail.

I remember once returning from overseas to be told we faced a very real risk of prosecution for contempt over an inadvertent breach—almost all contempts in major media are inadvertent, unless you're Derryn Hinch—of a court suppression order.

'But I was lying on a beach when it happened,' I said in exasperation to our lawyer.

'Doesn't matter,' he shot back, without a hint of empathy.

The long-standing principle under British law, and hence our law, is that the editor is held responsible for all contempts

committed by a paper. This means that you can suddenly find yourself charged without so much as a police interview. What other
profession demands that you show up around 9 a.m. with a completely clean slate and drive the creation of an entirely new product
that must be on the streets barely 12 hours later and meet the
expectations of more than 500 000 buyers? Oh, and you could go
to jail for doing it.

I've always likened an editor's role to that of a theatre impre-
sario. At the end of the day, you are simply trying to put on a good
show. And, like live theatre, it can be exhilarating. But disaster is
always close at hand.

Certainly I wasn't about to conspire to get such a position. My
attitude then was simple: do one job well and the next one will
look after itself. After 20 years in senior management, I now realise
that's naive at best.

As assistant editor (Features) at *The Herald*, I was responsible for
the opinion page of the paper, which carried columnists, letters to
the editor and the day's editorials, and the op-ed page, literally the
page opposite editorial used for feature articles examining the key
issues and people in the news.

In offering me the job, Beecher had called the pages the 'intellectual heart' of the paper, an oxymoron if I'd ever heard one. But
I caught his meaning—he was keen to make *The Herald* more intelligent. I had no problem with that; the challenge would be to stop
them sliding into intellectualism, a mistake made by many opinion
editors. I decided my pages would be smart and well written but
accessible.

I also had control of the editorials, which pose a challenge at
the best of times. But at 6 a.m.? I defy anyone to be a clear thinker
at that hour. Under Beecher's predecessors, Les Carlyon and Neil
Mitchell, *The Herald* had veered to the right of its traditional
conservatism; Beecher wanted it pulled back, almost to small 'l'
liberalism.

Some of these pre-dawn conferences between Beecher, me and a couple of other senior staff would have failed as high school clear thinking exercises. Somehow though we managed to make sense by the time the paper hit the street around 11 a.m. each day.

Beecher was a revelation. Until then, I had never worked with anyone who approached his energy levels or his enormous capacity for ideas. Day after day, department heads would receive typewritten notes full of possible stories for his or her pages. It was not unusual to receive 20 to 30 ideas in one memo, most of them well rounded and cleverly thought out. That said, he once memorably suggested I put a reporter on the trail of a stray dog for a day. Years later when I recounted the story for a senior commissioning editor at a major metro daily, he laughed along with me ... and then assigned the story.

Suddenly *The Herald* was a paper of ideas, no longer dictated solely by the events of the day. The price we all paid for this was extremely long hours—I rarely put in fewer than 12 in the office and often more—and meetings. Lots of meetings. The key ones were the 7 a.m. news conference and the midday planning meeting to plot tomorrow's paper while today's was still breaking around us.

At least we were only working five days a week, Monday to Friday. At its peak in the late 1960s, *The Herald* had been a six-day paper with its Saturday edition a standout. By the mid-1980s, it was the nation's sole surviving Saturday evening newspaper and its sales were slipping alarmingly. Carlyon oversaw its relaunch as a tabloid in 1985 but it did nothing to halt the slide. In December 1986, it ceased production.

If Beecher was intimidated by the prospect of failure, he rarely showed it. At 36, he had the audacity of youth, opting to take on *The Sun* and *The Age* within three months of arriving by doing a morning edition of *The Herald* that, in the words of a page-one pointer the day before, would detail Paul Keating's mini-budget 'as the sun rises over Melbourne'. Of course, *The Herald*'s readers were used to getting their news as the sun set.

Our battle to beat *The Sun* on Budget night was aided by one of the paper's production executives who caused a walkout of his sub-editors with a particularly vituperative attack on one of them. My pages in the historic morning edition of *The Herald* carried more words and columnists than I care to remember, prompting one of them, Mungo MacCallum, to observe: 'Geez mate, you've got more columns than the bloody Parthenon.'

The hiring of MacCallum had given me pause to consider my career path. Beecher and I had flown to Canberra to complete arrangements with our new columnist. While waiting for him to arrive, Eric briefly broke from his incessant observations about the paper and where it might be headed to say without warning: 'You know, Bruce, if you'd taken the job I offered you two and a half years ago, you'd be editor of *The Sydney Morning Herald* now.' I'm not sure I heard anything for several hours after that.

Although Beecher's impact on the paper had been immediate, the six-week evolution of *The 'Beecher' Herald* started in earnest on 1 June 1987. In a page-one note to readers, he announced the forthcoming changes would constitute 'the biggest, most ambitious program of development undertaken in *The Herald*'s 147-year history.'

Beecher spent many Murdoch millions, hiring new staff, expanding the number of pages devoted to news, boosting foreign coverage and launching slick new sections all designed by a team of specially contracted artists.

My new pages launched on 9 June, the left-hander given over to columnists including former Treasury head John Stone and one-time Goon, Spike Milligan. Letters took out columns seven and eight—the paper now had a rigid eight-column grid that you dared not break out of—while the day's editorials sat atop it all in a horizontal strip. The right-hander was given over entirely to a buy-in on Maggie Thatcher, who was about to claim her third UK election victory.

Bob Hawke was chasing an election win too, having in mid-May conveniently called the federal election for 11 July, meaning the evolution of the paper unfolded pretty much in tandem with the campaign. By 13 July, Hawke was back in power and the metamorphosis of *The Herald* was complete.

Expectations were indeed high. Most agreed the relaunched paper was immeasurably better, but would it sell? Afternoon papers were under pressure around the world, displaced by television news, traffic snarls and lifestyle changes in the same way morning papers are now under pressure from the internet.

Later that week Rupert Murdoch, who had come to town for the relaunch, hosted a lunch upstairs at Society Restaurant, the venerable Italian eatery in Bourke Street. Only senior news executives of *The Herald* were invited. I was seated alongside The Great Man and we talked briefly about the travails of American Senator Gary Hart, whose tilt at the presidency was being derailed by a sex scandal. Forgetting Rupert's long-running hatred of the Kennedys, I suggested that if the same scrutiny had been applied a generation earlier we would never have had JFK in the White House.

'That would have been no bad thing,' Rupert spat back.

He had arrived at the lunch with his Australian CEO, Ken Cowley, in tow. Despite his irritability over the Kennedys, Murdoch was otherwise ebullient. This could have been explained by either the relaunch of *The Herald* or his just-completed purchase of the London-based mid-market tabloid, *Today*, which he had snatched out of Robert Maxwell's hands in a furious bidding war. It was merely the latest component of a burgeoning media empire that seemed to grow bigger every day.

'Why did you buy *Today*?' asked Steve Price with his customary directness.

Murdoch, who was gaining a reputation worldwide as an acquirer of media properties, tellingly misheard the question.

Turning to Cowley, he asked: 'We haven't bought anything today, have we?'

As the table politely tittered, Price clarified the question.

'Oh,' said Murdoch. 'I thought you asked me "What did you buy today?"' Laughter all round.

Murdoch had bought the paper to give him a set. In the UK, he had the upmarket broadsheets—*The Times* and *The Sunday Times*—the downmarket red-tops—*The Sun* and *News of the World*—and now *Today*, a so-called mid-market riser, pitched at those people in Thatcher's England who imagined themselves to be on their way to the middle classes or better.

Sitting at that lunch it was hard not to think that for a moment at least you were at the epicentre of modern media. Murdoch was by now a bona fide mogul and we were all basking in his reflected glory. The warm glow didn't last long for me: as Rupert stood up to go, we all sprang to our feet, prompting him to utter a few words of congratulation over the relaunch and encouragement for the future. As everyone beamed I shifted uncomfortably as I realised my tie was sitting a centimetre deep in my dessert. I slowly extricated it as Rupert wound up his speech.

Flinders Street was certainly abuzz with new faces, including not only the marquee hirings Peter Smark, Terry McCrann and Ben Hills, but young cartoonist Mark Knight, reporter Kate Legge in Canberra, even Andrew Bolt, who had signed on as Shelley Gare's deputy in Features and would go on to become one of the nation's most controversial columnists. Although *The 'Beecher' Herald* had its critics, we undeniably brought to Flinders Street the talent that still largely sustains the *Herald Sun* today. The paper was producing some of its finest journalism and was capable of surprise, always a key ingredient of great publications. Without that element, you become dull and predictable; too much and you become dangerously inconsistent. Beecher had the mix about right, although I sometimes wondered about the paper's humanity.

Newspapers inevitably reflect the personalities of their editors. Or, at least, they should. Beecher was smart and clever and so was the paper he was creating, but he had no populist sense at all. My job in part was to pull him up whenever he got a little too egg-headed and to remind him that we would have to attract a broader audience than he was used to chasing on papers like *The Age* and *The Sydney Morning Herald*. We launched campaigns, polled our readers on everything from sex to euthanasia, and occasionally did crazy things. We bought a 10 000-word piece out of the United States on one reporter's search for the actor Marlon Brando and then ran it across five days—even though the author never did find Brando. When I occasionally look back on those relaunched editions of the paper, I am struck by the energy and ideas leaping from them.

My first six months flew by in a blur of innovation and sheer bloody hard work. In September Beecher took me to lunch—how would I feel about a change of role, he asked. 'What if I put you in charge of Features and News?'

I accepted the new job on the understanding that Beecher would make it clear to Steve Price that I had neither sought it nor conspired to get it. Despite the assurances from Eric, Steve concluded I'd 'stitched him up', resigned soon after, and went off to radio. On the day of Price's departure from *The Herald*, Beecher delivered a glowing speech about him, only to have Price attack me in reply. What Price didn't know was that I had written the laudatory farewell Beecher had delivered; it took us years to patch up our friendship.

One of my first moves as the new boss of News and Features was to be more aggressive in chasing stories. So, after weighing up with Beecher the appropriateness of pursuing a politician on holidays, I dispatched our 'On the Spot' columnist Bruce Dover to Hamilton Island, where the Victorian Opposition leader, Jeff Kennett, was holidaying with family while senior members of his shadow Cabinet were moving against his leadership back in Melbourne. If my relationship with Kennett had been built on shifting ground because of my years as a state political reporter, it would now become seismic.

It was not a decision taken lightly. Public figures are entitled to their privacy in strict family matters. But the circumstances here were compelling. Kennett's decision to take a full two-week break had been the subject of chatter among his shadow Cabinet; now there was serious number-crunching going on in his absence and a challenge to his leadership was almost certain. (He would survive a party-room vote just weeks later.) Beecher agreed we should go.

Dover was to ask Kennett once, and only once, for an interview. If he refused, he was to accept that refusal. I also asked him to photograph Kennett, but only in public areas. With camera in tow, Dover headed to Hamilton Island. We would publish his report in Monday's *Herald*. When it duly arrived it began with Kennett's refusal to comment on the leadership speculation, always a sure way to kill any reader interest in the story.

My new role meant I now sat at Beecher's elbow each morning as we pulled together the day's first edition on the backbench. After quickly reading Dover's copy, Beecher turned to me and said: 'Can you have a go at fixing this? It needs a completely new top.'

Dover had had more success with photographs, capturing an overweight Kennett in his bathers as he strode along the beach. The Liberal leader looked very much like a man who had spent too long at his job, and not enough time on his physique. I knew the feeling well.

I turned the 'no comment' intro into this: 'As the sun beat down on Hamilton Island, an embattled Jeff Kennett took to the white sands and demonstrated that, like his leadership, he is not in the best of shape.'

Beecher loved it. We ran the story on page one with three pictures of Kennett at play, including a main image that would look like a 'before' shot for a diet franchise.

I did not expect Kennett to like the treatment, but consoled myself that we hadn't badgered him. When the paper hit, Kennett's physique predictably became a talking point. Word gradually filtered back that the Liberal leader wasn't happy and that he had fingered me as the culprit.

It wasn't until several years later that the full force of Kennett's anger over the story and pictures hit me. During a visit by Steve Harris to the Liberal leader's parliamentary office in 1991, Kennett produced a printout of Dover's original report with its 'no comment' intro. As Harris would later tell me, Kennett was enraged by my rewrite.

This was alarming on several levels. Not only had Kennett not been appraised of the circumstances—when an editor tells a deputy to rewrite a story on deadline, you tend to do what you are told—where the hell had he obtained the printout? Newspaper publishing systems need to be sacrosanct; whoever obtained and then passed on the original version of the story had breached an article of faith.

Within months of my elevation to the News and Features job, Beecher stunned me by suggesting another promotion. He and Rupert had agreed in principle that he should become editor-in-chief of *The Australian* as well as editor-in-chief of HWT. He would be based in Sydney, but commute to Melbourne on a regular basis. I would edit *The Herald*. To say I was dumbfounded would be an understatement.

Quite apart from the question of my preparedness for the role, I felt strongly that Eric had attracted a lot of people to Melbourne on the strength of his commitment to *The Herald* and this would be seen as at least a partial abandonment of them and the paper. We talked the issue back and forth for days, with Beecher and Murdoch eventually shelving the plan when Rupert visited early in 1988.

That visit by Murdoch was notable for at least one other reason. After spending a day or two at Flinders Street in March—and hosting a small private dinner at the fashionable restaurant Mietta's attended by D'arcy, McCrann, Geoffrey Blainey, Des Moore and me—he flew out to visit company interests in Fiji. Within hours the phone rang on the news desk.

'Is that you, Eric?' said The Great Man.

'No, it's actually Bruce Guthrie here, Mr Murdoch.'

'Right, Bruce. I've got a page-one lead for your next edition: Robert Maxwell has put in a bid of $800 million for *The Age*.'

'*Really?*'

'That ought to fire them up at Spencer Street. You can go with it; it's absolutely right. See you.'

Of course it was right. Maxwell had rung Murdoch to prematurely boast that he had purchased *Today* only to have his Australian rival steal it out from under his nose. It was reasonable to assume that Rupert's source on *The Age* story was also Maxwell.

Murdoch was right about one other thing too. When our third edition appeared that day with a page-one headline that read '$800m firm bid for *The Age*' it certainly fired them up at Spencer Street. Especially when we added this second paragraph: '*The Herald* believes the John Fairfax group, owner of *The Age*, is likely to accept the offer. But acceptance of the bid is certain to cause a political furore.'

In no time, forces opposed to a Maxwell takeover came together. While the battle attracted leading Melbourne figures, the most notable combatants were the staff of the paper themselves. Quickly they formed a Maintain Your *Age* committee from which emerged a charter that was designed to protect the editorial independence and ethos of the paper. This was thought imperative because of Maxwell's reputation as an interventionist proprietor.

The charter enshrined the right of journalists, photographers and artists to report and comment without fear or favour and was quickly endorsed by staff, editor Creighton Burns and managing director Greg Taylor, before winning the support of the board. It was impressive brinkmanship, ultimately rewarded when Prime Minister Hawke blocked Maxwell's bid.

The uprising certainly saved *The Age* from falling into the clutches of a man destined to die with his business reputation in tatters. But the grim reality was that it preserved the ownership of the paper by young Warwick Fairfax who had launched his successful but ultimately disastrous takeover of the Fairfax Group a year earlier.

The staff's successful opposition to the Maxwell bid also changed the nature of Fairfax in the decades to follow. A series of managers and owners have complained of their inability to really affect the culture of *The Age*. Small wonder when, thanks to the Maxwell episode, many staff feel a greater sense of ownership of the paper than some of the shareholders who've come and gone in the years since.

By the time the ill-fated Maxwell takeover lapsed I had been back at *The Herald* a year. Now came another surprise: Rupert was having a confab in Aspen, Colorado, of his best and brightest and I was invited. It had been a heady 12 months, but this topped the lot.

9

Rocky Mountain high

Barry Diller's Fox Inc. jet had gold taps, sumptuous leather seats and couches, and a guestbook sure to impress. I remember being particularly taken by Sylvester Stallone's entry. The hottest box-office star in the world, thanks to the *Rocky* and *Rambo* franchises, Stallone had signed in with not one but two *Playboy* Playmates of the Month.

Diller's jet was just one of a small fleet of private planes provided for the 50 or so participants at Rupert Murdoch's June 1988 editorial gabfest in Aspen. The jets took us from LAX where editors and executives had assembled after flying in from four continents.

We had already been treated to a lavish welcoming dinner at the Murdochs' stunning Beverly Hills mansion—the purchase of which I had reported on as a humble foreign correspondent just 18 months earlier—and now we were being feted like generals from some all-conquering army.

Which, in a way, we were. As Murdoch wrote in his official conference welcome: 'Gathered together are people from four continents—members of our company, The News Corporation Limited, the largest publisher of English language newspaper titles in the world.' (News Corporation was the global empire; the Australian businesses were known as News Limited.)

As William Shawcross observed in his 1992 biography of Murdoch, if there was a high point in the spread and the confidence of the News empire, it was marked in part by the Aspen conference.

With the exception of the Murdoch children—Lachlan, James and Elisabeth attended—at 33, I was probably the youngest participant. I will admit that as I rubbed shoulders with the editors of *The Times*, *The Sunday Times* and *New York Magazine* I more than once asked myself: 'What the hell am I doing here?'

Flown in on Friday morning, we were immediately kitted out in a News uniform and offered all manner of recreational activities. Beecher and I chose a four-wheel drive and headed off into the surrounding hills to the Snowmass ski resort, now ablaze in summer wildflowers. Eager to stretch our legs, we took to one of the walking trails only to bump into Terry McCrann and Paul Kelly doing likewise. It was surreal, to say the least.

The conference officially opened on the Saturday morning with legendary News promotions man Graham King talking us through his marketing successes, including the famous Bingo, Bigger Bingo and Almost Too Big Bingo games that had so effectively boosted sales of *The Sun* in London.

Beecher was up next, walking the audience through the remaking of *The Herald*. His pitch was simple: we were repositioning the paper with quality readership that, in turn, would attract advertisers. It had to be simple—12 months after the official relaunch circulation was still falling, albeit at a slower rate than we had inherited. When in doubt, argue demographics.

Throughout these sessions, The Great Man sat at the front of the lecture hall at Aspen's Given Institute presiding like a proud father. At his side throughout was *Sunday Times* editor Andrew Neil, playing the role of facilitator and master of ceremonies. Murdoch clearly had drawing power—speakers included former US president Richard

Nixon, one-time Federal Reserve chief Paul Volcker and the leader of Britain's Social Democratic Party, David Owen.

By the end of the first day, attendees were muttering there was too little discussion of newspapers and far too much about geopolitics, most of it reflecting Rupert's peculiarly right-wing view of the world. For a man who made most of his money out of cheap populism, it was a pretty lofty agenda.

Sunday promised much. First up was Tom Petrie, veteran news editor of *The Sun* in London. It was supposed to be his legendary boss, *Sun* editor Kelvin MacKenzie, but he had begged off at the last moment, pleading an asthma attack. Petrie had been news editor of *The Sun* for eight years and boldly boasted: 'We don't report the news, we make it.' His presentation was wildly entertaining with its stories of chequebook journalism, general skulduggery and, ultimately, 'heavy lifting' of rival paper's stories if they were unable to match them. For anyone who took journalism seriously, it was appalling.

In one of the more serious misjudgements of my career, I decided to wade into this morass of *Sun* exaggeration, invention and character assassination. After Petrie's 30-minute presentation, Murdoch asked for questions from the audience. I slowly raised my hand, aware that I had better not stuff it up. (A significant number of attendees didn't speak for the entire weekend.)

'Tom,' I said. 'Do you have any ethical framework at all at the London *Sun*?'

Reflecting on it 20 years later, I'm proud that I had the guts to raise the issue. At the following year's conference the topic dominated the agenda and my question to Petrie was apparently cited. But at that moment, around 9 a.m. on Sunday, 26 June 1988, I might as well have asked about our host's sexual proclivities. The place simply erupted.

'Ethics? At *The Sun*? You've got to be joking,' shouted one of the execs from the London broadsheets. All around were shouts of derision, raucous laughter and general hysteria. So much so that Petrie claimed to have not heard my question. He called for calm.

'Sorry, mate, but could you repeat the question? And would you shut up, you blokes?' pleaded the harried news editor.

So I repeated the question. I don't remember looking at Rupert throughout any of this, which had lasted a good 90 seconds or so. But Beecher would later gleefully report that the proprietor had turned red when I first asked the question and blue when I repeated it. Soon Murdoch would have steam coming out of his ears as I was forced to ask it a third time.

'For God's sake,' said Petrie. 'Can you shut up? I'm sorry, mate, I missed it again.'

By now, I was wishing Aspen would disappear in some summer blizzard. My future at News Limited was going to be, well, limited.

I tried one last time, rushing the words to get the whole wretched thing over: 'Doyouhaveanyethicsat *The Sun*?'

Petrie came to my rescue with a thoughtful reply. 'To tell you the truth, we don't really have any kind of ethical framework at all,' he admitted. 'But we better get one, because if we don't Maggie Thatcher will give us one.'

To my horror, Murdoch himself weighed in at this point, in a voice clearly designed to warn off any other attendees stupid enough to continue this line of questioning. 'I would have thought it's news if the captain of the England cricket team is taking barmaids up to his room the night before a Test match.'

This was a reference to exclusive reports just weeks before in *The Sun* and *Today*, both owned by Murdoch, that England captain Mike Gatting had invited barmaid, Louise Shipman (presumably the recipient of a News cheque or two), up to his room during that summer's first Test against the West Indies. Gatting, who strenuously denied having sex with the woman, nevertheless lost his job over the incident after the two Murdoch tabloids fanned public outrage.

Having arrived at the conference feeling somewhat an outsider, I now was the social equivalent of a leper. No-one came near me.

I spotted Rupert and Ken Cowley in earnest conversation across the room. Much later Cowley confided to me that Murdoch had advanced on him, bemused by my question of Petrie, saying: 'I see we have a Fairfax wanker in our midst.'

I ducked out to get some air before Richard Nixon took to the stage. The once reviled president was undergoing something of an image makeover, bobbing up in various media as a commentator on global affairs. As I strolled the streets of Aspen I spied a T-shirt in a store window that read: 'He's fit, he's tanned, he's ready—Nixon in '88.'

As it turned out, the former president was first-rate, predicting a Bush landslide in the forthcoming presidential election and anointing the Soviet Union's Mikhail Gorbachev as a statesman of international repute. 'If Gorbachev has the will to choose progress at home over aggression abroad,' said Nixon, 'he will become not just man of the year, but man of the century.' History proved him right.

We marked the end of the conference with a dinner at Rupert and Anna Murdochs' palatial home. The house featured an indoor lap pool that ran through the main entertaining area. As the booze flowed, several high-ranking executives came dangerously close to tumbling in. Late in the night Anna Murdoch pulled me aside, saying: 'Eric, we haven't had a chance to catch up over the weekend.' People were forever mistaking me for Beecher. With any luck maybe they thought it had been him questioning Petrie.

10

The downhill run

Despite my tumble at Aspen, Beecher appointed me deputy editor of *The Herald* within weeks of arriving back. He had another surprise. Murdoch had decided it was time to launch a Sunday paper in Melbourne and planning was to start immediately—Eric would be spending increasing amounts of his time assembling staff and plotting the paper. I was sworn to secrecy about *The Sunday Herald* and one other key ingredient of the plan—Rupert was going to launch a *Sunday Sun* as well.

Two new papers? Three, if Spencer Street responded as expected? It was almost unthinkable.

For much of its history HWT and David Syme, publishers of *The Age*, had conspired to keep Murdoch out of Melbourne by effectively shutting down the Sunday market, his most logical entry point. In fact, for much of the twentieth century there had been a Victorian law forbidding Sunday publication. Later the two companies combined to produce one tabloid, *The Sunday Press*, sharing costs and profits. Newsagents remained closed and the paper was sold only out of milk bars; it was always seen as little more than a blocking action by two competitors who didn't have the heart to go up against each other. Here was Rupert flagging an end to that cosy relationship.

We did have a more pressing problem. Despite the obvious improvement in *The Herald*, the daily's sales were still declining and so were revenues. We had plaudits, but not profits. And Rupert always preferred the latter to the former.

It was not necessarily the best starting point for creating a couple of new papers. Still, we set about the task, Beecher hiring and plotting and planning, while I concentrated on the daily. Murdoch duly informed David Syme that he would be pulling out of *The Sunday Press* deal, throwing Spencer Street into apoplexy.

As the year drew to a close, several dramatic events unfolded. The first saw the demise of John D'arcy, the man Murdoch had left in charge of HWT when he had bought the company two years earlier. Inadvertently, I played a key role in D'arcy's removal.

D'arcy was no fan of Beecher's and never had been. The two men had very little in common. Around October 1988 I took a call from a Melbourne restaurateur who was also a good and close friend. D'arcy had recently dined there and, according to my informant, 'spent most of the lunch criticising you and Eric', telling his lunch companion that we were 'stuffing up' the paper. Ironically, 20 years later, I would receive similar intelligence about my managing director, Peter Blunden, who was heard more than once criticising to outsiders my efforts on the *Herald Sun*.

Beecher was enraged when I told him of D'arcy's conduct and promptly contacted Rupert, telling him it was untenable that the big Queenslander remain in the job. Murdoch promptly summoned D'arcy to London.

Days before he flew out for the fateful meeting D'arcy told the weekly management conference that he had been summoned by the boss.

'I don't know what it's about,' said D'arcy, adding with a laugh: 'Perhaps he's going to sack me.' I didn't look at Beecher, but I did shift uncomfortably in my chair. I wasn't privy to what fate awaited D'arcy, but I certainly knew it wasn't going to be good for him.

In the end, Murdoch did remove him from the post, delivering the blow within hours of D'arcy touching down at Heathrow.

If Beecher was pleased with the outcome, his celebrations would have been short-lived. Ken Cowley announced days later that D'arcy's successor would be Malcolm Colless, a Murdoch man to his bootstraps. Colless had been a political and industrial correspondent for *The Australian*, cutting his management teeth by running Murdoch's suburban newspaper chain in Sydney. HWT would be his first major management role. At the same time Murdoch installed his sister Janet as chair of the HWT board. The Murdoch takeover of Melbourne was complete.

If D'arcy and Beecher had had no chemistry, the Colless and Beecher partnership would be positively toxic. There was no way the relationship could work. It occurred to me that perhaps it wasn't meant to—Colless had been put in place to force Beecher out. Slowly and inevitably it began to happen. After just a couple of months, it was no longer a question of would Beecher go, but when. Colless even tested my patience with some of his observations about the paper.

'Why do the datelines on foreign stories always have the wrong day on them?' he asked one morning as the first edition was flying around us. 'It's always yesterday, not today.'

'Er, that's because it *is* yesterday over there now,' I explained helpfully. 'It's Monday morning here, but it's still Sunday over there. Or, at least, the story was filed on a Sunday.'

'Oh. I reckon we should make it the same day anyway,' said Colless.

The final straw for Beecher was the arrival in the office of a bearded and slightly dishevelled man who started appearing, almost Zelig-like, at key editorial discussions about the new Sunday. None of us knew who he was; only that he would sit quietly at the rear of meetings or perhaps poke an enquiring eye over the shoulder of designers while they worked away at dummy pages. Eventually,

Beecher summoned the man to his office while Shelley Gare, who had also peeled off from the daily to work on the Sunday, and I looked on.

'Who are you?' Beecher asked.

'My name is Arnold Ernshaw,' came the reply.

'Right. Well, who the fuck *are* you?'

'I told you, I'm Arnold Ernshaw and I'm here to help.'

'Help,' said an incredulous Beecher. 'Who sent you to help?'

'Rupert thought I might be able to help.'

'Oh, did he now,' said Beecher. 'Well, we don't need your fucking help. Understand? If I see you at any of our editorial meetings I'll have you thrown out, all right?'

'Very well,' said Ernshaw, who promptly turned and left, no doubt to brief Colless and then Murdoch. Ernshaw had been a trusted lieutenant for many years and had been used as something of a troubleshooter, particularly when Murdoch felt papers were in trouble. The portents for Eric and, by association, me were not good.

The end came sooner rather than later. In March 1989, Beecher turned up at our home unexpectedly, midweek around 7 p.m.

'I'm here to tell you that I'll be resigning tomorrow,' he said matter-of-factly. It was obvious from his tone that there was no point trying to dissuade him. Besides, I had witnessed first-hand the ebbing away of corporate confidence in his editorship of *The Herald*.

It was a double blow for me. He had taught me an enormous amount in two years and I would miss that terribly. Then there was a more practical element to all this: one of his key hirings for the new Sunday had been my wife Janne, who was the putative editor of the paper's planned colour magazine. If I were to quit in solidarity with Eric, it would no doubt cost us both jobs.

'What do you think they'll do with me?' I asked Beecher.

'You'll be getting the daily,' he said. 'You should be celebrating.'

I certainly didn't feel like breaking out the champagne. I had shared the Beecher vision for *The Herald* and, if there was to be a repudiation of it, it was as much a slap for me as for him.

The announcement of Beecher's departure was made straight after first edition the next day. Ken Cowley was in Melbourne and immediately started summoning key executives into the board-room to plan the succession. I got summoned about an hour after first edition.

'We need to put in place new arrangements because of Eric's departure,' said Cowley, pleasantly and in very measured tones. He was trying to appear very much in control, as if the Beecher res-ignation had been anticipated. No doubt it had been. I was later to learn that News offered Beecher the deputy editorship of *The Sunday Times* in London in a bid to keep him, but he'd had enough of Murdoch and turned it down.

'You've done very good work for us, Bruce, over the past two years and we'd like to reward that,' said Cowley.

At this point my mind raced with a mix of anticipation, self-doubt, excitement, perhaps even a little dread. Did I want this prize? After all, did *The Herald* really have a future? Yes, I decided, it did. It was my destiny to save it or, at least, have a good go at it.

'So we've decided to make you editor . . . ' said Cowley, adding after a dramatic pause, 'of the Sunday.'

'*Pardon?*'

'We want you to edit *The Sunday Herald*.'

'But what about the daily? I've spent my whole career on the daily.'

'Well, we think that's an easier job,' said Cowley. 'More a case of just continuing to pedal the bike. But the Sunday's a whole, new product. Massive challenges there.'

When I reflect on the conversation 20 years later, I realise that Cowley was right. But at the time I felt gutted. After all, who had worked harder for and on the paper?

'So, who gets the daily?' I asked, resigned now to my fate.

'Bruce Baskett.'

We had come full circle then. Baskett finally had the paper some thought he should have got two years earlier. Good on him. I had a weekly that didn't even exist yet.

As I struggled to comprehend all this, Cowley offered me the luxury of time. It wasn't a now-or-never situation, the common approach at News.

'Take your time over this, Bruce,' he said. 'If you have doubts, I'm sure we can find something else for you.'

I often reflect on the offer of *The Sunday Herald* and wonder whether, like *The Sydney Morning Herald* four years earlier, it was a great opportunity forgone.

In the end I turned it down, in part because I was exhausted from the effort of trying to rebuild *The Herald,* tired of trying to coexist with News Limited managers I had little in common with and because I had simply decided I had to get out of Flinders Street. It was time to break the ties that had begun 17 years earlier in 1972 when I had unexpectedly landed that copy boy's job.

It took me two weeks to say 'no' and it came after a fateful second meeting with Cowley, this time in his office at Holt Street, Sydney. I had been flown there so we could finally resolve *The Sunday Herald* editorship. The ever-polite Cowley gave it a big sell, urging me to grasp the opportunity with both hands.

'We would like you to complete the dummy in, say, three weeks and then fly to New York to walk Rupert through it,' said Cowley.

The timetable wasn't a problem because Beecher and his team had already done a great deal of work on the paper. It was almost ready to go.

'That shouldn't be a problem,' I told Cowley.

Then he said this: 'It would be good for you to get together with Rupert again because you upset him a bit with that question of yours at Aspen.'

'Oh, which question was that?' I asked, knowing the answer full well.

'You know, the one about ethics.'

In the same way a throwaway line by a corporate lawyer would convince me to take on the might of News Limited 20 years later, Cowley's confirmation of the Aspen odium I had stirred up convinced me to walk away. I decided that if a proprietor could denounce an editor for raising ethical issues at an editorial conference, it wasn't a company I wanted to be part of.

So, 24 hours later, as promised, I rang Cowley with my response. *The Sunday Herald* was a very attractive proposition, but I had decided it was time for me to leave Flinders Street. Who knows, I said, maybe one day I would return to News Limited.

What I didn't tell him was that I'd had an attractive offer from Spencer Street. It was time to become a Fairfax wanker.

11

Off to war

My decision to turn down a Murdoch editorship for a Fairfax deputy editorship confounded most of my peers and, at times, left me wondering too. Why would I want to be a number two again when I could finally ascend to the number-one spot on a paper? ABC broadcaster and columnist Douglas Aiton rang me days after my resignation to ask me just that.

'Doug,' I replied, 'I just didn't like them.'

He describes it as the best reason he's ever heard for turning down a job. It may have been naive, it was certainly idealistic, but two decades on I'm comfortable with the decision. I probably should have applied the same good sense when offered some other positions in the years since. More than money, conditions and seniority, what you should look for in an employer is shared values; my Aspen experience had only underscored that.

Ironically, the putative editor of *The Sunday Age*, Fairfax's response to Murdoch's plans, was Steve Harris. I had put him up to Beecher for the job I eventually took in Melbourne after Los Angeles.

Harris was soon ringing almost every night from California where he was spending a year at Stanford University on a Knight fellowship. He was determined to hire not only me but Janne as well. She had only recently left *The Age* to join *The Sunday Herald*, but was now disinclined to stay there, particularly if I turned down the editorship. Harris' pitch was simple: come over here and we'll plan and design the paper, then we'll launch and edit it together.

A delighted Harris greeted us at San Francisco airport. Over the next couple of hours it became obvious that while Beecher had been painstakingly putting together *The Sunday Herald*—we had even had a two-day planning session at Murdoch's central New South Wales sheep station and a full dummy of the paper existed—and *The Sunday Sun* was also well advanced, Spencer Street had done virtually nothing in response.

It appeared they were still hoping Murdoch would abandon his Sunday plans, so much so that my formal letter of employment had an 'out' clause, stipulating that if *The Sunday Age* did not go ahead I would be given a senior role on *The Age*. Clearly David Syme & Co, the Melbourne arm of Fairfax, was in denial.

Not that anyone could blame them. The takeover of the Fairfax group by young Warwick Fairfax on the eve of the 1987 sharemarket crash had stretched it to the limit. If the Murdoch takeover of HWT was the first great body-blow against the Australian newspaper industry in the modern era, young Warwick's disastrous bid to claim his birthright was the second. Rupert Murdoch's only real competitor was weakened by events that directly flowed from the takeover and the collapse that followed. In some senses, Fairfax has never been the same company since.

Saddled with enormous debt, the last thing they needed in 1989 was a protracted Sunday newspaper war, but they simply had to fight. At stake was not only the potentially lucrative Sunday market, huge in other states and essentially untapped in Victoria, but the Saturday market too. Fairfax's massive profits from classifieds flowed principally from the Saturday *Age*; if Murdoch could somehow shift those into the Sunday market, all bets were off.

By launching not one but two papers out of Flinders Street, it left Spencer Street with no real option but to go broadsheet on the Sunday. If Murdoch had launched only the tabloid *Sunday Sun*, *The Age* would at least have had the option of matching it. After all, that was the basis of the big-selling Sunday market in Sydney—two tabloids going head to head.

Murdoch's pincer movement on *The Age* was typical of the shrewdness he had demonstrated throughout his career. He knew that if *The Age* against all the odds went tabloid with their Sunday, it increased the possibility of the broadsheet *Sunday Herald* succeeding and eventually making a full-scale assault on the weekend classifieds. If Fairfax took the more predictable route of staying broadsheet, it would deliver the mass tabloid market to Murdoch. Either way, he couldn't lose. Ultimately Spencer Street decided to go broadsheet. Although the tabloid option was discussed, it was never seriously entertained.

The Age had paid our airfares to California and was putting us up in a hotel close to the Stanford campus. Each day we would head to Harris' modest campus lodgings and, with pens and paper in hand, plot *The Sunday Age*. The clock was ticking—it was already April and the papers were due to launch on 20 August. There was much to be done.

We drew layouts, played with alternative grids and headline fonts and discussed everything from mastheads to formats to philosophies. Then we drew up a list of staff we would target. The new paper would have more than 60 journalists, photographers and artists, many of them new hirings; inevitably most of them came from *The Herald*. This wasn't motivated by revenge; it was simply the largest pool of broadsheet talent on offer. As Charles Wright observed in a *Good Weekend* piece previewing the Sunday newspaper war:

For [*The Herald* editor] Bruce Baskett, the next few weeks were to be a nightmare. It was as if the sign on his office door had been surreptitiously altered to read 'Exit'. When the last echo of departing footsteps died away, there would be at least 30 fewer journalists on the staff. Seventeen staff and four columnists would be over at *The Sunday Age*.

Wright went on to note that, by hiring me, Harris had robbed News of momentum, key executives and, ultimately, talent. Wright noted: 'Guthrie became a beacon for disaffected *Herald* staff'. Ultimately, he observed, News Limited's decision to precipitate the row that would convince Beecher to quit and to then overlook me for the daily job amounted to serious miscalculations.

At one point a senior HWT executive bemoaned to one of the defectors that I seemed determined to gut *The Herald*. It wasn't true. I still had a great deal of affection for the paper and its editor, but people were keen to leave Flinders Street, probably as a result of the friction that inevitably comes from a big corporate takeover. Years later I was reminded of this when I heard Fox News boss Roger Ailes recount how more than 80 staff had left NBC to join him at the nascent Fox News channel. At the height of these defections an NBC lawyer rang Ailes to accuse him of tampering. Said Ailes in reply: 'You don't know the difference between recruitment and a freakin' jailbreak.'

Janne and I eventually settled in at Spencer Street in May. We arrived full of ideas and gusto, only to find chaos and resentment.

At News there was absolute respect for the proprietor; certainly there was never any doubt who was running the place. At Fairfax, the proprietor, Young Warwick, seemed to be an object of ridicule who should be grateful to those lending him their talents. This seemed to be an inevitable consequence of the staff seeing off the Robert Maxwell takeover bid.

A perfect symbol of the disarray we found was the fact that the new paper had no office. Eventually management commandeered what had been *The Age* gallery, a windowless exhibition area on

Spencer Street. They brought in trestle tables as desks and a handful of computers powered up by leads that criss-crossed the drab olive green carpet. We had all been attracted by the prospect of creating a bright and bold new paper but it was being hatched in decidedly second-rate conditions. As former *Herald* people arrived, I felt embarrassed to show them to their new digs.

Meanwhile, the intelligence reaching us was that *The Sunday Herald* was actually going to be pretty good. Alan Farrelly, a long-time Murdoch lieutenant, came from Sydney for the role I had turned down. He had remained faithful to our dummy, a classic broadsheet in the style of London's *Sunday Times*. It bore more than a passing resemblance to the short-lived *Sunday Australian*, launched in February 1971, closed in June the following year, but much lauded along the way.

Part of the solution to our space problems—the only solution on offer—was that we would take over *The Age* editorial floor on Saturdays. That meant we would commandeer reporters' room desks, sub-editors' terminals, even the daily's editor's office on publication nights.

As the first publication night loomed, we confronted an urgent problem. What the hell were we going to put on page one?

Our best hope came from our national political correspondent, Michael Gordon, who had somehow convinced Prime Minister Bob Hawke and Treasurer Paul Keating to be photographed together exclusively for our launch issue.

We dispatched our best photographer, Wayne Ludbey, to Canberra. Things quickly started to go awry. They were running late, then very late, and then there was a chance they would have to cancel the session. No, no, that would be unacceptable, we said, even hinting it could permanently damage the relationship between the paper and the pair. Gordon intervened, suggesting they give Ludbey 10 minutes rather than the 30 we had been promised. You can have five, they said.

In the end, Ludbey got three frames. He jumped on an early evening plane and headed straight back to Spencer Street. Harris and I waited anxiously as he shuffled into the hen house—our name for our Monday-to-Friday digs—and with furrowed brow headed into the darkroom. He looked anything but confident. Fifteen minutes later he emerged and laid down the three prints.

Two of them looked terribly staged, but the third had a quality that struck the viewer instantly. Both men had removed their suit coats in an attempt to look relaxed; Hawke had even rolled up his sleeves. Keating stood on Hawke's right, both hands shoved deep into the pockets of his grey suit pants, a half-smile breaking out on his face, almost in spite of himself. Hawke meanwhile had slung his right arm around his Treasurer, while cocking his left on his hip. His grin was full-face and unforced. They may very well have decided to campaign together for the greater good of the ALP, but Ludbey's picture revealed this was a marriage of convenience. Keating's uncomfortable body language said it all. Ludbey's shot had captured the tension in a relationship that would nevertheless define Australian politics for more than a decade.

We had not only a page-one picture, but a great page-one picture. Our relief and excitement were palpable. Mid-afternoon, Harris and I both visited the stone, the area where typeset stories and pages were spat out by machines and laid in by compositors before being sent off to be made into plates. As we wandered the area checking early close pages the phone sprang into life.

'Steve, there's a call for you,' said one of the comps. It was young Warwick Fairfax, calling from Chicago to wish us luck with our new undertaking. The call lasted about a minute. It was a rare exchange between the proprietor and one of his editorial executives. Warwick Fairfax had become something of a recluse as his bold bid to claim what he saw as his birthright faltered badly. In the end, *The Sunday Age* would last considerably longer than his ownership of Fairfax.

12

Out of the red, into the Black . . .

The Royal Melbourne Yacht Squadron sits on the shores of Melbourne's Port Phillip Bay, its whitewashed clubrooms somewhat out of place among the nightclubs and restaurants of St Kilda, just down the road from Luna Park. It was to its wood-panelled rooms the most senior executives of David Syme & Co, publishers of *The Age* and *The Sunday Age*, had been summoned in December 1990 to discuss the future of a once-great enterprise now desperately trying to keep the banks at bay.

By now, *The Sunday Age* had pulled well ahead of its chief competitor, *The Sunday Herald*. But despite winning this particular skirmish, Fairfax was losing a much bigger war.

Over four hours at the Yacht Squadron we heard from marketers, accountants and editors as we looked into the future of our great titles. We were treated to the frog-in-a-beaker metaphor: if you put a frog into a beaker of boiling water, he'll jump straight out; if you put him in a beaker of cold water and slowly heat it, he'll boil to death.

As yachts bobbed about on Port Phillip Bay, we shared a jolly lunch and swapped war stories and gossip. Then the afternoon sessions began and Steve Harris made a particularly strong denunciation of short-sighted newspaper management, urging Syme to be bold. It was a thinly veiled attack on both the management of the company and the editorial management of *The Age*.

Then, after more coffee, proceedings were halted by a short announcement: the banks had called in their debt and the John Fairfax Group was now officially in receivership. Our 'planning for the future' conference was suddenly a sad oxymoron.

So we all trudged back to Spencer Street. We had begun the day discussing our future and had ended it wondering if we had any at all. The frog was well and truly cooked.

The new 'boss' of David Syme was an accountant named Des. At least, he was the man we met regularly to discuss the immediate future of *The Age* and *The Sunday Age*. Installed by the banks to protect their investments, he was to make sure the group was in safe hands until it was inevitably sold on.

Because David Syme was much leaner than its Sydney counterpart, receivership didn't change things all that much at Spencer Street. The journalists imagined conspiracy theories everywhere they looked but that tends to happen at the best of times. We simply went about the business of building up *The Sunday Age* and we soon had a very significant victory.

Eighteen months after its launch, *The Sunday Herald* was fast running out of steam. Alan Farrelly had moved on and the content and pagination were thinning. Our circulation lead was now in the tens of thousands most weeks. So when it was announced in March 1991 that *The Sunday Herald* was shutting down, it was no real surprise. It was ironic: our paper in receivership had 'won' the great battle of the two Sunday broadsheets, while the Murdoch empire waved the white flag.

There were decidedly mixed feelings on the editorial floor of *The Sunday Age*. No-one, least of all journalists, likes to see a paper fail; besides, many of the staff now out of work were friends or former colleagues.

106

Six months earlier, in October 1990, Murdoch had shut down the daily edition of *The Herald*, merging it with *The Sun* to create the *Herald Sun*. Murdoch had also moved at the same time to shut down Sydney's *Daily Mirror*, merging it with *The Daily Telegraph*. The two new Melbourne and Sydney papers were marketed as 24-hour publications, published morning and afternoon. In time, the afternoon editions would disappear too.

Murdoch had long preached 'sensible competition' and now he had it in both the daily and Sunday markets. I found myself wondering whether *The Sunday Herald* wasn't always intended to be short lived. With the Sunday papers 18 months old and *The Sunday Sun* nudging 400 000 copies each day, it was now safe for News to shut down its Sunday broadsheet. The remaining two papers—a serious broadsheet and a mass market tabloid—would not be going head-to-head in an expensive battle as happened every week in Sydney. Sometimes though, these things aren't decided by market forces. In another example of 'sensible competition', a senior editorial executive at a company other than News Limited once confided to me that his company had agreed to stay out of one sector of the newspaper market if their rival stayed out of their sector. Almost two decades on, the two companies have avoided going head-to-head with print products.

Whatever his motivation, I will forever be grateful to Murdoch for giving us 20 August 1989. With experts now picking over the entrails of so many doomed newspapers, it seems extraordinary that three mastheads launched on the same day in Melbourne.

When news of *The Sunday Herald*'s demise came through, Harris, Janne and I promptly booked a table at a Chinatown restaurant to mark the occasion. I was conflicted because, after all, the last vestige of the paper that had given me my start was gone. It was to be a low-key event but as the guest list swelled, the wine flowed and the toasts grew louder, it turned into quite a night.

A group at a neighbouring table seemed to be taking great interest in proceedings.

'What are you celebrating?' asked a woman with the group. She was seated next to a man with a vaguely familiar face.

'We all work at *The Sunday Age*,' I explained. 'And today our direct competitor went out of business. It's one part celebration, one part wake.'

'Well done,' she said before passing on the news to her fellow diners, some of whom turned to us with raised glasses.

Then it came to me—the man at her side was Jim Leslie, a former chairman of Qantas and the man who was now heading up Australian Independent Newspapers, the Melbourne-based group bidding for Fairfax against Canadian Conrad Black (and at that stage Kerry Packer) and Irishman Tony O'Reilly.

AIN would consistently be referred to as the Melbourne Club bid, because key players had links to that famous Collins Street bastion of conservatism. As it turned out, it was broader based than that, but Bob Hawke and Paul Keating still despised them. If they were going to win control of Fairfax or, at least, *The Age*, they would be coming from a long way back.

The ongoing war for control of Fairfax and the strictures imposed on us by receivership would provide the backdrop against which the year would be played out. We had no idea who would win, but the demise of *The Sunday Herald* at least meant we would almost certainly still be around when new owners took over.

While at least one Fairfax editor was closely identifying himself with one of the bids, Harris and I stayed well out of the process. My preference was for a Melbourne-based owner but, given my history with Jeff Kennett, perhaps the worst outcome for me would be blueblood conservatives. So I watched from afar.

Most interest centred on whether Kerry Packer would succeed. His partnership with the Canadian media tycoon Conrad Black was very much a pragmatic exercise.

Years later Max Hastings, the respected editor of the UK's *Daily Telegraph* for a decade under Black, recounted to me over dinner in London the fateful meeting between his boss and Packer where the deal was done.

Black, accompanied by Hastings and his fellow Canadian, lawyer Dan Colson, had gone to Packer's suite at the Savoy Hotel where the mogul and his son James awaited them. Hastings would later observe in his 2002 memoir, *Editor*, that James was 'a lanky youth whose head appeared to have undergone some bizarre longitudinal experience in a cider press and who sat mute throughout the proceedings.'

As Packer and Black talked through the prospect of a joint bid for Fairfax, waiters moved about the Savoy suite, making a terrible mess of the simplest tasks. Finally, Packer could take it no more, unleashing on each of them the full fury of his appalling temper. As Hastings recalled, Packer barked: 'Put the fucking food down there, put the fucking bottles here and get your useless fucking asses out of here.'

Retelling this story over dinner in London in the northern summer of 1993, Hastings couldn't help but chuckle. But one wonders what was running through the minds of Black and his men as they contemplated working with this raging bull of a man. Finally, Hastings recalled, Packer summarised what he saw as the key elements of their partnership.

According to Hastings in both our conversation and later his book, Packer said:

Right, Conrad. We're all agreed then. I'll take a back seat on this one. You'll lead the band. I'll fix Canberra. I'll deal with the government. I'll square the banks. All I want out of this one is to see certain people's heads so deep in the shit that the tops of their heads will only be visible through a powerful microscope.

It is such an appalling assessment on so many levels it is difficult to know where to begin. Certainly it would have done nothing to assuage the view of both Black and Colson that Australia was some sort of banana republic where deals were done based on political patronage and our most successful businessmen were motivated by a deep-seated desire for revenge. Clearly there were scores to be settled at Fairfax and Packer couldn't wait for his chance to get even.

As it turned out, Packer would eventually be blocked from participating in the bid and Black would go it alone, winning the right to be the majority shareholder in Fairfax, but having his holding capped at 15 per cent under foreign ownership rules.

When Black's successful bid for Fairfax was officially announced, it naturally put the management and staff of the company into a spin. They were right to be nervous. Black's first full year at Spencer Street was one of great tumult. Editors and senior managers came and went, and the new majority shareholder launched a determined bid to smash the culture of Fairfax.

Although Packer had been forced to drop out of the Tourang syndicate that eventually won the Fairfax prize, there seemed little doubt that his low opinion of the company and its journalists had poisoned Black as well.

Pity that. Putting aside his grandiloquence, I always felt that Black had the makings of a first-rate proprietor, prepared to invest in his products and plant, back his editors, and stand up to those only too willing to attack *The Age* and *The Sunday Age*. I even came to like his turn of phrase, seen as pompous by most, but vastly entertaining when experienced first-hand. Besides, he had done a terrific job of resuscitating *The Daily Telegraph* in the UK.

Such was the antipathy towards Black that on his first visit to Australia he had to point out that, in fact, he had neither cloven feet nor horns. Despite the assurances, many Fairfax journalists remained unconvinced throughout his relatively short tenure.

Whenever a new proprietor arrives—or, for that matter, a new managing director—editors begin to consider their mortality. In the absence of any real strategy, the quickest way for the newcomer to give the impression of vision is to remove a hapless editor or two. So it wasn't entirely surprising that both Spencer Street incumbents—Mike Smith at *The Age* and Steve Harris at *The Sunday Age*—reflected on their futures upon Black's arrival.

Harris was particularly hopeful that somehow the change of ownership would deliver him stewardship of the daily. He had lost out to his long-time rival Smith when Creighton Burns had stepped down for personal reasons in 1989. If the opportunity was to arise again, there was no way he was going to miss out a second time.

Black's relations with his Australian editors and a few other senior staff had a very rocky start when a highly sensitive memo detailing the strengths and weaknesses of incumbents and aspirants somehow found its way into the public arena. *The Australian* gleefully published extracts.

Not that Black was a meddling proprietor. One of the things I liked best about him was how little he involved himself in the business. This was due in large part to his hatred of the long flight from London and his increasing disdain for our politicians, Paul Keating chief among them.

Black left most of the headaches to his trusted lieutenant, Dan Colson, who once asked me, when discussing Keating and Kennett: 'Where do you guys come up with these fucking lunatic politicians?' I could merely offer a Gallic shrug.

Kennett was now powering his way to what would be a runaway state election victory in October 1992. Our relationship showed no signs of improving.

In the midst of all this upheaval, our daughter Susannah arrived. At 37, I was a relatively late first-time father and I doted on her accordingly. Her birth gave me an important new perspective on my professional life, which was becoming more and more complicated. Soon another difficult career choice loomed.

On a quiet Tuesday afternoon in early 1992, while I was editing in Harris' absence, my secretary took a call from an American visitor who wondered if I might be available for a chat. He was working in the media and wanted to see first-hand what an Australian newspaper looked like.

'Yes, but who the hell is he?' I asked, not unreasonably.

Moments later my secretary returned. 'His name is Henry Muller and he is the editorial director of Time Inc. worldwide.'

'I'm available,' I said.

Twenty-four hours later Muller, a charming Swiss-born American who had once edited *Time* magazine and was now overseeing all the company's titles, was sitting in the cramped editor's office at *The Sunday Age*. I had blocked out 30 minutes for him; in the end we swapped stories, opinions and outlooks for more than two hours.

He left my office with a smile and this promise: 'If you ever want to work in magazines, give me a call.' Months later the conversation would bear fruit; years later it would provide me with a lifeline at one of the lowest points of my career.

Meanwhile, Black soon made two crucial appointments at the very top of his Australian operation. South African Stephen Mulholland would be Fairfax chief executive officer while his deputy and editorial director would be former News Limited executive Michael Hoy.

Mulholland was a very strange fish, given to rage and with an almost palpable hatred of those who made his money for him: journalists. On one occasion he famously kicked out at a media throng camped outside Fairfax headquarters in Sydney. Whatever the motivation for that episode, his conduct and general demeanour played to those who feared Black was all about crushing Fairfax journalism and its practitioners.

Hoy had the people skills that Mulholland lacked but his CV, which included stints as managing editor of *The Times* and, curiously, executive editor of the *National Enquirer,* the American scandal sheet published weekly out of Florida, left him open to charges that he was ill-equipped to oversee the great Fairfax broadsheets. Indeed, one editor worked tirelessly behind his back, denigrating him to Mulholland and others.

Although Hoy sometimes focused too much on design and too little on content, he was easy to talk to and placed great faith in me as an editor. His problems began with his first major appointments, replacing editors Mike Smith at *The Age* and John Alexander at *The Sydney Morning Herald.* The moves would reverberate for years.

Smith had been a career servant of *The Age*, beginning with a cadetship as a teenager in the late 1960s. He had first come to attention in the 1970s as a standout medical reporter and then smoothly made the transition into the executive ranks. He was a laconic bloke with superb news and investigative skills.

Alexander was a very different person indeed, a great delegator and a voracious collector, of both art and talent. He had surrounded himself with expensive staff at *The Sydney Morning Herald*, much to the chagrin of *Age* executives who marvelled at his budget. He had risen to the top at the paper by taking the route I had turned down: when Beecher had failed to get me over the line, he had offered the right-hand man role to Alexander. Known simply as JA, Alexander would eventually fall short of his ambition to run Fairfax but, instead, wound up running the Packers' gambling interests. Now, however, Alexander—and Smith—appeared to be in the firing line for no other reason than Black and his team wanted their own men.

In October 1992, Smith stepped down as editor of *The Age.* The change of ownership and some personal matters conspired to take the job from him; it must have been a bitter pill for one so devoted to the paper. He was put in charge of running foreign bureaus. As he made an emotional speech in the paper's main reporters' room, the guessing games started: who would succeed Smith? Would it be Harris, the logical internal candidate, or would it be some outsider?

I was more than a disinterested observer. After all, if Harris got *The Age* there was a good chance I would get *The Sunday Age*. As the days went by without any announcement, the speculation became distracting, to say the least. Hoy apparently had a list of preferred candidates, the scuttlebutt went, and, yes, Harris was on it, but so was Kerry O'Brien. Kerry O'Brien? He was a television presenter; what the hell was he doing on the list?

Harris was eventually summoned to Sydney by Hoy. Clearly this was the meeting at which he would be anointed. But hang on a minute—if Harris was going to get the daily and I was getting the Sunday paper, surely we would both be invited up, wouldn't we? That meant either I was going to miss out on my promotion or we both were.

It was a long day, constantly interrupted by speculative phone calls and gossipmongers. Finally, around 5 p.m., Harris rang with the news.

'Are you sitting down mate?' he asked.

This didn't sound good.

He went on: 'The next editor of *The Age* is Alan Kohler.'

'What? Who?' I asked, more than a little surprised.

'Yep, Alan Kohler. Don't ask me why,' said Harris. Kohler had been a well-performed editor of *The Australian Financial Review* some years earlier but had never edited a general news publication. Most recently he had been a well-respected business commentator.

'What about you? What do you get?' I asked Harris.

'Hoy wants me to do *The Sun-Herald* in Sydney, but I've told him to stick it up his arse.'

This was turning pear-shaped, to say the least: Hoy had chosen a business editor, admittedly a very good one, to run a broad-based daily and he had chosen a Melbourne editor to run a Sydney paper he neither knew nor cared about. *The Sun-Herald* editorship was now vacant because previous incumbent, David Hickie, had taken Alexander's job editing *The Sydney Morning Herald*. Just to complete the merry-go-round, Alexander had been put in charge of *The Australian Financial Review*. If Hoy was trying to make his presence felt, he had succeeded.

There was one more obvious question to be asked of Harris: 'What does this mean for me, Steve?'

'I'm afraid it's "as you were",' said Harris.

It was true. We would be forced to contemplate an extended future together even though we realised the paper was no longer big enough for both of us.

Worse, we now had a formidable political foe. Weeks earlier Kennett had been elected Premier of Victoria and he had already sounded his battle cry. *The Sunday Age*, he had announced, was 'the *Labor Star* in drag'.

Then, in the space of two phone calls, the mix changed considerably.

'Why don't you call Chris Anderson and let him know you're looking around?' said one caller. 'He's doing some headhunting now in the media sector. He could be useful.'

I shared the news with Harris, who was particularly interested that Anderson, a former editor-in-chief of *The Sydney Morning Herald* and a future CEO of Optus, was headhunting. News Limited was apparently one of his clients, I told Harris.

I never rang Anderson but Harris did, almost immediately. He learned that News was increasingly concerned about the *Herald Sun*'s performance. Would Harris be prepared to talk about that position?

Around the same time I took another call from a senior executive at Time Inc. The then managing editor of their incredibly successful *People* magazine was coming to Sydney and would like to meet me.

I flew to Sydney and on a hot early summer's night listened as Landon Jones, veteran editor of *People*, laid out an almost irresistible offer to move to *Who Weekly*, the fledgling news-celebrity magazine based on *People*, to replace founding editor, Jake Young, a towering American who would soon be taking over the editorship of *Time*'s Australian edition before he eventually returned to New York.

I wrestled with the offer for weeks. Even though I was tremendously impressed with Time Inc. and its most senior people and I loved *Who* for its sassy mix of news and celebrity, it wasn't the sort of journalism I necessarily wanted to spend a career on. How would I face all those people I had brought to *The Sunday Age* if I up and bolted? Besides, I loved the paper.

My deliberations were fraught but were helped tremendously when weeks later Harris announced he was leaving *The Sunday Age* to become editor-in-chief of HWT, a plum role by any measure. The news reverberated at both ends of town because Fairfax was losing a well-performed servant and News was enlisting an outsider, moreover, one who had taken potshots at *Herald Sun* editor Piers Akerman.

That only left one question: who would succeed Harris at *The Sunday Age*? After another week of speculation and rumour and one inscrutable phone call from Hoy—'What do you think of Kennett?' he asked—I was given the job.

It was December 1992 and I had already spent more than three years at *The Sunday Age*. I was determined to make it the best newspaper in Australia.

13

TV or not TV?

With *The Sunday Age* well established, I soon found myself caught up in a significant subplot in my professional life. As a young reporter I had had occasional approaches from television stations to consider switching from print to electronic but I had always resisted. This was partly due to my general cynicism about the medium and because I believed newspapers were still the crucible of great and important journalism. Besides, they had treated me well. But a phone call in April 1991 began a series of extraordinary events that almost saw me switch.

It came from the Channel Seven news director in Melbourne, David Broadbent, a former *Age* reporter who had crossed over to television in the mid-1980s after a distinguished print career.

He and I had enjoyed many battles as political reporters on rival newspapers in Melbourne and had become firm friends along the way.

'Scoop, can you talk?' he asked when he rang me on deadline on a Saturday night at *The Sunday Age*, just weeks after the demise of *The Sunday Herald*. Broadbent had nicknamed me 'Scoop' after a particularly good run of exclusives during the days when we had competed head-to-head; I called him 'Smokey' because of his propensity to disappear for days, only to return with his own exclusive. In the parlance of the industry, such absences were known as 'working on a smokey'.

'That depends on what you want to talk about,' I said. As always, Steve Harris was sitting at my left elbow as we worked our way through the first edition.

'I want you to host a new current affairs show,' Broadbent said with a chuckle.

'I'd better call you back,' I said.

Later that night he sketched out his plan: the Seven network wanted to take on Nine's *60 Minutes* with its own weekly current affairs hour and Broadbent had told his bosses I was the natural host of the program.

'Ri—ight,' I said, flagging my incredulity by drawing out the word as if it were a sentence. 'David, I've never been in front of a camera in my life.'

This wasn't a problem for Broadbent, who had landed his job at Nine without so much as a screen test.

'Television needs a few rough heads,' the legendary news director John Sorell had told Broadbent when hiring him.

I was delighted by David's support and his confidence but even he acknowledged there would need to be at least a screen test.

'Can you come in to the studio on Monday?' he asked. 'We can get you to read the news or something.'

There was one other problem—I already had a perfectly good job and believed I was on track to become editor.

'That's all right,' said David. 'You'll be able to do both. Edit the paper Tuesday to Saturday and front the show on Sunday nights.'

What could be lost by testing? I dropped in to Seven's Dorcas Street studios the following Monday and was promptly led into the studio where the 6 p.m. news bulletin was produced each day.

'Just read what's on the autocue,' said Broadbent, as I sat at the newsreader's desk, watched by the news director and a second man,

Peter Charley, who, I was told, was the putative producer of the new show.

On Broadbent's count the autocue started and two cameramen filmed proceedings. Charley watched silently throughout. I was soon in difficulties, tripping over words written for the previous night's bulletin—it's always preferable to write your own scripts and almost impossible to read someone else's perfectly first up—as the autocue rolled on remorselessly. I had never used one of the wretched things in my life.

'This autocue is going too fast,' I explained with embarrassment.

'Ah, it's actually following you,' Broadbent explained, with a chuckle. 'You might want to slow things down a bit.'

Five minutes later it was over. I had no doubt it was the worst screen test ever attempted; indeed, I actually apologised to Broadbent.

Moments later Broadbent, Charley and I crammed into a tiny booth as an editor ran the tape. 'Oh, God!,' I thought, 'I look like a startled rabbit.' How much was it going to cost me to have this thing destroyed?

As I squirmed, Charley, who still hadn't broken his silence, approached the small screen and, literally, put his large nose up against it. Bent over, so that his upper body was at an almost 45-degree angle to his legs, and with hands resting on his hips, he calmly watched the train wreck unfold. Then, as I grabbed Broadbent's arm and suggested lunch, Charley, without shifting position, said: 'Bruce, you have an aura.'

'Pardon?' I said.

'You have an aura,' Charley repeated.

'He's having a lend of me,' I thought. I looked to Broadbent, expecting him to expose the joke. His eyes widened and he spread his fingers in a 'I-told-you-so' kind of way. What was going on here exactly?

'Do you have a deal with any network?' Charley, now looking directly at me, asked.

Negotiating was never my strong point, so I simply blurted out: 'Why would I have a deal with a television network? They don't even know I exist.'

'Oh, they will once they get wind of this,' Charley said. It was unclear whether he was talking about the show or the screen test. Surely it was the show? Charley went on: 'I'd like to put you on a deal. We'll pay you a monthly retainer for the rest of the year not to sign with any other network, okay?'

'And what would I have to do for this money?' I asked.

'Nothing,' said Charley.

I was warming to television.

Deep down, I had no real expectations, but in mid-year the Seven program started gaining some momentum. First I was flown to Sydney to shoot a pilot of the show at a nondescript 'secret' location. For a full day, I read to camera, conducted interviews with real and imagined subjects—the tearful mother of a premature baby, a veteran jazz musician and a producer posing as a dodgy politician—while all the while crew darted here and there.

This was turned into a 15-minute pilot with the working title *Prime Time*. When it was screened for me, I was surprised at how professional I had become. 'My God,' I thought, 'this could actually happen.'

There was already an issue: the early promise of being able to do both *The Sunday Age* and the television show had evaporated. Seven had decided that, instead of taking on *60 Minutes*, they would prefer to take on *A Current Affair*. In other words, I would now be hosting a nightly current affairs program, not a weekly. As mild panic slowly crept in—why the hell would I want to be a current affairs host when I could have the dignified role of a newspaper editor?—I was flown to Sydney to meet the network boss, Bob Campbell.

To my astonishment, Campbell produced a specimen contract with a fat salary and benefits and a detailed job description: as host of a new current affairs program I would have to be able to report from the field, conduct celebrity interviews with the likes of Elton John and moderate a studio debate.

'Think you could do all that, Bruce?' asked Campbell.

'Don't see why not,' I replied.

'Then you're our man,' said Campbell. There was one caveat: Seven had signed former *60 Minutes* executive producer Gerald Stone to oversee the new show and he wouldn't be back in Australia for six to eight weeks. He had to sign off on my hiring; until he did, we would keep all our options open.

When Stone returned to Australia from a stint in the United States I was invited to a Sunday night dinner in Sydney where, presumably, Gerald would size me up.

The evening began well enough. 'You remind me of a young Ray,' said Stone, as we sipped our drinks in the bar of the Sebel Hotel.

'Ray? Who's Ray?' I asked.

'There's only one Ray,' said Stone. 'Ray Martin, of course.'

Of course. Former ABC correspondent Martin was a household name and a star of commercial television through his work on *60 Minutes* and his successful hosting of a daily midday talk show on Nine.

After swapping Martin stories and Willesee stories and Kerry Packer stories—the American-born newsman had enjoyed a close working relationship with the Channel Nine boss who would be none-too-pleased by his defection to Seven—we headed for dinner, but not before this from Stone: 'I've seen your tapes, Bruce, and I'm very excited. Together we are going to change the current affairs landscape of this country.'

Waiting for us at the Italian eatery were Stone's wife, and Peter Charley and his wife. Stone didn't drink, but Peter and I more than made up for that over the next three hours. If I had begun the evening conflicted, with each drink I became more convinced that television was for me. After all, there would be glamour, fame and wealth. I'd drink to that.

After three hours of war stories, gossip and the occasional diversion into the merits of certain stories, Stone rose to take his leave.

'It's been great to finally meet you, Bruce,' said a very sober Stone. 'And I'm very much looking forward to working with you.'

'Me too,' I stammered through an alcoholic fog, not helped by an incredible weariness brought on by my early morning finish at *The Sunday Age*, 600 kilometres away.

'In the next week or two we should do another pilot to clean up a few things. It's going to be very exciting.' And with that, Gerald Stone, a famed television newsman on not one but two continents, disappeared into the night. I found myself thinking, if I'm going to put my television career into the hands of any single individual, then this was a man I could trust.

Days, then weeks went by and I didn't hear from Stone. This was curious as it was now November and the show was due to launch in January. More importantly, Janne and I were expecting our first child in December. We were about to change from a couple into a family. Where would we be spending Christmas, much less 1992?

Then I spied a television magazine in a city newsagent boasting an exclusive: 'Revealed—Seven's new current affairs secret weapon'. 'Oh dear,' I thought, 'the jig is up. I'm going to be outed in the pages of *TV Week*. Fairfax won't be happy.' I quickly flipped through the pages of the weekly and there it was, Seven's new current affairs host and his show: Stan Grant and *Real Life*. Huh? What about Bruce Guthrie and *Prime Time*? And here was Gerald Stone singing the praises of Grant, an Aboriginal reporter who had first come to attention on SBS. Now he was going to host a nightly current affairs show on Seven. What gives?

I laughed out loud then and there, right in the newsagent. Was I angry? No, I was overcome with relief. Stone had promised everything and delivered nothing and I couldn't care less. Not only had I not heard from him, despite his promise that we would remake the landscape of current affairs in Australia, I've *never* heard from him.

In reality, Janne and I couldn't have cared less. For on 28 December we celebrated the birth of our daughter Susannah. Frankly, I'm not sure I would have taken the Seven job even if it had been eventually offered.

And I was to have another shot at television anyway. *Real Life* lasted only two years, replaced in 1994 by the state-based *Today Tonight*. In late 1993 Channel Seven executives in Melbourne, anxious to find a host for the Victorian edition of *Today Tonight*, had pulled out my original audition tape.

I was invited to Melbourne's Athenaeum Club where, over drinks in a wood-panelled room, I was offered the hosting job.

'I know we had a go at you a couple of years ago,' said station boss Brian Mellon. 'But we stuffed it up.'

'It did end badly,' I said.

'Yeah, sorry about that,' said Mellon. 'Anyway, I've had another look at your tape and I've got to say you really rattle my cage.'

Television executives, I decided, talked in soundbites. '*Real Life* ended up being pretty crappy, Brian,' I said. 'Is this going to be any different?'

'Definitely,' said Mellon. 'This is going to be serious current affairs. The bloke who's going to produce it has won Walkley Awards and everything.'

'Listen, I'll give it some thought,' I said. 'I'll come back to you tomorrow, okay?' I was being polite.

'Tomorrow? Bewdy,' said Mellon.

With that, I rose from my leather-upholstered armchair, downed my tumbler of Scotch and headed for the door. As I made my way down the Athenaeum's graceful staircase, Mellon came after me.

'Bruce, Bruce,' he whispered urgently. 'There's just one thing: you wouldn't be wearing those glasses on camera, would you?'

Did someone say serious journalism? The next morning I politely declined the offer.

14

Not your everyday newspaper

One of the first well-wishers to call on my first official morning in the chair as editor of *The Sunday Age* was former prime minister Bob Hawke. At least, I thought he was calling to wish me well.

It was December 1992 and I greeted Hawke warmly: 'Good morning, Bob.' No doubt he was calling to sing my praises, having learned of my promotion. 'What's up?' I asked cheerfully.

'What the fuck are you cunts doing down there?' asked Australia's longest-serving Labor prime minister in a tone he might have adopted at the height of his powers when dressing down, say, an errant backbencher.

'Pardon?' I enquired, more than a little taken aback. I had experienced his colourful language before, but this was a new low even for him.

'I said, what the fuck are you cunts doing down there?'

Hawke, who contributed a regular column to *The Sunday Age*, complained that his copy had been changed the previous Sunday and he wasn't happy. The changes were negligible, and as I had been weighing up the value of keeping him in the paper anyway, the phone call pretty much decided it then and there. Weeks later we parted company, along with another ex–prime minister, Malcolm

Fraser, who had also been contributing a regular column. Two prime ministers gone within weeks of each other—not even Sir John Kerr could boast that.

There were other considerations though. As I moved into the editor's chair I felt we needed to set the agenda more. What was the point of editing a paper like this without bringing about change?

We had critical mass, selling about 170 000 copies every Sunday, and we were able to boast that we were the only one of the three papers launched on 20 August 1989 to survive in its original form: *The Sunday Herald* was gone and *The Sunday Sun* was now the *Sunday Herald Sun*, a hybrid of the serious broadsheet and the populist tabloid.

In early January 1993, like so many Saturday afternoons before, I took a 4.30 p.m. phone call from our police roundsman reporting in on the usual mayhem in the suburbs—a car accident here, a milk bar hold-up there. And, as had happened far too often in summers past, a small child had drowned in a backyard swimming pool.

With my daughter having just celebrated her first birthday, the news affected me more than perhaps it had in the past. Victorian law did not require the fencing of backyard pools or spas and there was no doubt in my mind it should. That and my new status at the paper convinced me to mount our first serious campaign: we would work to change the law.

Our campaign was run through February and we pressed the new Kennett government for change by the next summer. Reporter Denise Ryan was stoic when assigned the story, which would have her talk to child safety experts, compare laws in other states, and track down the parents of 10 children who had died in Victorian pools to tell their stories. No journalist likes intrusions on grief but if this assignment succeeded, we could bring about real change and perhaps save lives.

Ryan turned the story around in three weeks, and on 7 February we devoted a large chunk of page one to her heartbreaking stories

126

of young lives lost and the emotional toll it had taken on shattered parents. Most of the parents we sought out agreed to participate and to a man and woman they supported change in the law.

On page one we ran headshots of nine children under a pointedly emotional headline that read, 'Wasted lives: the faces of children who have died in backyard pools and spas'. This wasn't normal territory for broadsheets, which tend to err on the side of intellectualism rather than emotion. That is less true today than, say, a generation ago, but generally speaking broadsheets think and tabloids feel. At *The Sunday Age* I was trying to create a paper that would do both because, frankly, the daily *Age* was way down on emotional intelligence, leaving vast numbers of stories and issues for us at week's end.

The effect of Ryan's story was immediate and profound. But not all of it was welcome. While the government did move on the law, eventually requiring perimeter fencing around pools and spas, some in the paper's marketing department thought the campaign ill advised.

'If you think this sort of stuff is going to sell Sunday newspapers you've got rocks in your head,' said a senior marketing manager on the Tuesday after publication. 'It's a definite turn-off.'

Eight weeks into what I hoped would be a bold new era of hard-hitting journalism, it was not what I wanted to hear and I told the marketing man what I thought of his opinions. Bob Hawke would have been proud of me.

There is often tension between the editorial department and the sales and marketing floors and for the most part it's contained. But there will inevitably be blow-ups over approach and tone. Even though expensive research is increasingly part of an editor's life, often you can only go with your gut. I had no doubt that the more we created journalism that couldn't be ignored, the better our chances of improving our sales trajectory. I still believed it 15 years later when explaining my *Herald Sun* philosophy to Rupert Murdoch.

To that end, I went in search of talent. We had already bolstered our strong reporting ranks with the addition of *Herald Sun* crime reporter John Silvester and in time went after Andrew Rule, his co-writer on a wildly successful series of books based on the letters from jail of Mark 'Chopper' Read. Rule had been producing a breakfast radio show in Melbourne and while he was very good and successful at it, his vast reporting and writing talents were largely going to waste. Both Silvester and his sometime writing partner were eminently capable of delivering the sort of story that would move papers at the newsstand. Decades later they would team up to deliver the books on which the *Underbelly* television series was based.

I also lured *The Age*'s Sports editor, Garry Linnell, from the daily, installing him as the paper's Features editor. Also a gifted reporter and writer, he would go on to edit *The Bulletin* and later Sydney's *Daily Telegraph*, with a turbulent stint as the Nine network's news and current affairs chief in between. In another significant move I appointed national political writer Michael Gordon deputy editor—we had started as cadets together the same year but at rival papers—replacing him with long-time Canberra observer Amanda Buckley.

With the likes of Caroline Wilson, future Walkley Award winners Paul Robinson and Paul Daley and future *Sunday Age* editors Gay Alcorn and Peter Fray, I was convinced we had more talent on our one-day-a-week paper than most dailies had in much bigger newsrooms. Much of the time my biggest challenge was trying to hang on to them as predatory publications attempted to lure them away.

Some of the predators were close to home. From his new post as editor-in-chief of HWT, Steve Harris was picking off key *Age* staff. While many weren't marquee names, at least one was: Ron Tandberg, the extremely gifted cartoonist and multiple Walkley Award winner who alone was reason enough to buy the paper each day. Harris lured Tandberg to Flinders Street with an audacious offer. It was a bitter blow for Spencer Street, especially as Kohler had already lost political editor and *Age* stalwart Michelle Grattan, who had accepted Kerry Stokes' offer of the editorship of *The Canberra Times*, becoming the first woman in Australia to edit a major daily.

Rightly or wrongly, the departures from *The Age* of two marquee names—Grattan and Tandberg—were seen by many as a repudiation of Black's ownership and Kohler's editorship. So much so that *The Age* felt moved to editorialise on Tandberg's shock exit:

> Ron Tandberg has gone to the *Herald Sun* and will be syndicated in other Australian papers owned by Rupert Murdoch. We hope that he will enjoy the same freedoms working for the Murdoch organization that he enjoyed here at *The Age* ... All things change, and so do newspapers.

It was a gentle dig at Murdoch's reputation for intervention, but the editorial was also, in some ways, a recognition of the turbulent times *The Age* had endured since the Black takeover. Perhaps it was also a line in the sand, a message to readers that their cries had been heard and the drift away from core values would be halted.

Relatively soon, both Grattan and Tandberg would return to the paper under Kohler's editorship but, in the short term, their departures contributed to a growing disquiet, a sense that the venerable broadsheet was unravelling. Harris and many others with scores to settle were happy to fan the flames.

Defections weren't the only problems at *The Age*. The change of ownership and editorship had altered the paper significantly; it had undeniably moved to the right away from its small 'l' liberal traditions and its forward news pages were increasingly filled with business stories, not surprising given Kohler's pedigree. This, coupled with a certain resistance to change common among *Age* staff, meant it was becoming an unhappy ship. When a redundancy offer was circulated, many long-serving staff took it.

All this cast *The Sunday Age* in a new light, at least internally. In little more than three years we had gone from bastard child to keeper of the flame. We were still very much a small 'l' liberal paper—despite the efforts of conservatives to paint us as rabidly left-wing—and despite our own occasional staff loss and continuing space limitations, a committed and happy group. Moreover, when considering the building blocks of any good publication—people, ideas, tone, pace, mix, look and, of course, content—*The Sunday Age* was well placed to really take off as a newspaper. But there's always another element needed too—good fortune.

Whenever Napoleon was presented with the name of a potential new general one of the first questions he would ask was, 'Yes, but is he *lucky*?' It can be the same with editors. Some have stories that fall their way, others don't. Paul Keating brought me a stroke of luck when he announced a March election—polls are always good for sales, particularly Sunday sales, because of their Saturday scheduling. This one delivered all that and more.

It was supposed to be the election the coalition couldn't lose, but Liberal leader John Hewson started talking in a sometimes-confused way about a goods and services tax and all bets were off. The campaign was lively as Keating, a wildly unpopular Treasurer whose voter appeal as Hawke's successor had never been tested at the ballot box, made inroads on the Opposition.

If the campaign was surprising, election night was wholly unpredictable. A lot of reputations suffered, none more so than that of the *Sunday Herald Sun* editor, Ian Moore. 'Cookie', as he was known, was a larger-than-life character whose favourite party trick was to remove his glass eye and drop it in your drink when you weren't looking. He was a long-time servant of News Limited who had moved down from Sydney to take the reins at the Sunday tabloid.

Election night coverage offers up rare and real challenges for any serious newspaper and particularly its editors. We planned ours with almost military precision, identifying all possible angles and placing reporters and photographers accordingly. I even remember doing provisional page layouts on the eve of the election—the trick is to prepare but also be bold enough on the night to switch direction if that's needed. We did at least five different page one treatments on election night as, first, Hewson looked likely to win, and then Keating surged to take the 'sweetest' victory of all. No doubt Moore and his team were chopping and changing just as much at the other end of town, but all anyone would remember—then and now—was the *Sunday Herald Sun*'s first edition.

In a blunder that would recall the *Chicago Tribune*'s infamous 'Dewey Defeats Truman' headline in the 1948 American presidential election, Moore sent his first edition with the splash head: 'Hewson in a photo finish'. Years later I would get to know Ian during a stint at *The Australian* and the subject inevitably came up. He believed the headline was at worst ambiguous and I can understand why he might think that. But unfortunately others didn't see it that way. As a Keating win became more and more certain late in the night, television panellists and pundits delighted in holding up Moore's front page. It must have been agony for him.

Days later I had T-shirts printed up that reproduced our page one—'How sweet it is'—and bought a stack of sweatshirts that someone else had printed bearing the *Sunday Herald Sun*'s infamous first edition front. Weeks after the election I found an excuse to call Steve Harris, now officially Moore's boss at Flinders Street. 'Not a good career move,' was all he would say about Moore's misadventures. Sure enough, not long after, Ian was replaced.

Having covered the election comprehensively and executed our pool safety campaign extremely effectively, we set ourselves another challenge: to change laws so that Australians who travelled abroad for the purposes of child sex could be prosecuted locally.

Veteran newsman Paul Robinson, recruited from *The Age*'s investigative team, travelled to Cambodia, which was attracting growing numbers of foreign paedophiles, many of them Australians, preying on poverty-stricken children forced into prostitution. Robinson's two-part series not only led to changes in federal law, it delivered *The Sunday Age* its first Walkley Award, the 1993 gong for best investigative journalism.

Newspaper campaigns such as these rarely sell extra copies but, if properly executed, they can certainly build a brand. But an editor has to be careful to pick a fight that is both winnable and in step with readers' expectations and aspirations. Probably the most successful newspaper campaign in Australia was Harry Gordon's 'Declare War on 1034', *The Sun's* stunningly successful assault in 1970 on Victoria's appalling annual road toll. It led to new seat-belt legislation, improved car safety, a review of speed limits—and a massive reduction in the number of people killed. Forty years on, the state's road toll is one-third of what it was.

Such campaigns are unlikely to attract too much opposition, for no-one is going to oppose a reduction in the road toll. Others are more inflammatory: *The Sunday Age* surprised many in 2005 when it launched a 'Bring Hicks Home' campaign, designed to repatriate accused terrorist David Hicks to Australia. It was far from the safe bet campaigns for road safety or pool fencing proved to be; after all, even if the paper was seen to win—Hicks was eventually returned to Australia in 2007—some readers would have seen it as a betrayal of their values.

The Sunday Age was now clearly a paper to be reckoned with, although some continued to have their doubts. As Kennett threw his weight around politically, shutting down schools, levying special taxes to pay off debt, and embarking on privatisation programs he had concealed during his election campaign, we voiced concern and opposition. We weren't alone in this. The daily *Age* was an occasional dissenting voice too.

Kennett, I soon learned, viewed with the utmost suspicion anything but outright support. He certainly had it at the *Herald*

Sun, which had advocated his election in the strongest terms and was now steadfastly behind him on almost everything he did. Soon Kennett, emboldened by the backing of Flinders Street and others, was making a great show of his distaste for the media in general and *The Age*, *The Sunday Age* and the ABC in particular.

In his inimitable style, Kennett worked the phones, complaining to senior Fairfax management about me and the paper. Fairfax editorial director Michael Hoy ran a lot of interference for me, convincing many on the Fairfax board that it was little more than the overheated rhetoric that often arises in politics. I was enormously grateful to him for backing me but a general lack of board understanding and support was a constant during these years. In its best years, *The Age* held governments and politicians accountable; during the turbulent 1990s, when the share register became dangerously volatile, Kennett somehow reversed that relationship.

The Kennett 'problem' came up again and again and was often discussed at board level, sometimes in my presence. On one occasion, while addressing the board on the progress of *The Sunday Age*—for their sins Fairfax editors got to do this once or twice a year—I was surprised when several knights of the realm, Sir Zelman Cowen, Sir Laurence Street and Sir Roderick Carnegie, all rounded on me asking why I 'couldn't get on with Jeffrey'.

'I'm not sure he wants to get on with us,' I ventured in reply. 'I've written to him suggesting we get together to air any grievances but he's not interested.'

'It's a great pity,' said Sir Laurence. 'We recently had dinner with him and [his wife] Felicity at Michael Hoy's house and he really was terrific company. We finished up around the piano singing songs in the early hours of the morning.'

Then, unexpectedly, the conference phone crackled into life. It was Conrad Black, phoning in from London. He had heard the exchange and my summary of the paper's performance and wanted to express his point of view.

'Gentlemen, gentlemen,' said Black in a disembodied voice weary from either lack of sleep or the tiresome business of Fairfax. 'May I remind you that we are not in the business of currying favour with politicians? Mr Guthrie is doing a first-rate job at *The Sunday Age*. I suggest we let him get on with it.'

Having addressed Fairfax boards more times than I care to remember, it was the one moment in such forums that I look back on fondly, almost reverently. Here was a proprietor speaking up for his editor. Conrad Black would later be jailed in Florida for fraud and obstruction of justice. No matter. If someone had asked me at that moment in the Fairfax boardroom I would have happily served as a character witness.

15

The poisoned chalice

As sales of *The Sunday Age* continued to climb and losses came down in almost equal measure, the Fairfax hierarchy were delighted. Michael Hoy recounted that on a visit to Canberra National Party leader Tim Fischer remarked that '*The Sunday Age* is the jewel in the Fairfax crown'. The comment soon found its way into a presentation delivered whenever I was asked to speak on the paper's fortunes.

We were suddenly hot. The ABC even wanted to do a television series about us. Cliff Green, the award-winning scriptwriter of *Picnic at Hanging Rock*, drove the project, calling it *Mercury*. It starred Geoffrey Rush as the campaigning editor of a Sunday newspaper forever at war with the premier of his state. Rush was then largely unknown but on the verge of major film stardom, thanks to the just-completed *Shine* for which he would win a Best Actor Oscar.

And if any further confirmation of our burgeoning reputation was needed it came with John Alexander's return to *The Sydney Morning Herald* and an extraordinary offer he made me weeks later.

While Alexander's move to *The Australian Financial Review* had energised that paper, his replacement at *The Sydney Morning Herald*, David Hickie, was seen to be faltering after two years in the job.

The story doing the rounds at Fairfax at the time was that Stephen Mulholland had bumped into Kerry Packer in the Sydney suburb of Paddington one Saturday morning only to have the billionaire turn on him.

'You've got to bring that little cunt Alexander back to the *Herald*,' Packer was reputed to have told Mulholland, adding: 'It's going down the toilet.'

Given that Packer owned a sizeable chunk of Fairfax and had strong support at board level, he was not a man to be ignored. Within weeks Alexander was back in his old job and Hickie had left the company, destined for success as a publisher of independent magazines.

Knowing that he had the whip hand, Alexander negotiated to keep both jobs—*The Australian Financial Review* and *The Sydney Morning Herald*—and, it was said, the two paypackets that went with them. Then he called me.

'Bruce, I'm ringing to offer you the editorship of *The Sydney Morning Herald*,' said Alexander matter-of-factly. It was extremely flattering, so why was I overcome with dread?

The answers lay in my personal life. Susannah was approaching her third birthday and Scott had just been born. I loved my work but saw my family as my first priority. Weekly publications allowed you a life outside journalism, daily papers didn't.

I was once offered some advice, ironically by Jeff Kennett, when he was a young and brash Victorian Opposition leader in the mid-1980s and I was a state political reporter. I had spent a day following Kennett as he went about the business of opposition. It included a stop-off at his son's primary school and Jeff couldn't remember which classroom his son was in. He had had to ask a passing teacher.

I questioned him about this when he returned to his chauffer-driven car and he said something that often came back to me during the long nights at an editing terminal or in a newsroom.

'Whatever happens, Bruce,' he said with a wisdom that belied his youth and his image, 'don't let your kids become little heads on pillows.'

For many newspaper executives that's exactly what they become. In one egregious example, I had an editor once confess to me that he had become so estranged from his family that he hadn't been invited to his own son's twenty-first birthday party. In another, the editor of a major metro daily admitted to me he had begun to have serious doubts about his role when he kissed his daughter goodbye one Monday morning only to have her say: 'See you Saturday, Daddy.'

Others, who had worked before the days of remote computer terminals that at least allowed you to be in your own home while working late at night, told heartbreaking stories of family dislocation. One used to wake his infant son at 2 a.m. just so he could play with him.

But could I really turn down the editorship of *The Sydney Morning Herald* a second time?

Alexander and I talked it back and forth over several days. He was, by turns, flattering and challenging. 'You're the best packager of news in Australia,' he said during one telephone call, only to add in another, 'but you're editing in a backwater ... the only papers that matter are *The Herald* and *The Age*.'

In the end, I turned down the offer, mainly for personal reasons but also because I had no wish to return to being someone else's number two. Any doubts that I had made the wrong decision evaporated when I rang Alexander.

'John,' I said. 'I'm going to have to say "no" because at this point in my life I just can't leave Melbourne. We've got a new baby and I've got an ailing mother.'

'Let me get this straight,' said an exasperated Alexander. 'You're turning down the editorship of *The Sydney Morning Herald* because of "personal reasons"?' He spat out the words.

'Yes, John,' I said, my back now well and truly up. 'That's exactly what I'm saying. Besides, *The Sunday Age* might be a backwater, but it's *my* backwater.'

Alexander was a man used to getting his way; I'm sure my refusal harmed our relationship in the long term.

During the week-long discussions I had gone to Fairfax editorial director Michael Hoy for his advice on whether I should take *The Sydney Morning Herald* editorship. Incredibly, the man responsible for the fortunes of all Fairfax papers knew nothing about Alexander's approach. With Packer in his corner, Alexander felt the normal hierarchies didn't apply to him.

With that difficult career decision behind me, I looked forward to the paper's fifth birthday. The anniversary edition was an immensely satisfying moment. Wherever my career might take me in the future, no publication would have as much of me in it as did *The Sunday Age*. To get to this point I had turned down three editorships and a nightly current affairs show. It had been worth it. We were now averaging 180 000 sales per week and had even recorded a couple of 200 000-plus sales. We were a committed and highly energetic bunch, proud of what we had achieved and anxious to make a mark.

Around this time I was invited to dine with Fairfax CEO Stephen Mulholland in Melbourne. Assuming Alan Kohler would also be invited, I mentioned it to him on the morning of the dinner. To my surprise, Kohler knew nothing about it. 'Maybe they're going to offer you my job, mate,' he said, with only half a chuckle.

Joined by Stuart Simson, the managing director of the Melbourne arm of Fairfax, and Hoy, it quickly became obvious to me at dinner that, although Kohler was joking about a possible job offer, it wasn't entirely out of the question. Mulholland bore into me, asking deliberately provocative questions, about Kennett, *The Age* and newspapers in general. It became obvious he was testing me; this was a job interview, and there was little doubt what the job was. In his customary way, Mulholland brought the evening to an abrupt end—he suffered from a chronically bad back and hated sitting for long periods.

I remember Mulholland most for his constant mantra: we want commercially minded editors at Fairfax. For me it ushered in a sometimes-uncomfortable era at the company and its papers; previously journalism was the sole focus of editors and commercial responsibility extended only to staying within budget. Mulholland appeared to be talking about something different entirely, where editors were drivers of profits first and journalism second. Simson continued the theme on the way home that night, warning me in a gentle way that 'you'll be judged as much on your budget performance as your editorial performance.' It was a line in the sand, to be sure.

Weeks later I was formally offered the editorship of *The Age* about 30 000 feet above the Murray River border towns of Albury–Wodonga. The offer came from my travelling companion, Stuart Simson, but he spoke almost in a whisper because the incumbent, Kohler, was sitting in the business–class seat directly in front of me on the same flight.

Not that Kohler would have minded all that much because, under the Simson plan, he was going to get a promotion. Simson was hoping to put together what he called 'a dream team': if I said 'yes', I would be editor of the paper, pulling it together on a day-to-day basis, and Kohler would be given the title of editor-in-chief, working the boardrooms of Melbourne and beyond. It was the same working relationship I would have had if I had accepted Alexander's offer to go to Sydney. Put simply, I would get to do all the work, while the other bloke would get all the glory.

I didn't blame Simson for trying. The plan made a lot of sense: for a start, Alan had a better relationship with Kennett than I ever would; he would relate much better to the big end of town than me; and I liked him a lot. I had no doubt we would get on. Indeed, if I hadn't promised myself I would never be a number two again, I might have gone for it. In the end, I couldn't bring myself to do it.

For the time being, we all went back to doing what we had been doing before. To the best of my knowledge Kohler never knew of the plan; certainly he wasn't aware of it at the time. I have no doubt he would have embraced it warmly though. Just weeks away from celebrating the third anniversary of his appointment, he was now doing the job hard and his relationship with his deputy, Michael Gawenda, was fracturing.

After weathering the inevitable ructions brought on by the ownership change that had ushered him in, and then withstanding staff defections—Michelle Grattan and Ron Tandberg were now back 'home'—Kohler was still fighting flagging circulation and mutinous staff.

Word had reached me at *The Sunday Age* which, after all, was just a few steps away from *The Age* across a narrow corridor, that a number of very senior staff were contemplating going to Kohler or perhaps Hoy and expressing a lack of confidence in the direction of the paper. With sales of the Monday to Friday paper hovering around the 190 000 mark, despite a hefty subscription discount, there was cause for alarm; *The Sunday Age* was well placed to overtake it. But moving against the editor? That was going too far.

By coincidence, Kohler and I were attending a lunch on 25 August thrown by organisers and sponsors of the annual Walkley Awards. At its conclusion, Alan offered me a lift back to *The Age*. As he played Lou Reed's *New York* album at an uncomfortable volume on his stereo, I reflected on whether I should tell him about the malcontents on his staff. He swung the car into *The Age*'s Lonsdale Street garage, parked and shut down the engine and, with it, the stereo. I seized the moment's silence: 'I'm sorry to bring this up, mate, but do you know what's going on behind your back at the paper?'

It has to be said that some of the more ambitious newspapermen I've worked with would have been appalled by the question.

After all, just two weeks earlier, I had been offered the editorship of the paper and clearly the prize was probably going to fall to me if I simply let things take their course. But I honestly believed Kohler deserved better. Editing newspapers is a demanding task at the best of times, but it is almost impossible without the loyalty of your key staff and executives.

Kohler had no idea what was going on behind his back. I've learned from bitter experience since that editors rarely do. The jobs are so all-consuming that you have little time for politics unless you're an editor-in-chief with a hardworking editor directly beneath you.

Kohler and I sat for almost 20 minutes in his four-wheel drive in the relative darkness of *The Age* garage and at the end of it he seemed physically diminished by the discussion. Certainly he had lost the effervescence that had characterised his editorship even in its darkest hours. He wondered aloud how best to deal with the discontent and decided he would seek the loyalty of those closest to him. If they wouldn't pledge it, he would move them on—and that was what he did.

It was all too late. Little more than a month later, Hoy announced that Kohler would be stepping down and about a week after that I was given the job.

I was brutally frank with Michael Hoy about the challenge that lay ahead. Circulation of *The Age* was in danger of slipping under 190 000 despite discounting. It was no longer the prize it had once been.

Hoy agreed and gave me a broad mandate for change. I would need new products, new people and, despite Conrad Black's conservatism and Kennett's bluster, I would have to restore the paper's small 'l' liberal values. Yes, yes and yes, said Hoy. I had just one request: could I have a week's break before I formally took over? I owed my family that, at least. After all, even though we would be remaining in Melbourne, they would definitely be seeing less of me.

Hoy was reluctant but agreed if Kohler would. When I approached Kohler, I knew the answer even before he opened his mouth.

'I'm sorry, mate, but I'm gone,' he said, the exhaustion in and around his eyes convincing me he truly was. Then he added, almost desperately, 'I can't wait to get out of this bloody place.'

So I headed off down the corridor where the most senior editorial executives sat. Perhaps someone could pinch hit for a few days until I took over. It was like entering the village of the damned. The first office was the deputy editor's, empty now because of Michael Gawenda's decision to return to writing; next was assistant editor Simon Mann, packing for a long promised junket to Ireland; then came Alan Morison, another assistant editor, his broken arm in a sling from a cycling accident and about to fly out to Bali on an extended holiday. I had never seen such exhaustion; what was I letting myself in for?

In the end, Kohler and I compromised: he would see out the week, which gave me a whole two days off between gigs. And with that I became editor of *The Age*, once described as one of the 10 best newspapers in the world but now slipping down the list.

After addressing *The Sunday Age* staff, I started fielding calls and messages of congratulation. One, from a *Mercury* scriptwriter, jumped out at me: 'It's a marvellous achievement, Bruce, but I fear you've been handed a poisoned chalice.'

On the Monday morning, I took my place behind the desk occupied by only 16 other people in 141 years of *The Age*. Then, just when I thought history couldn't weigh any more heavily upon me, I looked at the desk diary. It was 16 October 1995—exactly 20 years to the day the greatest editor of the paper, Graham Perkin, had died suddenly at home. The portents weren't getting any better.

16

'If the boss rings, can you get his name?'

It had been more than two decades since I had wandered nervously into the Flinders Street offices of HWT at one end of Melbourne's CBD and here I was now standing at the other, addressing some of the biggest names in Australian print journalism, telling them, with only slightly more conviction, that I believed better times were coming for *The Age*. But first I wanted to warn them of our enemies.

'There's this band of critics and criticism that starts at Spring Street with Jeff Kennett, heads across to Flinders Street and the *Herald Sun* then south to 3AW,' I said to staff at *The Age*. 'We have to stare them down.'

Kennett's hatred of *The Age* and *The Sunday Age* was now almost gothic, and he had enlisted both the *Herald Sun* and Melbourne's top-rating talkback radio station to indulge it. They were willing participants because Kennett was good copy and good talent on radio.

Radio 3AW gave Kennett nearly unfettered access to the airwaves, so much so that the premier had developed almost a sense of ownership of the place. In one instructive incident, Kennett clashed with 3AW's program director, Steve Price, when he dared invite then Opposition leader John Brumby onto the station to take calls from listeners. As Price told me days after the incident, Kennett grabbed him in a corridor, pushed him into a room, slapped him across the face, then grabbed him by the scruff of the neck, asking him: 'What about loyalty, mate?'

If anyone was going to hold this government accountable, it had to be *The Age*. This wasn't driven by any desire to derail Kennett; it was more an attempt to reclaim what had made *The Age* great—an unflinching scrutiny of power.

We also needed to restore a desire in readers to *want* to buy the paper. I had no doubt that they felt they *should* read it, but this was a long way from a genuine desire to go out and hand over money for it. To me, *The Age* had become the newspaper equivalent of broccoli: we all knew we should consume it but, frankly, we really didn't want to.

One of the most important tasks for any editor is to argue for and win sufficient resources for journalists to do their jobs to the best of their abilities. I promised my colleagues I would be pressing management for as much as I could get. But we had to be realistic. There would be ongoing pressure to get by with less.

Back at my desk, my personal assistant Lorna Earl put through a call from John Lyons, my former cadet on the state politics round at *The Herald* in Melbourne who was now one of four assistant editors under John Alexander at *The Sydney Morning Herald* fighting for the job I had turned down.

'I gather you've just addressed the staff. How did it go?' asked Lyons.

'Pretty well, I think,' I replied.

'Did you say something about the budget and how you expected cuts?' asked Lyons. Boy, news travelled fast, I thought.

'No, no, I said I'd be asking for more but sometimes you didn't get what you wanted.'

'Well, you didn't hear this from me, but [he named the editor of another Fairfax paper] is walking around up here saying,

"Guthrie's fucked already, he's telling people he's going to cut the budget", said Lyons.

Perhaps I should have confronted the culprit then and there, but I stored it away. Clearly there were people at Fairfax who didn't want me to succeed and most of them were in Sydney. As I would learn in often painful ways, Fairfax's Sydney editorial executives liked nothing better than to decry their Melbourne brethren and, if possible, damage them. Not for the first time I found myself thinking that Fairfax would be a better company if senior executives directed their energies away from internal wrangling and into their jobs and external competitors. I could just imagine Rupert Murdoch rubbing his hands with glee.

Within days of starting in the job there was more upheaval; Stephen Mulholland was stepping down as Fairfax CEO to be replaced by former McDonald's boss, Bob Mansfield. Mansfield had absolutely no publishing experience but that didn't seem to bother the new Fairfax regime one little bit.

Mulholland had been far from perfect as CEO but at least he understood newspapers, having worked at the highest editorial levels in his native South Africa before crossing over into management, a move he had always said he had regretted. Editorial was more fun, he had often said, and I had to agree with him.

That said, Mulholland had been less than supportive in the ongoing row with Kennett. During my time at *The Sunday Age*, he had chided me after the Victorian Premier and I exchanged testy notes. In one of these Kennett had suggested 'your mighty organ [*The Sunday Age*] is very limp indeed'. My response suggested this was undignified language for a premier, yet Mulholland chose to rebuke me after apparently being shown my reply.

The announcement of Mulholland's departure left me ambivalent. The more worrying development was the likely resignation of Michael Hoy who, despite having detractors across the business, had been a strong backer of mine. As Mulholland's designated deputy throughout the South African's tenure, Hoy probably expected to succeed him. Now he appeared to be surplus to requirements.

Sure enough, within weeks of Mansfield beginning his role in November, Hoy was gone. He had decided, he said, that there were too many hands on the steering wheel and he had best move on. I was now worried: where did all this leave my mandate for change?

My first meeting with Mansfield was curious indeed. I had never met a manager quite like him. I liked that he was relentlessly upbeat, energetic and talked frankly. I also knew he had been holding meetings behind my back, roundtables with various people in Melbourne, asking their opinions of me. To his credit, he admitted it, saying the general consensus was positive. Ultimately his view of me came down to this: 'Bruce, I'm a big believer in chemistry, and I sense the chemistry between us is pretty good, so let's move forward.'

Did that mean I was safe in the job? What if the chemistry suddenly went awry? It was all very unsettling. Still, I seized the opportunity to walk him through quite sweeping changes to the paper. He embraced them all.

Then he offered up a metaphor to support his belief there should be a redundancy program. In his new role, he said, he was a gardener. 'We all are really. We identify the flowers and plants that are doing well, nurture those, and then weed out the ones that are holding the garden back.' So, he said, he would stump up the money to weed out the non-performers and I could replace every two staff who left with one new plant, er, person.

Finally, we discussed a looming $2 subscription offer. This bargain basement approach had been introduced after a particularly disastrous audit the previous year. It offered *The Age* seven days a week for just $2. As a sales driver it was a guaranteed winner, but I believed it did untold damage to the brand. What sort of quality product sells for $2 a week? Besides, if recent experience was any guide, the new subscribers dropped off as soon as you tried to up-sell them.

In the end we reluctantly agreed it would go ahead the following February because it had been budgeted, television ads had been shot, and space had been booked across the networks. It would have been a nightmare unravelling it all. I pressed for two things: that we wouldn't declare the bulk of the circulation in forthcoming audits (I wanted to claim only a realistic component we could sustain long term); and fast-tracking of the editorial changes so they were in place by the time the offer launched in February.

As first meetings go, it had been productive, but I wasn't entirely convinced this was going to be an enduring partnership. I also had the cloying feeling that someone in Sydney was getting into Mansfield's ear. My suspicions only deepened when weeks later, as Christmas loomed, Mansfield rang to ask how I would react if he gave Hoy's old job of editorial director to Alexander.

In the end, I supported the move, if only because I'd prefer to have Alexander with me, rather than against me. If his success as editorial director depended in part on improved fortunes at *The Age* then I felt he would have to help me in that. As things stood, there was no incentive to assist me in rebuilding the paper because, frankly, he liked *The Sydney Morning Herald* being perceived as the company flagship. There was almost a disincentive to help.

Good Weekend boss Anne Summers certainly opposed JA's elevation. At one point she rang me asking in high dudgeon why on earth I had supported Alexander's potential appointment. It was well known within Fairfax that the two were barely on speaking terms. *The Sun-Herald* editor Andrew Clark was similarly distrustful of JA and would have also opposed the appointment. Not surprisingly, Mansfield dropped the notion. In future, we would all report to him.

In the second and final week of my Christmas break my successor at *The Sunday Age*, Jill Baker, rang with some disturbing news. Mansfield had been in town asking some searching questions about Simson, pushing her for an assessment of his standing and his abilities. She said, 'If I didn't know any better, I'd say he's going to sack him.'

The last thing we needed was even more disruption but, back at work, it didn't take long for Baker's prediction to come true. On 15 January 1996, a brief announcement came out of Sydney that Stuart had decided to move on. Mansfield had clearly moved against him and it was already apparent that some board members, including Mulholland, were unhappy about it. Mansfield had set in train his own demise.

Circulation director Derek Holt couldn't resist some gallows humour. Collecting me for lunch one late January afternoon he turned to my secretary. 'If the boss rings,' said the wise-cracking Holt, 'can you get his name?' It was to be one of the great running gags of my editorship.

In the midst of all this Fairfax upheaval, Paul Keating called an election. We were glad of the distraction.

We also launched new sport and education sections around this time. We were building some genuine momentum. And the timing of the $2 offer turned out to be inspired. Tens of thousands of new subscribers took it up, so much so that our problem in the September to March audit wasn't whether we would go up, but by how many. Some managers argued that we should declare the lot, which would have given us a sales figure of more than 220 000, a massive increase over the previous year. In the end, the more conservative view prevailed—we would go up, but we would hold back most of the increase so we could avoid disruptive peaks and troughs in the future. The challenge in the months and years ahead would be to hold onto a fair percentage of our new subscribers as we upsold them. To do that, the paper just had to be more compelling.

As the election campaign rolled on, I had an important decision to make. Labor had been in power since 1983, and *The Age* under Kohler had written off Howard as 'yesterday's man'. I had taken a different view at *The Sunday Age*, arguing Howard would be a good leader of the Liberals, who instead opted for Alexander Downer. Howard eventually won back the Liberal leadership in

January 1995. If anyone pointed to the apparent contradiction of
The Age backing a leader it had once dismissed as 'yesterday's man',
I could always argue that hadn't been my view. Whatever concerns
I might have had about backing a conservative, there was this simple
reality: Labor had run its race and Howard was going to win. Better
to be in step with your audience than out of step.

After a spirited editorial meeting, I decided to go with Howard,
and ran an editorial saying he deserved a chance. Australia obviously
agreed, the next day delivering him government. I'm sure few of
them were swayed by our editorial. Certainly, it didn't seem to win
me any friends in Liberal ranks.

Within days of Howard's victory, Kennett announced Victoria
would go to the polls on 30 March and, in no time, the paper and
I were being attacked for our Labor bias. Two elections in the same
month? I didn't know whether to laugh or to cry.

We had another, more pressing, problem: all through the federal election campaign we had been sitting on a huge story that we
couldn't possibly hold any longer. But mere publication of it would
be seen as political. What to do? Publish, of course.

Within weeks of my taking up the editorship of *The Age*, the
paper's news editor, Sean O'Connor, a hugely energetic and savvy
South African with superb news instincts, appeared at my office door
with a large bound book. Could he see me on a matter of some
delicacy, he said.

The book, as it turned out, had been left at the paper's front
desk more than a year earlier by a building worker who had found
it while working on renovations to the premier's office at Spring
Street. It had been abandoned and left in a bin that was sitting in
open space. O'Connor certainly had my attention.

'We believe it belonged to Ken Baxter,' said O'Connor, as he
opened the book to reveal extensive handwritten notes under diary
dates. Baxter had been the head of Jeff Kennett's Office of Premier
and Cabinet during its first tumultuous years when Kennett and

his team basically retooled the state. Added Sean: 'We think it's his Cabinet diary.'

O'Connor went on to explain that a former senior editorial executive of the paper had chosen not to pursue the story, believing it was nothing but 'old history'. I took a very different view. If O'Connor was right, he was holding the definitive account of the Kennett government's first 100 days in office.

But we had better be bloody right.

The first thing to do was match the events recorded in Baxter's diary against published news events: did the dates tally, were the people involved and discussed within Cabinet eventually appointed, and so on. I immediately pulled our state political reporter Shane Green off his day-to-day duties and told him that for the next month, longer if necessary, he would be working from the library, matching event against entry. Three weeks later he reported back: everything checked out. If the diary were a forgery, it was an extremely elaborate one.

Now we had to check the handwriting. Before we could do that, we had to locate another example of Baxter's script. Mike Richards, whom I had made executive editor of the paper, remembered that during his days as a political consultant working out of Keating's office there had been correspondence from Baxter, including handwritten margin notes. Within 24 hours he somehow produced it.

O'Connor then called in the handwriting experts: not one, but two. They independently assessed the margin notes and the diary entries as almost certainly being written by the same hand. Right, that was two out of three. Now for the big card.

I had first worked with Paul Austin when I was state political reporter for *The Herald* and he was a cadet at the paper. He had rung me soon after I was appointed editor of *The Age*, saying that if I was looking for a deputy editor he was most definitely available. I jumped at the offer. He was reliable, understood Melbourne and Victoria, particularly its politics, and having worked at *The Australian* at a very high level, grasped federal politics too. On top of everything, he had terrific people skills and the energy of youth.

Together we hatched a plan to determine once and for all whether the Baxter diaries were as they seemed. He would contact Baxter, who was now working for the Carr government in Sydney, and tell him it was imperative he see him on a matter of great importance and some delicacy. He would then show Baxter the diary and offer to return it to him then and there but only if he confirmed its authenticity. Intrigued, Baxter agreed in a heartbeat.

Throughout all this Shane Green was busy preparing a three-part series: 'The Baxter Diaries—Inside the First 100 Days of the Kennett Government'. It was a marvellous package, detailing Cabinet discussions on everything from choosing a new police commissioner to the $100 levy imposed on all Victorians to get the state out of hock. It was written, the photographs had been taken, dinkuses prepared; all we needed now was Baxter's confirmation. By mid-afternoon on the day before publication of part one, we had it. Austin rang in saying he had handed over the diary to Baxter at his Sydney home after he had confirmed its authenticity.

Months of hard and detailed work was about to pay off. This would put *The Age* right at the centre of debate again. It would be not only a defining piece of journalism for *The Age* but also a defining moment in my editorship. We would be reclaiming the paper's reputation for scrutiny.

There was a twist. With the first instalment laid out, subbed and ready to run on page one and inside the paper, my phone rang. It was right on press time.

'Mr Guthrie, it's Ken Baxter here,' said the voice at the other end of the phone. 'This diary you've given me is fake.'

'What do you mean fake? You accepted it on the basis it was genuine,' I said, now concerned we would have to junk the whole thing, at the very least causing long delays on our first edition.

'Well, much of it is,' said Baxter. 'But there are large chunks that aren't. Bits have been added in that weren't written by me.'

He then made an offer: if we delayed publication he would actually write a three-part series on the Kennett government's first 100 days. I wasn't interested. In my hand I had one of the great finds of the recent political past. Why would I trade that for what would inevitably be a solid, but ultimately boring recounting of Cabinet's good governance? There would be none of the colour and movement contained in Baxter's daybook, including interjections from ministers that he had dutifully recorded in his neat hand.

After I had spent 15 minutes in conversation, the paper's chief sub-editor, Gavan O'Connor, Sean's brother and, like him, enormously skilled, appeared at my doorway. 'Do I send the paper or not?' he asked.

We were already 20 minutes late, the presses were on hold and the drivers would be getting antsy in the loading dock. I had to make a decision.

We had done all the work; there was nothing we hadn't checked and rechecked. I couldn't blame Baxter for wanting to wrest back control of the diaries but that's all this was—an attempt to talk me out of publishing. If I acceded to his request anything could happen the next day—we could wind up in court fighting an injunction or the bloody diary could turn up at the *Herald Sun*.

I took a very deep breath. 'I'm sorry Mr Baxter but I believe the diary is yours and we are going to publish tomorrow,' I said. 'You are most welcome to write anything you like about its contents and its context, but I'm not holding off in the meantime. Goodnight.'

In a career spanning almost four decades, I never had the chance to say 'Stop the presses!' Even if I had, it couldn't possibly have matched the adrenalin rush of saying to Gavan that night: 'Run the presses. Run them!'

I barely slept that night. When my alarm went off at 7 a.m., I had probably only grabbed an hour or two at best. Naturally, our revelations were leading the radio bulletins. And, just as predictably, there was Jeff Kennett berating the paper and me.

Significantly, he wasn't disowning the diaries, conceding they were genuine and only attacked us for publishing 'irresponsibly'. Never had I been so pleased to receive a Kennett outburst. (Sixteen years later I would have cause to reflect on our painstaking efforts to substantiate the diary and its contents as News Limited papers shamefully published fake pictures of a young and scantily clad woman they wrongly claimed was Pauline Hanson.)

As all the polls and pundits predicted, Kennett was storming towards an electoral rout of Labor leader John Brumby. In the midst of the campaign a local filmmaker, Richard Keddie, asked if he could record our election editorial conference for a documentary he was making on Brumby's tilt at power. I agreed, theorising that any publicity—the documentary was to be screened post-election on the ABC—was good for the paper. I also felt that news organisations that made their money out of public scrutiny could hardly run and hide when the spotlight was shone on them. The decision would come back to haunt me.

The subsequent footage showed associate editor Mike Richards, deputy editor Paul Austin and me workshopping possible approaches in the editorial. At one point I wondered aloud whether we could support a vote for Labor, and ticked off the Kennett government's failings, including a struggling public hospital system, deficient ambulance service, high taxes, and a renowned arrogance and lack of inclusiveness. Like any editorial conference, it was an exercise in clear thinking, going through the possible arguments and seeing which one held up best. After a brief discussion we rejected the notion of backing Labor and acknowledged the Kennett government should be returned, even though we felt he had trampled many of the small 'l' liberal values we championed. A reduced majority would be no bad thing, we decided.

It wasn't enough for Kennett. Come election night he delivered a victory speech short on humility. Watched by a beaming James Packer he called it 'probably the most profound election result in this country, state or federally, in the past 50 years.'

I watched his landslide win unfold at a Richmond hotel where Geoffrey Rush and the entire cast and crew of *Mercury* were celebrating the completion of the show's 13 episodes. It was clear to all that, given the conservatives' clean sweep of government at both the federal and state level that month, there wouldn't be another series of a program that painted as heroes a probing newspaper and its journalists, while reducing an arrogant premier to villain status.

On Sunday, as we prepared the post-election edition of *The Age*, Mike Richards pulled me aside to tell me he had taken a call earlier that day from a senior Liberal who wanted it known that Kennett had vowed to get me during his second term.

'He told me to tell you it's not going to be pretty,' said Richards. It didn't take long for his informant to be proved right.

Although the Fairfax board usually met in Sydney at Fairfax's Darling Point offices, the 16 April gathering was set down for Melbourne in *The Age* boardroom. I approached the meeting with the enthusiasm of a trip to the dentist, but at least I had a good story to tell: we had covered two elections magnificently, completed a redundancy program without any real rancour, introduced some accomplished news executives, broken one of the stories of the year (The Baxter Diaries), were well advanced in planning on a new daily section, and were on budget. But I had saved the best for last—on current projections we should be able to post a circulation figure of around 206 000, up dramatically on a year earlier.

Throughout my address, I couldn't help but notice that several board members were writing notes to each other. They seemed terribly distracted. At the end of my short speech, there was some polite applause and I was spared the usual uninformed questions, although there was a brief, curious exchange with chairman Sir Zelman Cowen.

'You mentioned that you want to restore the paper's reputation for scrutiny. Is that right, Mr Guthrie?' the former governor-general asked.

'That's correct, Sir Zelman.'

'That's all very well but it will be positive scrutiny, won't it? We don't want any of this negative stuff.'

Positive scrutiny? What the hell did that mean?

With Hoy gone and Black incommunicado, there was no-one to pick up the journalistic cudgels; in fact, one or two board members muttered 'hear, hear'. I thought about quoting Phillip Knightley's rule that the best journalism is that which 'someone somewhere doesn't want published', but thought it would be wasted on this room. So I simply replied: 'Uh-huh.' Then I respect-fully exited, only to find a strangely subdued Bob Mansfield sitting directly outside the boardroom.

'Why aren't you in there, Bob?' I asked. All I received in reply was a rueful shrug.

Moments later the board summoned him back to tell him his services were no longer required. Mansfield was out, fewer than five months after he had taken the job. Was there no end to this turbu-lence? As word spread throughout the building, so did the theories. The most popular was that the Black camp suspected Mansfield was too close to Packer; another suggested he had exceeded his brief by removing Simson. Hours later Mansfield rang me during celebra-tions of the AFL centenary at the MCG. As I stood on the ground's hallowed turf in light rain, he theorised that Black simply didn't like him acting first and asking the board second, rather than the other way around.

'They just wanted someone to take the phone calls from London, and I'm not that sort of bloke,' said Mansfield. I wished him well, told him honestly that I had enjoyed working with him, and hung up wondering if this merry-go-round was ever going to stop.

Meanwhile, Black's right-hand man, lawyer Dan Colson, was already flying back to London. He had left the board meeting straight after Mansfield's sacking, jumped into a waiting BMW and sped off to the airport. Somewhere along the Tullamarine Freeway, the car's mobile phone rang and an animated voice asked to speak to Colson.

The Canadian lawyer took the phone from the driver only to hear a slightly hysterical middle-aged man shouting down the line: 'You sacked the wrong man, you sacked the wrong man.'

An exasperated Colson asked: 'What are you talking about? Who the hell is this?'

'It's Kennett,' said the voice. 'Jeff Kennett.'

'Oh. So who should we have sacked, premier?' asked Colson.

'Guthrie, you should have sacked Guthrie,' said Kennett.

It had been exactly six months since I had taken over *The Age* and already I had had two CEOs, two managing directors—one of Mansfield's last acts was to appoint former Bell Publishing chief John Reynolds as Simson's successor—and two elections. Despite all the turmoil, we were building real momentum. Yes, we had our critics, Kennett chief among them. But I took heart from those attacks as well, often reflecting on the old Middle Eastern saying: 'Everyone will stone a tree full of fruit but no-one will touch a fruitless tree.' Our efforts were clearly bearing fruit. If my masters could just keep their nerve, all would be well. I was kidding myself, of course.

17

Drip, drip, drip

Jeff Kennett wasn't the only man capable of delivering a force-five verbal assault. As an editor, you quickly learn they can come from anywhere. Paul Keating was particularly adept at them, once promising in an early morning phone call to 'cut you and your paper dead' after we published something not entirely to his liking.

I gave Keating points for ringing me directly and having it out. Kennett tended to skulk around, working the board or, at least, senior management. However, some of the worst attacks came from readers, many of them nasty and anonymous. During his stint as *The Age*'s editor, Alan Kohler opened his mail one morning to find a letter of complaint from a reader: it consisted of an *Age* masthead, ripped from the paper and used as toilet paper.

I had a standard letter of reply for anyone who forgot their manners when writing. It usually began:

Dear Sir/Madam,
    I feel compelled to bring to your attention that someone posing as you has recently written to me complaining about our journalism. Given the intemperate tone of the letter and

its general mean-spiritedness, I refuse to accept it could have come from you. Hopefully you can track down the culprit and put matters right.

If I was really put out by some correspondence I would simply adopt the same approach John Lennon took when Paul McCartney wrote complaining of Yoko Ono's presence at The Beatles' 'Let It Be' sessions. Lennon replied to McCartney's tirade with 'Dear Paul, Get well soon.'

With the pressures of *The Age* job building, our small farm south-west of Melbourne became a much-needed refuge. We had bought a 20-hectare block on the outskirts of Anglesea and put a kit home on it. Janne would typically head there late afternoon on a Friday with our two young children and I would drive down and join them later that night whenever I could get away from the office. Often I would arrive and everyone would be asleep; I would kiss the cheeks of my son and daughter and remember the words of Kennett: don't let your children become little heads on pillows. It was troubling on many levels, not least that this pearl of wisdom had come from him. My mother's health was also improving and we'd managed to find her a place in an aged care facility, which meant she—and my brother and I—finally said goodbye to Widford Street, Broadmeadows, 40 years after we'd moved in.

Scott's second birthday fell midweek two days after Mansfield's shock sacking, so I decided to take the morning off to spend it with my son. My plan soon came unstuck. Kennett was a guest every Thursday on Neil Mitchell's radio program, fielding questions from the host and listeners. Mitchell inevitably asked Kennett about the week's upheavals at *The Age*, but also sought his reaction to the news the paper was apparently about to post a substantial circulation increase.

The premier, fresh from telling Dan Colson I should have been sacked, couldn't help himself, launching an extraordinary attack against the paper—'absolute crap'—and me—'a boy trying to do a man's job'. They were little better than the taunts of a schoolyard bully.

Publicly, I tried to shrug it off. 'Politicians have been attacking *The Age* for more than a century, so we are all used to it,' I said in one of many interviews the Kennett attack spawned, adding: 'Usually they do it with a little more intelligence and grace than Mr Kennett could muster today however.' There was no way I was going to blink in the face of his chest thumping. Privately though, I was feeling increasingly isolated.

When our home phone stopped ringing with requests from media for interviews I looked at the clock—it was after 1 p.m.; I had spent the entire morning defending myself against another intemperate attack from the premier. So much for spending time with Scott. I grabbed a couple of hours with him—the photos taken that day still leave me with a sense of anger and regret—before heading into the office.

A strong news organisation would not have left an editor to defend himself or herself against such mean-spirited attacks. But Fairfax was no longer strong. For a start, we had no CEO; it would be months before Mansfield would be replaced. And, although our new managing director in Melbourne—John Reynolds—had been announced, he had barely put his feet under his desk; he wasn't interested in getting into a war of words with the premier. Kennett would have been emboldened by the lack of response from the company.

The 'boy trying to do a man's job' jibe washed over me, but I was deeply concerned at what was happening to democracy in Victoria. With massive majorities, Kennett controlled the upper and lower houses of parliament, had the *Herald Sun* and 3AW in his thrall, and wanted desperately to silence *The Age* and the ABC.

It would be tough enough at the best of times to run a paper like *The Age*, but the combination of Kennett's overweening arrogance, Fairfax's then lack of direction, and much of the media's subservience to the premier, made it increasingly difficult. I was worried I was becoming the de facto leader of the Opposition. Certainly Labor wasn't landing any blows even though I sensed Victorians were becoming increasingly concerned about Kennett's 'my way or the highway' approach to government.

Still, there was an upside to his attacks: in a perverse way Kennett was making *The Age* relevant again. Every time he attacked us, our sales went up.

★ ★ ★

Ironically, I often drew on some other Kennett advice whenever momentous news stories were breaking around me. The premier had once confided to me that he had learned during his army service that a leader had to appear most in control when he felt least in control. I had seen him use it to great effect many times. Whenever his leadership seemed ready to fall over because of a challenge or some apparent scandal, Kennett would emerge at a press conference or doorstop smacking his lips or rubbing his hands with glee, perhaps saying: 'What a wonderful day.' His message was: I'm on top of things here, even if you expected chaos. Steering the coverage of big stories can be a little like that.

Given the tumultuous events of April I repaired to the farm for the last weekend of the month with more than the usual relief. I walked the paddocks with the kids, chopped some wood, read books and papers before a blazing fire at night—I had never needed a quiet weekend more. About 3 p.m. on Sunday, we loaded up the car and headed for home. I had the radio tuned to a football broadcast on the ABC when the first news of the shootings at Port Arthur broke. A lone gunman had opened fire at the former penal settlement in Tasmania and already the death toll was in double figures; it would eventually climb to 35.

I rang the news desk immediately to ensure we had coverage on the ground—they were already booking flights to Tasmania—and had a brief conversation with deputy editor Paul Austin to ensure we had enough pages allocated to cover the story properly. We headed straight to Spencer Street where Janne dropped me off in my grubby jeans and flannelette shirt and I stayed there till the first of what would become almost continuous editions of the paper was off the press late that night.

In truth, it's almost impossible for a newspaper not to be compelling when recording a story of the magnitude of the Port Arthur massacre. Readers turn to papers in extraordinary numbers when events such as the 9/11 attacks or the death of Princess Diana happen. Perhaps they are looking for context; perhaps, they are looking for a memorial they can reflect on years later. The sheer volume of stories, angles, eyewitness accounts and photographs meant we were bound to publish a first-rate paper the next day. The true test of a newspaper is not the volume of stories, but the defining one. Sometimes I can wade through dozens of pages of coverage and still feel disconnected; the challenge for a good editor is to search out and publish the one piece that captures the essence of the story: a survivor interview perhaps or the final hours of a victim or culprit. It would take us a week but eventually we would publish it. In the meantime the challenge was to stay abreast of an extraordinary story that was throwing up new angles for days. Apart from our first-rate news coverage, we were also quick to identify the issue that would dominate debate for weeks after the massacre—gun laws.

An early key decision on that Sunday was whether to publish a photograph of the alleged gunman, Martin Bryant. An image of him had emerged within hours of the massacre; in normal circumstances, given the laws of contempt, we would have held back, but the scale of the story was such that I felt compelled to publish the picture, albeit thumbnail size. In the end, just about every major Australian newspaper did likewise, with Paul Kelly at *The Australian* attracting severe criticism after someone at the paper apparently coloured Bryant's eyes to give them a demonic redness. It was foolishness because the story was already compelling enough.

On the Monday morning we kept the presses running, producing an 11 a.m. edition. It was a groundbreaking move for *The Age*. My biggest decision saw us publish on the Friday after the shootings a special 8-page, ad-free broadsheet section devoted entirely to a single 10 000-word narrative of the massacre, written from *Age* reports and other supplementary material by the paper's former deputy editor, Michael Gawenda. Featuring our best photographs, it was a tour de force that ultimately won us the 1996 Walkley Award for best application of the print medium. Our coverage, the special section and the multi-edition approach delivered *The Age* its highest Monday to Friday sales figure in almost 15 years—236 674.

Kennett could decry us all he wanted, but the evidence was clear: we were a rapidly improving newspaper and Victorians were rewarding us at the newsstand. We were even outstripping the *Herald Sun*, whose circulation was stagnating, even falling under Harris and his new number two, former Adelaide *Advertiser* editor and lifetime Murdoch man Peter Blunden.

My problem was that Kennett wasn't playing to a Melbourne audience; he was playing to one based in Sydney—the Fairfax board. At the time, the only Melbourne board members were former governor-general Sir Zelman Cowen, and Sir Roderick Carnegie, a former McKinsey consultant who had driven mad my predecessor, Alan Kohler, by continually asking him to 'write down' what was good journalism and what was bad. When Kohler quite reasonably responded that it wasn't as prescriptive as that, Carnegie was perplexed. Now he was trying the same tactic with me. Then there were his political leanings; suffice to say he seemed to be more a supporter of Jeff Kennett than he was of me.

Because of the tension between the government and the paper I was becoming something of a regular on the talk circuit. Kennett had painted me as some wide-eyed lefty and the more audiences I fronted, the quicker I could blunt false perceptions. (I recall at one gathering Melbourne football legend and former *Herald Sun* columnist Lou Richards remarked after we had spent about an hour in each other's company: 'Kennett reckons you're an arsehole, but you're not a bad bloke actually.')

In mid-1996, Dick Denton, one of the city's more eminent research professors and a former member of the David Syme board, invited me to address a group at that bastion of conservatism, the Melbourne Club, at the very top end of Collins Street. It was a prestigous gathering with several knights of the realm in attendance and a number of prominent business leaders also on hand. The night began well, as we gathered in an anteroom and exchanged pleasantries around an open fire. Then John Elliott walked in.

'John, we haven't seen you at one of these in years,' said the host.

'Editor of *The Age* speaking? I wouldn't miss this for quids,' said the former IXL and Foster's boss with more than a trace of mischief in his voice. Elliott was on the downslope of his once-illustrious career, and was just weeks away from being acquitted of fraud charges brought against him by the National Crime Authority. I had never met him before this cold July night, but I could see he hadn't come simply to exchange pleasantries. We shook hands though and adjourned to the dining room where the group of about 40 took their seats.

After a pleasant meal I rose to speak. Elliott had shaken my confidence somewhat, but I soon hit my stride, recounting some of *The Age*'s history and, anticipating a likely Elliott attack, explaining our attitude to the Kennett government: we had urged his election at the past two elections but were increasingly concerned at the lack of process and consultation. This was, after all, a government, not a corporation. At question time, Elliott slowly and very deliberately raised his hand, like a naughty boy in class bent on mayhem.

'Do you have a question for the editor of *The Age*?' asked Dick Denton.

'Yeah, I've got a question,' said Elliott with his customary gruffness. 'Why don't you just give up?'

I was now growing used to these performances.

'I have no intention of giving up, Mr Elliott,' I said, somewhat combatively, adding: 'Because at *The Age* we sense our vigilance is needed more than ever.'

And with that, we went at it, swapping barbs, insults and observations until almost midnight. Eventually Professor Denton wound things up.

'Well, we've had prime ministers, Nobel Prize winners and heads of state address this gathering,' said Denton. 'But I don't believe we've ever had such a robust discussion as we have had tonight.'

While several diners made their way to me to apologise for Elliott's behaviour, I assured them I had enjoyed the night. Then Elliott himself appeared at my side.

'You did all right mate,' said the former Foster's boss. 'Can I buy you a beer?'

Over the ensuing drink, he made an extraordinary offer. 'I know you and Jeff don't get on, but I can fix that if you want me to. Do you want me to fix it?'

I replied that I thought it 'unfixable', only because it served Jeff's purposes to be at war with *The Age*. With a huge backbench, most unoccupied by the business of government, a limp Labor opposition and a compliant *Herald Sun*, Kennett had to create an enemy somewhere and *The Age* was a perfect fit.

'Yeah, you're probably right,' said Elliott as we bid each other goodnight.

Despite the ongoing attacks by Melbourne conservatives against me and the paper, we had much to celebrate. The 1 July launch of the new 'Metro' section, which brought together arts coverage, daily features and service components such as the television guide and crosswords, had exceeded our wildest expectations. Editor Jonathan Green, who a decade later would edit Crikey.com with great distinction, had done an outstanding job of marrying *Age* sensibilities, wit, words and style to create the groundbreaking new daily section that had an almost immediate positive effect on sales. We had already been able to boast circulation increases in the first two quarters of the year and Metro would almost certainly give us more in the future. At the very least it would build frequency of purchase and, we thought, attract new readers as well.

I had also taken control of our website which, over the next decade or so, would become an increasingly important part of the Fairfax business. When I arrived at the paper, it had existed only in the research library, updated when and if the library staff could find time in their busy work schedules. After discussions with Sydney management, I convinced them to let me oversee it as an editorial product. With their agreement, I brought it onto the editorial floor, appointed former News Extra editor, Alan Morison, as the first editor of theage.com.au and gave him staff to run it as, if not a 24-hour site, at least one that was updated regularly.

As the first anniversary of my editorship approached, Fairfax also finally acquired a new CEO, former News Limited number two, Bob Muscat. The word was that he had realised he would never jump Lachlan Murdoch for the top job at News and had opted for Fairfax instead. Like Ken Cowley, he had come from the production side of the business. I remembered Muscat from my Melbourne *Herald* days. At least he understands newspapers, I thought. This may have been true; the problem was, as I would learn to my cost, that he didn't understand editors.

High on Muscat's to-do list was 'the Kennett problem'. Several times he raised it in a fairly clumsy fashion; while he didn't expect *The Age* to soften its stance on what we saw as the government's failings, perhaps we could 'overpraise' them when we thought they had done well. Was he really suggesting we use our editorial columns to curry favour with a politician? We would be crossing the Rubicon if we adopted that course. I chose not to.

When my first anniversary came around the senior editors and I had a quiet celebratory lunch in the fifth-floor dining room at Spencer Street. As it drew to a close I reflected on hugely increased circulation and readership, a strong showing in that year's Walkley Awards, and the decision by industry newsletter, *Mediaweek*, to name me Newspaper Executive of the Year.

Yet I couldn't shake the feeling that we were putting on a first-rate performance for an audience in Sydney that didn't appreciate the stagecraft on show. This disconnect was becoming a bigger and bigger problem for all of us at Spencer Street. *The Age* had started becoming a Sydney satellite when Fairfax bought a controlling interest in David Syme in the early 1970s and then acquired the rest of the company a decade later. Along the way there had been guarantees of editorial independence but it was becoming increasingly clear to me that we were almost an afterthought for Sydney management. This was despite *The Age* rivalling *The Sydney Morning Herald* in revenue and profits. Then, unexpectedly, there were more ructions.

The first hint came when senior executives were asked to attend a meeting in the little-used television studio on the Spencer Street side of the building. There, late in the afternoon on 16 December, we watched Dan Colson on video link explain that Conrad Black's Hollinger International was giving up control of Fairfax by selling its 25 per cent interest to Brierley Investments of New Zealand. 'We just got sick of banging our heads against a brick wall,' explained Colson, who with Black had failed to convince successive governments they should be allowed to own more than the 25 per cent—increased from the original 15 per cent—they were limited to under foreign ownership regulations.

We barely had time to digest the momentous news when Bob Muscat announced that two senior executives from the new owners would be in the building the next day at 9 a.m. to hear presentations from all senior managers. I would be up first, Muscat told me.

The two executives turned out to be Rod Price, an Australian who oversaw Sir Ron Brierley's investments far and wide, and Sir Roger Douglas, the former New Zealand Labour treasurer famous for his 'Rogernomics', an almost radically conservative form of economics. Moments before I entered the boardroom, Muscat pulled me aside, suggesting I talk directly to the Kennett 'problem' as they were sure to raise it. Better to get in first, he said.

Price and Douglas entered without fanfare, shaking hands with each of us, before taking their seats side by side. Sir Roger pulled out a notebook and pen and immediately started writing as I began my short address. Price, who would file for bankruptcy a decade later, eyeballed me throughout. I was matter-of-fact: I had had the job 14 months; had in that time boosted circulation and readership by more than 5 per cent; substantially improved the product; motivated the staff; launched an internet site; we'd recently taken out more Walkley awards than any other paper.

I should have stopped there, but mindful of Muscat's advice, I ploughed on. If we had a problem, I said, it was a political one— the premier didn't particularly like us, but it probably wasn't in his best interests to anyway. He needed an enemy and he had decided it was us. End of two-minute presentation.

Muscat asked Price and Douglas—who was still writing in his notebook at a furious rate—whether they had any questions. Douglas didn't even look up from his notepad; Price, who was buffed and tanned within an inch of his life, had clearly been waiting for this very moment.

'Why are you waging war against a politician of international standing?' he asked provocatively.

'Who are we talking about?' I asked, equally provocatively.

'Why, Jeff Kennett, of course,' said Price.

'We're not waging war, Mr Price. If anything, he's the one waging war.'

'Well, I disagree,' said Price.

At this point I wanted to say this: 'Who the hell do you think you are walking in here when you don't even own a bloody share yet and questioning me about the paper's relationship with a politician when frankly it doesn't even matter if we do or don't get on with him. Instead you should be bloody grateful that we are in good shape again or presumably you wouldn't be buying the shares.'

But I didn't say any of that. Instead I merely looked to Muscat who, realising I was seething, intervened and invited the next manager to speak. I took my leave soon after, pleading a news conference. Muscat followed me out, apologising as we both walked. He had been wrong to raise Kennett with them and with me.

I took the lift back to the third floor and immediately called in a couple of my more senior editors, Shane Castleman and Sean O'Connor, who had known of my appointment with the new majority shareholders upstairs.

'Boys,' I said to them. 'I've just met the new owners and I'm here to tell you: I'm officially on the drip. I'll be lucky to last another six months.'

As it turned out, I was unduly pessimistic; I actually lasted another seven months.

18

Outnumbered

Newspaper editors are never far from power or, at least, the people who wield it. This can be quite seductive if you forget one simple fact: it's not you they're really interested in, it's the machinery you sit atop. Lose the job tomorrow and most politicians will want to cosy up to your successor, regardless of the circumstances or their qualities.

This goes both ways. I've seen editors who mine the role for every contact it can bring, ruthlessly seeking out politicians and business leaders. At the very least it might produce a story or two and, at best, enduring networks that could benefit an ex-editor should employment circumstances change. But it's amazing how quickly such relationships can founder.

I was reminded of this during my time at the *Herald Sun*. After dining with Prime Minister Kevin Rudd midway through 2008, I was suddenly receiving all sorts of text messages from him, including several after a particularly tense Brisbane Lions game at the Gabba that saw the home team get up in the final minutes as Rudd looked on.

You could begin to take yourself a little too seriously and over-state your importance in the affairs of the nation when you're swapping text messages with the Prime Minister on a Sunday after-noon. Janne and the kids thought it great fun as football observations from him lobbed on my mobile. I long ago put such exchanges in perspective. If there was any doubt, I was reminded of the editor's true place in the world when, six weeks after my sacking, on a whim I sent Rudd a text message wishing him and his family a merry Christmas. There was nothing in return. By then I was merely a former newspaper editor, about as stale as yesterday's news.

My final months at *The Age* in 1997 seemed to be dominated by politicians. The Howard government was still less than a year old and so was busy building relationships that might serve them well throughout their term. Better to have newspapers—and their editors—with you than against you.

There's another element to these relationships. Politicians, whatever their persuasion, seem to think editors have some unfail-ing gift for knowing what the public thinks and wants on any given issue. This can be useful to a government, particularly a new one, wanting to chart a steady course through choppy waters. Truth is, while we might be better placed than most, we are still relying largely on letters, emails, sales figures and general feedback to arrive at our positions.

As Peter Costello's second Budget loomed in February 1997, I was offered the chance to sit down with him in Canberra. Clearly I would be able to use the session to get a sense of what might emerge and he would be able to get a sense of what readers of *The Age* might be expecting. And it would be an opportunity for us to bond: he with the editor of an important masthead and me with a man who might one day be prime minister.

While we weren't close, the Treasurer and I did have some things in common. We shared a boyhood fondness for the tele-vision series *Get Smart*, a love of the Essendon football club and a growing disdain for a certain state premier. For about 30 min-utes we swapped stories and opinions on these and other subjects,

Costello pausing at one point to admire my cufflinks: one read 'yes', the other read 'no'. I was impressed by his powers of observation; he would have made a good journalist.

'I should get a pair of those,' said the Treasurer. 'Except mine would have to say "no" and "absolutely not". They'd be useful at Budget time.'

As I left my meeting with him I was intercepted by a man waiting for me in the corridor outside Costello's office. Could I spare a few minutes for Communications Minister, Richard Alston, he asked. Within seconds I was sitting opposite the minister who, like Costello, represented a Victorian constituency. Melbourne's eastern suburbs' conservatives read *The Age* in vast numbers, making it an important element in the lives of their elected representatives.

Alston explained he would have to leave in five minutes for the airport, so he would come straight to the point: 'How would you feel if we broke up Fairfax?'

Gobsmacked, I could only utter an incredulous, 'Excuse me?'

'How would you feel if the Fairfax papers were owned by different proprietors, rather than just one?' clarified Alston.

'Well, that would depend on who ended up with *The Age*,' I said.

'What about a group like the AIN bid?' asked the minister. This was a reference to the consortium that had lost out to Conrad Black five years earlier. Costello's predecessor Paul Keating had loathed them as Collins Street Tories, never making any secret of it.

'Oh, you mean the Melbourne Club group,' I said, by way of clarification.

'Yes, someone like that,' replied Alston.

As a Fairfax editor I had learned to live with almost constant speculation of takeovers and new owners, most of it focusing on Kerry Packer's ambitions. There had even been talk that the company's new majority shareholder, Sir Ron Brierley, was merely holding the shares for Packer because the Australian billionaire was forbidden to own the company under cross-media restrictions.

The current ownership of Fairfax was certainly doing me no favours and, like most Australian journalists, I had long harboured concerns at the concentration of media control in this country. So a government policy that had the effect of bringing in more owners may not be a bad thing. But I played a straight bat with the minister.

'I could see how a few new owners in the industry might be a good thing but, overall, I think the benefits of having one proprietor across *The Age*, *The Sydney Morning Herald* and *The Australian Financial Review* probably outweigh the disadvantages,' I told Alston. And with that we parted on the best of terms.

After a few further meetings with members of the government, including South Australian Senator Nick Minchin, I dined with members of our Canberra bureau. Michelle Grattan had again resigned from *The Age*, this time to join *The Australian Financial Review*, forcing a significant reshuffle of the team. But after promoting Nikki Savva to Michelle's role and hiring long-time Canberra observer Laura Tingle as Savva's deputy, I felt we had emerged in good shape.

Grattan's decision to join Greg Hywood at *The Australian Financial Review* absolutely confounded me and for a long time the gossip around Canberra was that I had somehow precipitated, even orchestrated it. Steve Harris even sent me an email when her departure was announced applauding me for a 'very deft' manoeuvre. The simple fact was Grattan made the move for her personal reasons; I would have preferred she stayed but could do nothing to prevent it.

The next morning I flew back to Melbourne and after checking in at the office was driven straight to Government House, nestled behind the beautiful Royal Botanic Gardens. *Age* editors have been invited to dine with the governor of Victoria throughout the paper's 150-year history. These are usually dull affairs attended by a diverse group of a dozen or so, dominated by stilted conversation and an unstated anxiety that you might forget your manners in some egregious way. When I received my second invitation in 15 months, I was less than enthusiastic. It would have been bad form to say no, so I accepted. When *The Age* driver deposited me at the steps of Government House we agreed he should return in 90 minutes. We both expressed surprise that ours was the only vehicle in sight; perhaps I had the day wrong.

Within moments, one of the governor's aides appeared, welcoming me warmly. I was directed to a much smaller lunchroom; the table was set for only two. Soon Governor McGarvie arrived. A former Supreme Court judge, McGarvie had been appointed by Premier Joan Kirner, just before Labor lost office in 1992. He had been a long-time member of the ALP but had resigned from the party after being appointed to the bench.

To my surprise, McGarvie and I were dining alone; to my astonishment, after extracting from me an understanding that our conversation was confidential—McGarvie passed away in 2003 so I no longer feel bound by the agreement which I have honoured until now—he steeled me for the fight against the premier. *The Age* was an essential part of democratic life in Victoria and we must not be cowed by Kennett, he said, adding: 'More power to you, Bruce.' Given that the governor sat down every week with senior Kennett ministers as the governor-in-council to sign off on government business, this was extraordinary. I left Government House feeling, if not uplifted, then certainly a little less alone. Soon the pressure was back on again though.

In early March, about a week after my meeting with Senator Alston, I was called to the phone at the Australian Club in William Street, Melbourne where I was dining as a guest of Mike Richards.

Founded in the late nineteenth century, the Australian Club was historically the gathering point for Melbourne Club members in winter. In those days Elizabeth Street, which divides the city's central business district into east and west, was prone to flooding and business people and graziers on the western side of the city often couldn't ford the flood. So they formed a second club they could reach when the weather turned bad—or so the story went.

Like Government House, such clubs often made me uncomfortable with their rules, stated and unstated. Apparently it was unusual, even bad form, for a guest to take a call while dining but journalists are rarely troubled by such things. When I picked up the phone in the booth at the front of the club, Anne Davies of *The Sydney Morning Herald* was on the line. Soon I was silently cursing whoever had divulged my whereabouts.

'Good afternoon, Mr Guthrie,' said Davies, the paper's well-respected media reporter at the time. 'I'm doing a story on all the lobbying that's going on in Canberra over Fairfax at the moment and John Alexander has asked me to include you as advocating the break-up of the company.'

'What was that?' I asked in high dudgeon.

'You met with Richard Alston last week, didn't you?' asked Davies.

'Yes, but it was unscheduled. His offsider grabbed me in a corridor for a five-minute chat with Alston,' I replied.

'Well, the minister says you urged the break-up of Fairfax.'

'That's not true,' I said. 'I certainly didn't do that.' I then explained the conversation, how Alston had bowled up a proposition that I considered and then rejected, telling him that while there might be some upside in selling off the group's papers to different proprietors, on balance it would be best to keep them together in one entity.

'Well, I've got a quote from him saying you did. All I can do now is carry your denial,' said Davies.

We were both caught in the middle of some extraordinary politicking, both federal and corporate. How to deal with this latest development? The next 24 hours would certainly be embarrassing and possibly career threatening. The board would hardly appreciate any suggestion by an editor that their company be broken up, particularly with a senior government minister telling them I had.

Back in my office I tried to call Alexander several times to set the record straight, but he wasn't available. Funny that. I was forced to deal with *Sydney Morning Herald* editor John Lyons, who sympathised with my position but explained the paper had a direct quote from Alston.

It seemed clear that I would be on page one of *The Sydney Morning Herald* the next morning advocating the break-up of the company or, at least, being reported as having done so.

Then, miraculously, fate intervened.

'Bruce, I have Peter Clemenger on the line,' said my PA, Lorna Earl. 'Do you want to take the call or should I tell him you're unavailable?'

I was tremendously fond of Clemenger, the doyen of Melbourne ad men whose eponymous agency held *The Age* account. He was semi-retired and I saw him only over the occasional lunch. His sunny disposition might be just what I needed.

In seconds Clemenger, then a very sprightly 69, was on the line asking how I was.

'Well, I've had better days,' I said. 'But you sound fighting fit, Peter.'

'Why wouldn't I?' he replied. 'I've just been in Fiji for three days on Kerry Packer's yacht.'

'Nice for some,' I said.

'Yes, it was very pleasant,' said Clemenger. 'Your little mate from *The Sydney Morning Herald* was there.'

Suddenly small talk was becoming much, much bigger.

'Which little mate is that?' I asked.

'John Alexander.'

'Who?' I said, scarcely able to believe my ears and seeing deliverance looming.

'That's his name isn't it? You know, the bloke who does your job on *The Sydney Morning Herald*.'

'The editor, yes. A small, thin bloke; very intense. Who else was there, Peter?'

'Bob Mansfield was there too and so was Brian Powers.' Powers was CEO of both Australian Consolidated Press and Publishing & Broadcasting Ltd, Packer's two main companies, at the time and would later become chairman of Fairfax. Mansfield had been a short-lived CEO of Fairfax.

Now incredulous, I asked: 'And what did they talk about all this time you were on Kerry's boat?'

'What else?' said Clemenger. 'What they'd all do when they got control of Fairfax.'

I almost dropped the phone, but quickly went into reporter mode, distilling the conversation down so I could pass it on.

'Let me get this straight, Peter,' I began. 'You just spent three days on Kerry Packer's yacht off Fiji with Bob Mansfield, Brian Powers and John Alexander discussing what they'd all do when they got control of Fairfax. Is that right?'

'Yes,' said Clemenger, who had no reason to be anything other than frank. 'That's exactly what we did.'

In a rush, I brought the conversation to an end: 'Peter, I've got to go. Sorry, let's speak again soon.'

Whatever Alexander's motivations for pursuing the Fairfax lobbying story and trying to put me in it front and centre, he was now in the thick of it. I immediately tried calling him once more but, again, Alexander was unavailable. So I asked for Lyons, telling his secretary it was extremely important. He was quickly on the line.

'John, do you know where your boss was at the weekend?' I asked.

'No,' said Lyons, his voice suggesting something was about to ruin his day.

'Well, I do,' I said. 'He was on Kerry Packer's boat off Fiji, discussing a carve-up of Fairfax with Bob Mansfield and Brian Powers, so if I'm in that bloody story tomorrow and he's not, it will be a bloody disgrace.'

'Ah, you've put me in a difficult position,' said Lyons. 'Can I get back to you?'

'Sure,' I said. 'But let me make this perfectly clear: if you don't put the record straight on this in *The Herald* tomorrow, I'll put it straight in *The Age*. Tell your boss that.'

Needless to say, it was a highly charged evening at *The Sydney Morning Herald*, ending with a threat by the paper's House Committee to stop work if the paper didn't record Alexander's weekend frolic. I put one of my own Canberra reporters on the story to increase the pressure on *The Sydney Morning Herald* to clean up its act; in the end, the paper carried a story on page two of the next day's edition detailing Alexander's trip and I held off, in line with my pledge to Lyons to give him first shot at putting his house in order.

That decision was misinterpreted within Fairfax, even by Lyons himself, who rang the next morning accusing me of letting down readers of *The Age* by not running the story. I was taken aback, believing I had simply honoured my undertakings to him to let *The Sydney Morning Herald* put the record straight in the first instance.

The broader story of lobbying on behalf of Fairfax or, at least, my alleged role in it, never ran in *The Sydney Morning Herald*. To his credit, Alston rang Fairfax CEO Bob Muscat to refute any suggestion I had advocated the break-up of the group.

Having survived the near-death experience of being accused of trying to break up Fairfax, I was pleased to escape for a family holiday to Tasmania in April, but in my absence, all hell broke loose. It was during this two-week period that my fate was sealed.

In what amounted to an extraordinary act of intimidation, lawyers threatened separate legal actions on behalf of two Victorian ministers, Marie Tehan and Alan Stockdale, over *Age* stories. Then lawyers acting on behalf of Felicity Kennett had a go too, over a *Good Weekend* article. Lloyd Williams' legal representatives also chimed in at this time, again over a *Good Weekend* piece. (The fact that I had no editorial input or control over the magazine apparently escaped them.)

But the best—or worst—was yet to come. In an unprecedented move, the Victorian government solicitor wrote 'on behalf of the state' accusing us of 'malicious and spiteful journalism' designed to 'besmirch the reputations' of ministers. The letters of demand were sent, not to me as was the usual practice, but to the Melbourne managing director, John Reynolds, and Fairfax CEO Bob Muscat. Our lawyers had never seen anything like this level of intimidation; clearly there was some undeclared war underway.

Editors become used to such letters of demand. Normally, you pass them straight on to lawyers who, without exception, respond in the coolest of terms, rejecting the demands as fanciful. Managing directors or CEOs rarely get involved unless the paper is dangerously exposed. When they are pulled into the net, they invariably turn to jelly. It was imperative that Muscat stare down what I believed was a misuse of government legal muscle and stand behind his journalists and editors. Instead, he was straight on a plane to Melbourne for meetings with Williams and Jeff Kennett in order to placate them. It wasn't the strongest position to take. Worse, he never consulted me; I only learned of the meetings from a third party.

As luck or, rather, misfortune would have it, Richard Keddie's documentary on John Brumby's failed attempt to unseat Kennett, *Outnumbered,* was shown on the ABC around this time. Muscat flew to Melbourne for separate meetings with the casino boss and the premier while I was on holidays. Williams, citing footage in the documentary, apparently asked the new Fairfax CEO how on earth I could continue as editor of *The Age.*

Muscat, who admitted to the meetings only after I confronted him, told me, 'Don't take this the wrong way, Bruce, but I told Jeff that every time he attacked you, it made it harder for me to get rid of you.'

'Gee, thanks for your support, Bob,' I said derisively to Muscat. Was there any other way to take it?

Worryingly, Kennett did indeed go quiet for several weeks, resisting the urge to attack the paper or me. Then came the official opening on 9 May of Crown Casino on Melbourne's Southbank. As events unfolded that night and in the weeks following, it became clear some sort of fix was in.

The casino's opening was telecast live on the Nine network, perhaps not surprising given the principals' and the premier's links to the Packers. Kennett spoke and couldn't help but take a shot at me and *The Age* when he spied me in the audience.

I knew when I accepted the invitation that we would be damned by our critics but we would have attracted even more criticism if I had turned it down. No doubt there would have been accusations—and phone calls to board members—alleging boycotts or worse. Despite my deep misgivings about the processes that had preceded the granting of the casino licence, we were actually quite measured in our editorial the morning after the opening, more generous than my private view.

The night itself was glamorous in the extreme with endless champagne and headline acts including Ray Charles, Kylie Minogue and John Farnham. The fireworks alone probably would have paid for a new hospital ward if not the entire hospital.

Organisers clearly had had fun with the seating arrangements on the night: Janne and I were put in Siberia with a tableful of Channel Nine personnel. I took it as an indication of the burgeoning importance of the Packers in our lives. Meanwhile my *Sunday Age* colleague, Jill Baker, was seated at the ALP table alongside John Brumby and future attorney-general, Rob Hulls. A Crown executive was also at the table with his wife. At one point I walked past their table, nodding genially. At that moment the wife of the Crown executive leaned over to Baker and whispered: 'Does Bruce Guthrie have any idea he's about to be sacked?'

When Baker rang me the next morning to tell me the story, she was angry and appalled. 'I'm sick of all this, Bruce. Maybe we should just resign,' she said.

I assured her there was no prospect of me being sacked because things were going too well.

The pressure built even more just four days later when Costello brought down the Budget. The night after the Treasurer handed it down, the ABC's *The 7.30 Report* opened its program with a story on its selling, detailing the many interviews and appearances Costello made after the event. It featured overlay of him talking with me in *The Age* room during the budget lock-up while we looked at my hand-drawn layout of page one. At one point we laughed and joked as the cameras rolled. Hours later Costello's Canberra phone rang—it was Kennett.

'Peter,' Kennett said. 'It's all right to like *The Age* and Bruce Guthrie, but I'm still going to kill both of them.' Costello relayed the story to Nikki Savva and urged her to call me. Neither Savva nor Costello could believe that Kennett had rung—the Treasurer and the premier rarely talked—or that he had expressed such sentiments.

Despite all the turmoil, we still managed some first-rate journalism during this time. We won a swag of Walkley awards later that year in a range of categories, but by that time I was gone. Investigative reporters Gary Hughes and Gerard Ryle won for 'Suffer the little children', a series of stories establishing that wards of the state had been used as guinea pigs in experiments conducted after World War II. The stories reverberated worldwide.

It was another example of the enormous rewards papers can reap if they give talented reporters time and resources to follow their instincts. Sadly, as the revenue base for newspapers shrinks, it's the sort of journalism that is most under threat. I was actually questioned about the public interest of the Hughes–Ryle series at a formal dinner at one of Melbourne's few all-female clubs, the Alexandra, in July 1997. One audience member felt history should be left alone.

During my address I had spied Fairfax board member Sir Roderick Carnegie at the back of the room listening with a kind of half-smirk. I had a curious relationship with Carnegie; we got along quite well but he was forever bemused by the ways of journalists and journalism.

As I fielded questions at the Alexandra Club, to my surprise Carnegie raised his hand. I gave him the floor, alerting the audience to his status as a Fairfax board member. Why did I think *The Age* was viewed by so many people as anti-Melbourne, he asked.

I called for a show of hands: who thought we were anti-Melbourne? Up went the hands of Carnegie and his table of guests and not many more besides. Who thought we were a positive and respected part of Melbourne? Up went the rest of the room. The vote was at least 10 to one.

'There you have it, Sir Rod,' I said with some satisfaction.

His reply? 'I think it was a close-run thing.' I walked out into the cold winter's night, thinking I wasn't long for this world.

I had three weeks left. The countdown began with the resignation of David Syme managing director John Reynolds. After an uncertain start, we had developed a very good relationship—the long and lean Reynolds was a sure and steady hand on the commercial tiller who left me alone to worry about the content of the paper. He would have no doubt preferred we had a better relationship with the Kennett government, but he had long ago factored it in as part of newspaper life.

When he called me up to his office to tell me about his impending departure, he uttered a fateful observation: 'I'm afraid your job is going to get a lot harder, Bruce.' Whether or not he knew about the machinations going on in Sydney, Spring Street, Southbank and elsewhere is unclear, but he would soon be proven right.

After several weeks' silence on a successor, I flew to Sydney to talk to Muscat about who might replace Reynolds. We met in his office at Sussex Street. Without committing to anything, Muscat was extremely sympathetic. He had no-one specific in mind to replace Reynolds, he said. I did extract from him a promise that, no matter whom he appointed, I would still report to him, not the new managing director in Melbourne.

His assurances lasted fewer than 24 hours.

The next morning I was leaving for work when Janne came running from the house, saying: 'Bob Muscat's on the phone, he says it's important.'

Muscat had flown down from Sydney that morning and was gruff, asking how far away I was. 'Come to the fifth floor—I have something important to discuss with you,' he said.

There are obvious parallels between my experience in July 1997 and what would unfold at the other end of town 11 years later at the *Herald Sun*. But there was a very significant difference: I had anticipated my demise at *The Age* since the change of ownership seven months earlier; I had no inkling of the treachery that would unfold at the *Herald Sun*. Both ways hurt.

As it turned out, Muscat didn't want to sack me. He was more creative than that. He simply wanted to advise me of an announcement the company would be making to the stock exchange later that day: Steve Harris, former *Sunday Age* editor and HWT editor-in-chief, would be returning to Spencer Street as managing director. That might be workable, even productive. But there was a sting in the tail.

'I've also appointed him editor-in-chief of *The Age*,' said Muscat. 'You remain editor, Bruce. That doesn't change,' said Muscat.

'But Harris can overrule me?'

'I suppose,' said Muscat.

'So I'm editor in name only. I go from senior editorial executive to number two. It's a downgrade, Bob.'

'No it's not, you're still the editor.'

At that point, I thought I would remind Muscat of his assurances less than a day earlier. 'Why didn't you tell me all this yesterday?' I asked him.

'Because,' he said, 'it wasn't finalised.'

'So you lied to me Bob,' I said.

'No, I just didn't tell you the whole truth,' said Muscat.

'That's the same thing, Bob.'

That night, after putting out the paper and dealing with the scores of queries from puzzled staff members, I faxed Henry Muller at Time Inc. in New York. As a 43-year-old father of two young children, I was in a precarious position. The job market was tough. Because of Kennett I would almost certainly have to leave Victoria. Where the hell would I find a position?

If Muller was true to his word, perhaps New York would be an option. After a restless night, Janne woke me with a faxed reply from him that said he would be delighted to discuss opportunities if I could get myself to New York. It wasn't a guarantee of work, but it was a potential opportunity. I went into *The Age* that day thinking that if events unfolded badly, I might now at least have a career option that hadn't existed the previous day.

The key to my future was Harris. If the editor-in-chief's title was only a kind of reserve power, I could put aside my misgivings and work on. But if he really was going to try to edit the paper, there wasn't much future for me. Besides, such a scenario would amount to a complete repudiation of *The Age* charter, which vested control of the content to the editor and control of the commercial side of the business with the managing director.

Years later former Fairfax advertising director Nick Jones recounted a story that illustrated the inherent conflict perfectly. During his time at Sussex Street, Jones had pulled off a coup by convincing Holden to launch their new Commodore through the pages of *The Sydney Morning Herald*. The sale was worth millions to the paper, then edited by Alexander. There would be wraparounds, double-page spreads, consecutive right-handers, you name it.

Yet, 24 hours before the in-paper launch, Alexander published a review of the car that was less than enthusiastic. Outraged, Holden immediately pulled their ads, and took their business elsewhere. Jones stormed into Alexander's office to register his protest in the strongest possible terms. Alexander pointed out to him that, although he regretted the loss of revenue, editorial could not be qualified because of it. The so-called church–state divide meant that sometimes content could endanger revenue. It was a price that occasionally had to be paid.

In time Muscat imposed his model on every Fairfax paper, eventually making Alexander a managing director and editor-in-chief in Sydney. It was a marriage of church and state designed, I believed, to make editors more commercially minded and, hence, more compliant.

As Jones asked me years later when we were both working at News Limited: 'Do you think the editor–managing director would have published that Commodore review if he knew it was going to stuff up his revenue figures that month?'

Harris and I spoke around midday and within seconds it became clear to me that, whatever successful partnership we had had in the past, he wasn't interested in renewing it. He would be 'all over the paper' in his new role, he said, and I wouldn't like it. Besides, he had a very different view of Jeff Kennett and the combined role of editor-in-chief and managing director. I appreciated his honesty, at least.

I couldn't bring myself to undo all the work I'd done the previous two years, so late on Thursday, 31 July, I finally left the place ostensibly on three weeks' leave while I considered my future. I never returned.

My final edition of *The Age* appeared on 1 August, the first five pages turned over to the Thredbo disaster in which a landslide levelled two ski lodges in the Snowy Mountains village, killing 18 people.

The next day former Victorian premier John Cain rang to say he and former Labor senator John Button were keen to galvanise staff and readers to wage a campaign against my treatment and the marrying of the editorial and commercial functions under Harris. He was disappointed when I told him I had already signed the 'divorce' papers; if I hadn't been exhausted by months of turmoil and intimidation, I probably would have wanted to fight too. But I was spent.

I did summon the energy to ring Fairfax board member Sir Laurence Street to tell him I was appalled that the board had given Muscat the power to force me out.

His response stunned me: 'But we didn't, Bruce. You were supposed to run the paper and Harris and Bob were to run the company.' Clearly, I had been outmanoeuvred.

In the end, I concluded I just happened to be in the wrong place at the wrong time. I had had eight very successful and happy years at Fairfax and, because of a few people who just happened to be passing through, a few lousy months. Within a year, Muscat was gone and so was Rod Price, the man who had goaded me over Kennett at our first meeting. By December 1998, Brierley Investments was gone too, selling back its stake in Fairfax. Even Kennett exited, thrown out by the voters of Victoria in September 1999. The church–state divide between editorial and commercial was eventually restored too.

The final say went to our golden retriever, Rosie. We had successfully trained her to retrieve the three daily papers we had home delivered each day—*The Age*, the *Herald Sun* and *The Australian*. On the morning after my exit she dropped the editions of the tabloid and the national daily at our feet as we sat down to breakfast.

No *Age*. After repeated attempts to get her to retrieve it, I decided to do the job myself. When I walked out the front door, I found it in pieces all around the garden where she had shredded it. She stood proudly at my feet, brown eyes looking up at me in supplication. I burst into laughter and patted the top of her head.

'Good dog, Rosie,' I said. 'Good dog.'

III
___

Sixth Avenue to Southbank

19

New York, New York

Our glamorous new life in the world's most exciting city began on the footpath outside Scores gentlemen's club around midnight in mid-September 1997. Janne and I had our two small children in tow as the cab-driver deposited us and our luggage outside the strip club, watched by about a dozen men queuing to go inside. Some years later, Scores and its pole dancers would come to national prominence for having hosted a drunken Kevin Rudd and *New York Post* editor, Col Allan, on one of Rudd's overseas study tours before he became prime minister. Our travel agency must have liked the place too, because they had booked us into an apartment virtually right above it.

I had come to New York for a series of job interviews with senior editorial executives of Time Inc., the largest magazine publishing company in the United States, which took its name from its flagship, the weekly news magazine *Time*, established by company founder Henry Luce in 1923. Time Inc. was now part of the huge Time Warner media conglomerate.

Eventually I would do four interviews, the first with Henry Muller, then his boss, Norman Pearlstine, the former *Wall Street Journal* managing editor overseeing all Time Inc. magazines as editor-in-chief, and then Landon Jones, the long-time *People* editor who had offered me the *Who Weekly* job four years earlier in Sydney. Finally I was ushered into the office of Jones' successor at *People*, the highly formidable—and highly successful—Carol Wallace, like me a former newspaper editorial executive, who had moved from New York's *Daily News* to *People* with great success. We hit it off, even though many others didn't. At one point during her tenure, the *New York Post* carried a gossip item on the hard-driving Wallace and her occasional clashes with staff. It was head-lined, 'Editor is not a People person' and asked: 'Is Carol Wallace the "editor from hell"?'

Time Inc. was very much an Ivy League company, full of Brooks Brothers suits and proud of its arcane traditions. Its great appeal to me was that it took immense care over its journalism, believing that if you got that right, the audience would follow. In that sense it was closer to Fairfax than, say, the News empire, which just went for numbers. If News could get there through journal-ism, that was a happy coincidence; if they couldn't, they would try nearly anything else to build an audience.

Henry Muller had decided that *People* was a better fit for me than *Time*. I was happy either way: while my head said *Time*, my heart said *People,* particularly as I was fond of popular culture. In the end, we agreed I would come over for two weeks in the new year and 'kick the tires' to see if I liked the place. It would also give them a chance to size me up.

The enormously successful *People* had started life as a column in *Time* that delivered bite-sized information about prominent people, especially celebrities. After launching in March 1974, *People* quickly became the most profitable consumer magazine in a group that also boasted *Sports Illustrated*, *Entertainment Weekly*, *Fortune*, *InStyle* and scores of others.

I had been a fan of *People* since our Los Angeles days. I loved the depth of its reporting, the pace, density and structure of its writing and the quality of its photography. Most of all I liked its core philosophy that every story is best told through a person. While it put celebrities on the cover, at its heart it was a news magazine, and a very good one at that. It also demanded—and got—extraordinary access to the United States' most prominent people. It was usually a condition of interview that subjects allow *People* reporters and photographers into their homes for what was known internally as the 'spaghetti shot', usually a candid snap of 'extraordinary people doing ordinary things', like making pasta for dinner.

People's founding editor, Dick Stolley, a former assistant managing editor of *Life* magazine who famously negotiated the rights to the Zapruder film of the JFK assassination, had clearly enunciated his formula for success at the weekly. It was based on years of watching sales rise and fall according to what was on the cover. Unlike *Time*, which was sold mostly by subscription, *People's* profits relied heavily on newsstand sales. About two-thirds of its average weekly sales of 3 million-plus came from newsstand purchasers. Given these could fluctuate by millions—1 million being barely acceptable and 3 million cause for celebration—there was tremendous pressure on editors to get their covers right. 'Stolley's formula', as it came to be known, went like this:

> Young is better than old
> Pretty is better than ugly
> Rich is better than poor
> TV is better than music
> Music is better than movies
> Movies are better than sports
> And anything is better than politics.

In time it was further refined by Stolley's successors. Landon Jones, who successfully ran the magazine for eight years until Wallace's ascension in 1997, once told me that he had eventually concluded that the ultimate *People* story was: 'Young woman struggling with problem.' But it couldn't just be any young woman—it had to be someone the public admired or at least liked and, ideally, the problem would be God-given rather than self-induced. In other words, buyers would flock to read a story about a young actress battling a serious illness but would be less inclined to buy a cover devoted to someone battling a drug problem.

Not surprisingly, *People* spent a lot of time and money trying to pick cover subjects that would sell. They were forever testing concepts—celebrity slimmers, sudden-money winners—and potential covergirls. Women almost always outsold men.

The magazine also spent a lot of money figuring out why covers *didn't* sell. In 1999, *People* pulled out all stops for a cover story on Dr Jerri Nielsen, the medico who had diagnosed her own breast cancer while working at the South Pole. The diagnosis prompted an extraordinary rescue story with the US Air Force pulling off a high-risk landing to get Nielsen out of Antarctica and back to the United States for cancer treatment. As was its custom, *People* swarmed the story, throwing huge resources at it and producing a first-rate cover ... that didn't sell. Weeks later, the magazine's marketers convened a focus group and asked them why they didn't buy the issue. Incredibly, while they acknowledged Nielsen's bravery, they resented her decision to take the posting in the first place, leaving her three children at home in the care of others.

It reminded *People* editors of another aspect of the formula: readers need to empathise with their cover subjects. Without empathy, there would be no sales or, at least, the millions *People* needed to keep the cash flowing in.

People editors had lots of theories on what would and what wouldn't sell an issue. Cover lines were an art in themselves and taken very seriously. Wallace would convene special meetings to finalise them every Tuesday morning and they would often run more than an hour as senior editors argued over verbs, nouns and adjectives. They would also try to tip the sales potential of the forthcoming issue, and back up their predictions with a dollar-in, winner-take-all sweep.

While I was mostly an onlooker the first week I was there, I managed to edit two stories into the next edition of the magazine, which featured *Titanic* star Leonardo DiCaprio on the cover. It did well. This illustrated another element of the *People* formula—catching the wave. It was vital when profiling stars that you picked your moment: if you went too early, no-one would buy it because they weren't sufficiently interested; too late, and they would be sick of reading about them. The timing of the DiCaprio cover was perfect.

After my two-week stint, Janne and I had a huge decision to make: should we stay or should we go? In the end we chose New York. It was a courageous decision because although I would be a senior editor at *People,* my contract was only for one year and it promised nothing more than a plane ticket home if I bombed out. My absence would last nine years.

★ ★ ★

In my first weeks at *People,* I had to recalibrate more than 25 years of newspaper learning. I also had to check my ego at the door. The Australian newspaper industry—and the people who inhabit it—has long believed its journalism to be pre-eminent and that other mediums are little more than noise. Most Australian print journalists are dismissive of the electronic media—television is sourceless and senseless, radio little more than news ripped and read from papers—to the point of barely concealed disdain.

At least radio and television are part of the conversation— unlike, say, magazines. There have been exceptions in Australia. *The Bulletin* was a journalistic and cultural icon for more than a century before its closure in January 2008 after 128 years of publication. One or two business magazines and the local edition of *Time,* now also defunct here, have made important contributions too. But it is newspapers that have traditionally dominated journalism in Australia.

Indeed, they have even encroached into core magazine territory over the last 25 years with the launch of various first-rate inserted magazines, glossy supplements that come free of charge with Saturday and Sunday editions of newspapers. The standouts here have been *Good Weekend* and *The Weekend Australian Magazine*, each contributing terrific journalism, photography and design over an extended period. They have, in turn, accelerated the demise of the relatively few newsstand magazines that sold on journalism rather than gossip or special interests.

This mirrors the publishing landscape of, say, Britain, which is also a newspaper stronghold with only a relatively few serious magazines, including *The Economist* and *The Spectator*, finding traction in the market. Elsewhere it's left to private passions—fishing, boating, motoring, whatever—and celebrity gossip and women's magazines to drive magazine sales in the UK.

But it's a very different landscape in the United States where the country's finest journalism has long been found in a vast stable of first-rate magazines. By contrast, relative to population and the scale of the market, the United States has only a few newspapers that can continue to claim true excellence and profits: *The New York Times, The Washington Post* and *The Wall Street Journal*.

America's finest magazines have included—and continue to include—*The New Yorker, Time, Newsweek, Harper's, Vanity Fair, Esquire, New York* and *The Atlantic*. Over the years they have produced some great journalism and continue to command an audience, albeit one in decline. At their heart is first-rate writing and reporting.

At the very core of this rich magazine history sits Time Incorporated, the biggest and most profitable magazine publisher in the United States. From its headquarters on New York's Sixth Avenue, directly opposite the famed Radio City Music Hall and

My father Bob was a widower trying to raise two daughters on his own when he met young nurse Ruby Thornley at a postwar dance in Rockhampton, Queensland.

Mum and dad married in 1950, moved to Melbourne and settled in Broadmeadows where my brother Ross (rear, centre) and I (front, centre) grew up. There was no shortage of friends on the Housing Commission estate.

I have no recollection of my two years in the Austin Hospital, which is probably a good thing—my days were spent on my chest on a frame, my nights on my back. No wonder my birthdays were joyous affairs.

I was saved from paraplegia, or worse, by young medical officer Dr Loris Figgins, who chanced upon using blood transfusions to successfully treat TB sufferers.

My stint covering Victorian politics in the mid-1980s (including a trek to China with Premier John Cain and reporters David Broadbent, left, and Jean Walsh) helped me become US west coast correspondent for the HWT.

Based in Los Angeles and armed with an LAPD press pass—and a healthy travel budget—I could go pretty much anywhere I wanted.

After the Murdoch takeover of the HWT, New York correspondent Bruce Baskett and I were both summoned home to Flinders Street. We had a 'celebration' dinner with our wives (Janne, left, and Taz in Honolulu, March 1987).

No-one could accuse Fairfax of rushing into the launch of The Sunday Age *in 1989. Just a few months out the senior staff charged with getting the paper off the ground (Janne, Steve Harris, Wendy Bowler, Geoff Slattery and me) had nowhere to sit, unless you counted upturned rubbish bins and builders' scaffolding.*

When police raided The Sunday Age *in the mid-1990s in search of leaked documents, I was secretly pretty chuffed. It was another step in our coming of age.*

Greg Taylor was farewelled at his retirement dinner in May 1993 by (from left to right) former Age *editor Les Carlyon, incumbent Alan Kohler, Conrad Black, editorial director Michael Hoy, CEO Stephen Mulholland, me, chairman Sir Zelman Cowen, Greg Taylor's successor Stuart Simson, Kohler's predecessor Michael Smith, Taylor, Smith's predecessor Creighton Burns, and* BRW *editor Robert Gottliebsen. The Conrad Black takeover of Spencer Street was complete. (Michael Clayton-Jones/Fairfaxphotos)*

The first edition of The Sunday Age *in August 1989 rolled off the Spencer Street press to a waiting (from left to right) John Jennison, Peter Davies, Steve Harris, his* Age *counterpart Creighton Burns, me and Greg Taylor. (Fairfaxphotos)*

The first edition's memorable and defining front-page pic of Paul Keating and a beaming Bob Hawke almost didn't happen after minders tried to cancel the shoot. (Wayne Ludbey/Fairfaxphotos)

Believe it or not that slogan on the lectern—'Melbourne's Newspaper'—was the result of hours spent in marketing meetings discussing brand positioning and elements. (Andrew De La Rue/ Fairfaxphotos)

Judging by the smiles, the story list must have been a good one at this Age *news conference in 1996. On my right is Paul Ramadge, who would become editor 12 years later.*

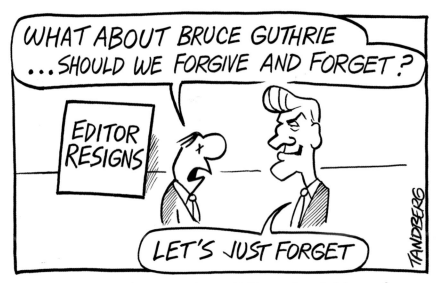

My resignation from The Age *in August 1997 caused much debate at Spencer Street and great celebration at Spring Street. Tandberg's take was perfectly pitched. (© Ron Tandberg)*

In October 1996 the ABC moved into Spencer Street for a 'day in the life' special. 3LO's Drive *host Douglas Aiton (interviewing me outside my office) did his entire program from the editorial floor. (Fairfaxphotos)*

One of the traditions of Time Inc. publications was the introduction of new editors in the pages of their magazines. Soon after we arrived in Sydney from New York in January 1999, Who Weekly publisher Marty Gardner published this photograph and penned a letter for the magazine, noting I was Who's first Australian-born editor. In the end I had four happy years there and took the title to its first Magazine of the Year Award. (Photo: Michael Amendolia)

Jeff Kennett's antipathy towards the media was well known. He famously confirmed it at the start of work on Melbourne's CityLink project (in 1996) by shovelling dirt over a waiting press pack. (Simon O'Dwyer/Fairfaxphotos)

The Weekend Australian Magazine *had struggled to match the success of Fairfax's* Good Weekend *since its launch in 1988, but its readership exploded in 2004 after a redesign and relaunch. The extra readers meant extra advertisers, and in November that year we were able to publish its biggest ever issue (pinned page by page on my office wall).*

Newspaper of the Year editors usually get to bask in the glory for at least 12 months. But nine weeks after I accepted the prize (on 8 September 2008 with Andrew Leighton of paper manufacturer Norske Skog) I was sacked. (PANPA)

Rupert Murdoch delivered the annual Boyer lectures on 2 November 2008, three days after he congratulated me on our website of the year win and eight days before my downfall. (AP/Rob Griffith)

Janne and I managed to put on a brave face most days as we walked the gauntlet to the Supreme Court. (Craig Abraham/Fairfaxphotos)

News Limited CEO John Hartigan struggled in the witness box despite the presence of his two key minders, corporate affairs boss Greg Baxter (behind Hartigan on 28 April 2010) and the company's chief general counsel Ian Philip. (Craig Abraham/Fairfaxphotos)

Norman O'Bryan, SC, tore apart the News Limited witnesses during his cross examinations. The son of a retired Supreme Court judge, he was particularly effective in his questioning of HWT managing director, Peter Blunden. (Craig Abraham/Fairfaxphotos)

Although News would deny it played any part in my dismissal, things started to go awry from the moment (23 October 2008) I splashed with 'Beverly Hills Cop'.

Murdoch's sister Janet Calvert-Jones (above, with husband John at John Elliott's wedding in 1987) became the first woman on the HWT board soon after her brother completed his takeover. She would later go on to chair the company. (Craig Abraham/Fairfaxphotos)

HWT managing director Peter Blunden (dining on 30 April with News chief general legal counsel Ian Philip, on his right) wasn't on News' witness list when the trial began on 27 April 2010, but he made a 'surprise' appearance, spending all of the fourth day in the witness box. By lunchtime that day he was already looking defeated. He fared no better that afternoon or in the subsequent judgement. (Craig Abraham/Fairfaxphotos)

Former HWT managing director Julian Clarke (leaving court on 28 April 2010) and I worked together well during my first year as editor, but you wouldn't have known it from his testimony. (Craig Abraham/Fairfaxphotos)

Given the trial and its lead-up I thought I was magnanimous in victory. Solicitor Tony Macken (on the steps, above my right shoulder) had sensibly urged it. The inner man was pumping his fists in triumph though. (Rebecca Hallas/ Fairfaxphotos)

After losing our court battle, News' CEO John Hartigan was reported to be trying to negotiate a way of avoiding court action by independent Melbourne Storm directors. Once again, Ron Tandberg made his point perfectly. (© Ron Tandberg)

next door to Rupert Murdoch's corporate base, dozens of the world's best weekly, fortnightly and monthly magazines emerge. It is, if you like, the epicentre of American magazine publishing; quite probably a global centre too.

And *People* sits very much at the centre of Time Inc. This is despite a slightly uncertain beginning, when many of the company's more conservative employees and executives questioned not only the wisdom of launching such a title but also the very propriety of it. What was Time Inc. doing getting into celebrity journalism? Answer: creating a whole new category of magazine that would very quickly bring millions of dollars in profits to the company and inspire dozens of imitators.

Time Inc.'s answer to the internal and external criticism levelled at *People* in its early days was to apply the same searching and strict editorial standards that it applied to its other more 'substantial' titles, including *Time* itself. Hence, although the magazine might be reporting on, say, the rise of Leonardo DiCaprio or the breakdown of the Tom Cruise–Nicole Kidman marriage, it would do so with unparalleled standards of accuracy, balance and research.

Celebrities weren't its only story subjects. *People* cast its net far and wide, searching for 'ordinary people doing extraordinary things and extraordinary people doing ordinary things'. It meant that in one issue you could read about the world's biggest box–office star or a mid-west librarian with a talent for sculpting the Last Supper out of a pumpkin. It was an extraordinary compendium of well-written and scrupulously reported human stories.

By the time I arrived in April 1998, *People* had become a publishing phenomenon with average weekly sales of more than 3 million and a readership of more than 10 times that. With a cover price of around US$3 and advertising page rates in excess of US$100 000, it was pretty much a licence to print money. *Rolling Stone* founder Jann Wenner had been trying for years to grab market share with his *US Weekly* but *People* was still very much the king of the jungle.

The first thing I noticed about my fellow senior editors and assistant managing editors was their age. There were about a dozen of us in all and many, if not most, were older than me. This was not the way journalism was playing out in Australia where, increasingly, anyone over 50 was being offered redundancy. At *People*, they were prized as the best and brightest, bringing tremendous experience and talent to the table.

Henry Muller had warned me that the sometimes curious ways of Time Inc. could be stifling. 'For better or worse, not everyone has the stomach for the bureaucracy and hierarchy,' he had cautioned me in a letter before I got there. Its approach to journalism was certainly multi-layered but I accepted it because it was designed to deliver better and more accurate reporting and writing.

Unlike the generalism of Australian journalism, where reporters gathered facts, wrote their stories and then fact-checked them along the way, each of those elements was done by different people at Time Inc., beginning with reporters reporting and writers writing from the reporters' source material. Senior editors entered at the next level, before handing their final stories to assistant managing editors, three or four trusted lieutenants who were the gatekeepers of the magazine's content. Then there was the managing editor herself who, depending on her mood, could send the whole thing back to its starting point.

After clearing all those hurdles, the fact-checkers would enter the picture. Usually smart young college graduates or long-time staffers, it was their job to literally stand behind you and tick off every fact, as you sought to close the story and send it to the copy desk. If they were in dispute—say, a descriptive passage that was neither black nor white—this process could seem interminable. Story subjects loved that fact-checkers actually called them to check quotes that were going to be used in the magazine. No wonder *People*—and its Australian counterpart, *Who Weekly*, which had the same editorial standards—was trusted implicitly.

In my first week at *People*, Carol Wallace surprised me by suggesting I write before I edited. That was all perfectly fine, except I hadn't really written since my Los Angeles posting, more than a decade earlier. It was one thing to have to pick up writing again after a 10-year lull, but in another country and for an audience I was largely unfamiliar with? That was a tall order. Worse, the *People* style was quite complex. It had an extraordinary energy and density to it that propelled readers along at a very fast clip. There was no such thing as a naked noun at *People*; everything had to impart information, even when attributing quotations.

So, for instance, when Wallace informed me of my duties on the magazine, I would have recorded it thus: Wallace, a stocky 43-year-old single woman from Chicago, told me I would be writing for my first few months at *People*, adding: 'It will help you understand the magazine's DNA.'

Like all writers at *People*, I was assigned to a pod or team that worked for a senior editor, in this case former *Washington Post* reporter Rob Howe. He was responsible for commissioning, running and editing stories under particular headings that might include everything from politics to parties. Other senior editors included Max Alexander, a former editor of showbiz bible *Daily Variety*, Jim Kunen, author of the late 1960s book—which later became a film—on student radicalism, *The Strawberry Statement*, and Larry Hackett, a former *New York Daily News* reporter whose name was appropriated by Michael Keaton's character in the Ron Howard film *The Paper*. They were a talented and endlessly entertaining bunch.

In the first instance, a senior editor was required to fill out an 'assigning wire', a detailed note that went electronically to reporters throughout the *People* network both nationally and, if necessary, internationally. It would detail what the senior editor required from reporters and could assign tasks to dozens of reporters in dozens of places depending on the scale of the story. The resources of *People* seemed limitless. The assigning wire would finish with a copy deadline that had to be observed. On a big, breaking news event like a celebrity death or mishap or major disaster story, the turn-around time could be 24 to 48 hours. But often it might be weeks.

Once reporters filed from various outposts, their contributions would be assembled into printouts and given to a writer who would be given a strict line count. Once the writing was complete, he or she would also furnish captions, a headline and a brief summary of the story, all of which would appear on all *People* stories. Then the editing would begin; like any organisation, some editors had a light touch and some were heavy-handed. If you were lucky your story would sail through to the next link in the chain, an assistant managing editor. But it could also come back at you very quickly, especially as the senior editor had read—in fact, was required to read—the same reams of reporting on which you had based your story.

In my first weeks at the magazine my writing efforts came back at me thick and fast. I did up to four rewrites on some pieces, a soul-destroying experience for someone who thought he was reasonably good at his job. After about a month of this, I trudged home to our apartment on Manhattan's West 60th Street one Friday night telling Janne I feared I had made a terrible mistake.

'I'm not sure I'm ever going to get this,' I admitted, before sitting down with a dozen editions of the magazine and reading them cover to cover so I could unlock their 'DNA'. At 4 a.m. the next day, I went to bed thinking I was finally making some sense of things.

Unlike newspaper reporting, essentially an inverted pyramid that has the most salient facts in the intro and the less important material at the bottom, a well-constructed magazine piece has to have a start, a middle and a finish. If you graphed it, it would look less like a pyramid than a straight line with regular peaks. Road-mapping is everything in magazines. I was rushing my writing because that's almost a requirement of newspaper news sections.

A *People* story had five basic components: the intro, a compelling fact, incident or anecdote that essentially 'turns on a light in a darkened room', as one senior editor described it; the billboard paragraph, where you flag what is to follow so readers will stick around; the body of the story, where you detail your best stuff; the subject's bio—where he came from and what he did before this newsworthy point in his life; and finally, the tagline or outro, a fact, anecdote or incident that ties up the whole piece, often completing a circle that began in the intro.

By Monday morning, I went to work at Time Inc. with a whole new confidence—and nailed a three-page piece first time; it eventually found its way into the magazine pretty much untouched. Within weeks, having proven I understood the magazine's basic story structure, I assumed my senior editing duties.

At all times the senior editor was working on two fronts at *People*: the issue that was coming at them at great speed and future editions, up to three weeks away. Hanging over them at all times was the all-in Wednesday morning story conference where, having sent the issue the previous night, they would be expected to offer up completed stories for future editions of the magazine. This process would be presided over by Wallace and you better not fall short.

A certain cold chill would come over you when she turned to you in front of the 50 or so people gathered in the conference room—senior editors would sit at a central table, watched by other staffers seated around the tennis court–sized room—and say: 'C'mon guys, I need a three-pager that's upbeat. What have you got, Bruce?' It was character-building, to say the least.

I quickly grew to love my time at *People*. It was demanding, but the staff and executives were great and the product was exceptional. More importantly, I felt I was learning again.

The family was happy too. We had moved out of Manhattan after our two months in midtown and headed for the suburbs of Westchester County. Each day I would walk a kilometre or so from our rented house in suburban Larchmont to the railway station and then board an express train to Grand Central, about half-a-dozen blocks from Time Inc.'s headquarters. The 43-minute train trip was like stepping into some secret society. Commuters, most of them bankers, brokers or lawyers, would grab the same seats every day; they would even stand on the same part of the Larchmont platform. I made a fool of myself my first morning as a commuter when I stood between two clusters of passengers. They knew exactly where the train doors would be opening and I was left stranded as the train pulled in.

Sometimes it felt like a Neil Simon farce. Conversation was frowned upon, as riders preferred to read *The New York Times* or *The Wall Street Journal* in peace. At day's end, I would grab any number of Time Inc. magazines or page proofs, and settle in for the ride back to Larchmont, where Janne and the kids—Susannah and Scott would often be in their pyjamas—would be waiting for me. It was a wonderful interlude in our lives.

I especially enjoyed Tuesday closing nights at the magazine, probably because it recalled my newspaper days. If you were working on a cover or a major forward story, you might not escape the building until well after midnight. Time Inc. provided limousines home on these nights—they would take you from their door to yours. It was almost worth the long hours.

As the months passed, rumours began to swirl, mainly out of Sydney, that I would soon be prevailed upon to return to Australia to run *Who Weekly*. It had been more than five years since I had first turned the job down. In that time, the magazine had succeeded in many ways but fallen short in others. Its sales had struggled to get above 200 000, well short of the mass-market *New Idea* and *Woman's Day*, but it carried more ad pages than any other Australian weekly. *Who*'s audience of young women and a surprising number of men had proved attractive to marketers. But sales were falling.

Sure enough, in the first week of December 1998, Henry Muller invited me to lunch in the Rainbow Room, the restaurant that sits atop Rockefeller Centre. Would I return to Sydney to take over at *Who*, he asked.

My mind flashed back to a similar lunch with Rupert Murdoch a decade earlier when, again, I was being asked to give up life in the United States for an opportunity in Australia. Then—and now—part of me wanted desperately to say 'no', but I knew that I really couldn't.

20

Bound for Botany Bay

Despite the success of *People* magazine, Time Inc. had never tried to export it. This was in contrast to, say, *Time* magazine, which was available in nearly every corner of the world. In the early 1990s, that all changed when it was decided to launch the fabulously successful celebrity–news title in Australia.

There was one immediate problem though: the name was already taken here, by a magazine that was as far removed from mainstream values—a hallmark of *People*'s American success—as could be imagined. Owned and operated by Kerry Packer's ACP Magazines, in Australia *People* was a 'tits and bum' publication. No problem, thought the bosses of Time Inc., we'll simply buy the name from Mr Packer. Clearly they hadn't done their due diligence. If they had, they would have known that he would drive a hard bargain. Sure, Packer told them, you can have the name . . . if I have half the business.

And, so, unable to use the name of its parent magazine, *Who Weekly* was born, the first offshore edition of *People*. The name had been suggested in a staff poll by Nancye Alexander, a famously gruff New Yorker who was one of an army of *People* employees flown out to Sydney months ahead of launch to ensure the magazine's success.

Local hirings could only marvel at the largesse heaped upon these visitors—harbour-side apartments, company credit cards, lavish entertainment budgets that even included something called the 'keeping current' allowance. This allowed staff to claim hundreds of dollars a month on movies, music or, say, visiting concert acts on the basis that they needed to stay abreast of popular culture. If that wasn't enough, it was said one New Yorker even continued to conduct weekly appointments with his shrink by phone to Manhattan, at company expense.

If Time Inc. had underestimated Packer, they left little else to chance. Their planning was otherwise meticulous, beginning with test issues overseen by a small New York advance party headed by a legendary Time Inc. editor, Hal Wingo. When those issues tested well, they went into full launch mode—lavish, staffed to the max and endlessly expensive. In typical Time Inc. tradition, they were prepared to wear losses for five years, confident the magazine would eventually pay for it 10 times over, just as the mothership had done.

When the magazine finally launched in early 1992, it was eye-catching, to say the least. Compared to the dowdy titles it was up against—*New Idea* and *Woman's Day*—it was positively edgy with a modern design and brilliant use of black-and-white photography. But more than anything it was well written; hell, up against the dross being pushed out at ACP and Pacific Magazines, it was almost literature. Time Inc. backed it up with an aggressive marketing campaign, built around The Who's 1978 hit, 'Who Are You?'

Who quickly attracted a young, hip crowd, both male and female. Survey after survey revealed that men read *Who*; they would never be caught dead with any of the older, established weekly titles that were our 'competition'. This was because of a certain Time Inc. alchemy, known within the organisation as 'permission to read'. Put simply, the multi-page do-ups on, say, Vietnam war veterans or real crime stories gave buyers subliminal permission to read about the dating habits of Lindsay Lohan or Pamela Anderson.

Yet despite successes in some reader categories, overall *Who* sales fell well short of what Time Inc. bosses had been assured the magazine would attract—hundreds of thousands short. Instead of a circulation of 500 000 or more, which is what the original business plan envisaged, *Who* struggled to get to 200 000. All of which may have seen it shut down after a year or two. But a curious thing happened, entirely unexpected in midtown Manhattan or at Lavender Bay, the picture-postcard, harbour-side setting of Time Inc.'s Australian operation. Advertisers flooded to the magazine, attracted by its dominance of the 18 to 25 market. They came in such numbers that it almost offset the relatively poor circulation of *Who*, ensuring its survival but leaving it in a kind of financial purgatory, never quite turning a profit, but too close to kill.

Tom Moore, the launch deputy editor who had landed the top job after I had turned it down, had got himself into hot water in June 1994 when he had put a picture of accused backpacker killer, Ivan Milat, on the cover of the magazine before Milat had even gone to trial. Moore claimed to have received legal advice that it was safe to publish but with identity clearly going to be an issue in the case, it was fraught with danger. Sure enough, Moore and the magazine soon found themselves charged with contempt. The magazine would be fined $100 000 and Moore $10 000.

He recovered from the setback to become a successful editor of the magazine, but there was another legal mishap in the late 1990s when *Who* carried a picture of journeyman actor David Carradine and his wife in its 'Star Tracks' pages, the popular pictorial spreads that opened the magazine. It should have been safe ground but, in pulling together the captions on the page, a young reporter identified the wife of the *Kung Fu* star as a porn actress. This was untrue and highly defamatory. Carradine sued.

I had twice been drawn into the mess during my stint at *People*. In mid-1998 the editor-in-chief of Time Inc., Norm Pearlstine, sidled up to me while I waited for a lunch companion in the foyer of the company's Sixth Avenue headquarters. (It was a great place to people-spot because you were never sure who you might bump into: in one three-day period I spied First Lady Hillary Clinton, baseball's home-run hero, the since disgraced Mark McGwire, and author Tom Wolfe.)

'I've just spent the past couple of hours with Mr Carradine,' said Pearlstine, shaking his head ruefully. 'We've been trying to find a way through the "porn star" problem.'

'Any luck?' I asked.

'Well, put it this way,' said Pearlstine. 'He wants a two-picture deal and a few things besides.'

As Time Inc. was now part of an entertainment conglomerate that included Warner Brothers movie studio, such things were possible, I guess. Some months later, in my final days as a senior editor at *People*, I was asked to issue an assigning wire for a piece the magazine would be doing on Carradine's, ahem, career resurgence.

Despite these stumbles, Moore's exit from the magazine—Time Inc. found another role for him in Sydney—was a matter of regret in some sections of the media. Sydney's *The Daily Telegraph* put it on page three of the paper, complete with a picture of him being farewelled over a beer at a Lavender Bay pub. Clearly it had been a quiet news day. *The Telegraph* reported that there were tears in the corridors of the magazine as its 'beloved' editor was moved on for a 'sacked' *Age* editor. Another News title, *The Courier-Mail*, called my appointment the most surprising of the year 'after that of Fred Hilmer as John Fairfax Holdings' supremo'. Ah, it was nice to be back home; clearly the standards of reporting hadn't improved.

I started in the role on Australia Day 1999 and very soon learned there was a stark difference between the local and American markets. In New York, the *People* approach to its journalism was richly rewarded week after week at the newsstand. In Australia fiction masquerading as fact outsold us week after week. Eventually it dawned on me that a strange sort of compact existed between other local weeklies and their readers; it was not unlike the unstated understanding that is at the centre of, say, professional wrestling—you know it's fake and we know it's fake, but let's not admit it to each other. It will be much more entertaining that way.

This curious attitude to celebrity journalism meant most readers ignored ours—scrupulously gathered, checked and double-checked—for the deception routinely peddled by our competitors. Worst here was ACP's *NW,* Kerry Packer's response to *Who* after Time Inc. had politely turned down his demands for half their business in Australia. Starting life as *New Weekly,* it briefly flirted with quality before descending into the usual morass of celebrity lies and half-truths. It was about as far removed from journalism as one could get, but it was slowly building its circulation.

We had to face an unpalatable truth: the journalism that we so prided ourselves on was actually dragging us down at the newsstand. We had to somehow break away from the pack. We began workshopping possible new approaches. While we would never compromise the journalism—it was an article of faith within Time Inc.—there were other levers we might be able to pull.

But there were distractions. First, Time Warner and internet provider America Online had announced a merger of the two companies, an astonishing development that reportedly had Rupert Murdoch wondering what the deal-makers had been smoking when they struck it. While we were thousands of kilometres away, it didn't take long for news to filter in from New York that this was not exactly a marriage made in heaven, particularly with AOL's share price plummeting as the internet bubble slowly deflated.

The deal had been the brainchild of Time Warner boss Gerald Levin and AOL's Steve Case. Levin had got lucky when he backed the future of cable television and now he was putting all Time Warner's bets on the internet. I had met him once during a New York visit and he had completely disarmed me by exclaiming when Pearlstine introduced us that '*Who* is just about my favourite magazine in the whole company', before adding *sotto voce*: 'I probably shouldn't say this, but I think it's better than *People*.' Levin would eventually be forced out of the boss's chair when the AOL deal went sour and with him went my chance to dine out on the story.

Then there was the Sydney Olympics. Time Inc. was a major sponsor so there was a steady stream of visiting executives from all parts of the empire. Advertising clients were also in town from various American markets, many of them housed on an ocean liner the company had leased for the duration of the Games and parked on Sydney Harbour. Ever thoughtful when it came to its revenue streams, the company made sure the boat was turned around each day so that if you missed out on a view of the Harbour Bridge and Opera House through your porthole one day, you wouldn't the next.

Some guests got even better treatment. The company flew in Leonard and Evelyn Lauder and put them in a five-star hotel in the eastern suburbs. Despite the luxury surrounds, some of the furniture fell short of the cosmetic tycoon's expectations—so the perfumed pair insisted that Time Inc. also fly in their bed from New York. Given Estée Lauder's spend in Time Inc. titles, Time happily complied and it was waiting for them when they checked in.

Once the distractions had passed, I pushed through an idea I had been developing almost since I had taken on the job—we would bring forward our on-sale day by 72 hours. Since launch, *Who* had always come out on a Monday, along with *New Idea*, *Woman's Day* and *NW*. I proposed we bring it forward to Friday, allowing us clear air in newsagents and supermarkets all weekend but, even more importantly, stamping ourselves once and for all as a magazine with unique qualities. We would break out of the muck ruck.

We would also use the switch to relaunch and to that end renewed our deal with Pete Townshend—at a cool $150 000—to use 'Who Are You?' in an ad campaign that recalled the edginess of the original. Soon after it would also be bought by the producers of the hit television series *CSI*. We saw this as a positive, the music reinforcing our brand across the week.

In late 2000 I flew to London with *Who*'s publisher Karim Temsamani to walk management through the proposal. Eager for the magic bullet that would help deliver the mass sales they had long been promised, they went for it. We won permission to make the switch in 2001.

Our final Monday sale was the year-end issue that hit newsstands in mid-December 2000. As always, the cover was devoted to the 25 most intriguing people of the year. It was an eclectic bunch, to say the least, including axed *60 Minutes* reporter, Jeff McMullen, manufactured pop group Bardot, Olympics sweetheart Nicky Webster, former *Today Tonight* anchor Stan Grant and his new love Tracey Holmes, *Wog Boy* Nick Giannopoulos and radio's Roy Slaven and H. G. Nelson, who had wowed audiences with a very funny nightly television segment during the Games.

'Wouldn't it be great,' I told our picture editor, 'if we could get all these people together in one cover shoot and do a gatefold?' The exercise would give me new insights into the difficulties of managing celebrity expectations and egos. We had immediate success—yes, everyone wanted to be involved and, yes, everyone could make the shoot. But then it started to unravel as Roy and H. G.'s 'people' insisted their clients be on the newsstand side of the gatefold—one half is folded back away from public view. We might be able to manage that, we said. Oh, but there's one other thing, they said: the boys don't want to be on the same half as Nicky Webster. Huh? That meant that she would be on the back flap, even though she had clearly been one of the stories of the year, appearing prominently in both the Games opening and closing ceremonies. Not only that, there wasn't a young girl anywhere in Australia who didn't adore her. She would definitely drive sales.

As negotiations between our picture department and Roy and H. G.'s people became more protracted and difficult, I pulled the plug on their involvement. Instead we would use the wombat that had become the symbol of their segment. And so that's what we did. It worked: the intriguers issue was our biggest seller of the year, even though Becky the wombat disgraced itself by peeing on people midway through the shoot.

When we returned from the Christmas break we had everything in place for our relaunch. All we needed was a big story. It came in early February when Tom Cruise and Nicole Kidman announced they were separating after 10 years of marriage. The announcement was made early enough in the first week of February for us to turn it around and make it our cover story. It sold out. *The Daily Telegraph* found itself back in my good books by running a photograph on its front page of a visiting Jennifer Lopez and her soon-to-be-husband, Cris Judd, reading the issue as they waited to begin a harbour cruise.

The story ran and ran and we were always ahead of the pack because of our three-day break on the opposition. In the end we did at least half-a-dozen covers on aspects of the break-up. Our sales were booming, advertisers were queuing up to be in the magazine and competitors were even flirting with their own Friday on-sale to match us. We were finally on our way to mass-market success, or so it seemed. But we hadn't factored in the disastrous merger of AOL and Time Warner.

The deal had been formally ratified in the United States about the time we began our bold new sales approach. By mid-year the merger was proving to be a disaster and it quickly scuttled our plans. As the company's share price plummeted on Wall Street, Time Inc. managers worldwide were pressed for cost savings and more. We were certainly not immune. In quick order we lost our marketing money, promotions budget and our advertising campaign. Print runs were slashed too. The magic bullet quickly became a blank as the circulation gains levelled off. Soon we were back in purgatory again.

Not all was lost though. We found ourselves nominated for a Magazine of the Year award among the annual gongs handed out by the Magazine Publishers Association of Australia. Despite its excellence over almost a decade, *Who Weekly* had never picked up a prize at the awards. Nominated in the general interest/news category our competitors included *The Bulletin* and *Time*.

I also scored an Editor of the Year nomination but believed myself an outsider given Jackie Frank, long-time distinguished editor of *Marie Claire*, was also nominated. Somehow *NW*'s editor, Phil Barker, also made the list, even though the magazine hadn't garnered a nomination in any other category.

When the big moment arrived, the editor of the year was … Phil Barker. 'How the hell did that happen?' I thought to myself. Never mind, I gritted my teeth, managed a thin smile and applauded politely. Then, to my absolute bemusement, in his acceptance speech Barker launched a thinly veiled attack against *Who Weekly*, before quickly exiting the stage and the room.

As the audience variously hissed, booed, cheered or tittered, the host announced the Magazine of the Year nominees in our category. Seconds later the room erupted as *Who* got the gong. Suddenly the other shoe dropped; Barker was angry because he knew we had won the category. There had obviously been a leak at ACP.

The incident had a hilarious denouement in the bar afterwards. *Who* senior editor Larry Writer, one of the most respected and well-liked people in the Australian magazine industry over a very long time, took extreme exception to Barker's remarks.

'Phil Barker,' Writer said as he stood over the newly crowned editor of the year. 'What you just said in there was one of the most ungracious things I've ever heard.'

Barker, a pugnacious Kiwi, was taken aback.

'What did you say?'

'You heard me,' said Writer.

Barker was suddenly on his feet but Writer wasn't backing down. To the astonishment of many, the gentlemanly *Who* senior editor invited the former *Daily Telegraph* sub-editor outside, only to be informed he was 95 kilos and a trained martial artist.

'Nevertheless,' replied Writer. 'Outside!'

Years later Writer would recall that on their way out to George Street, Barker asked him whether he had had any fight training.

Replied the father of two: 'Yes, I box.'

Which wasn't exactly true. Writer *trained* to box but he had only ever had one fight in his life—against another 50-year-old dad whom he beat narrowly after three one-minute rounds.

When the pair hit the street, they had an audience of revellers peering through windows and from the hotel's revolving doors. Then the midwinter chill hit them and they realised how silly they were being. After some heated conversation about what had transpired at the awards, they both, with obvious relief, smiled, shook hands, and returned inside.

Barker finally demonstrated a small measure of the class he had lacked on the night, when he rang the next day to apologise to Writer. The incident—and the subsequent apology—eventually made it into the gossip column of *The Daily Telegraph*. So did my assessment of Barker's antics: 'I've met some sore losers in my time, but I've never met a sore winner.'

Despite our victory, celebrations were short lived. Still reeling from the AOL merger, our New York bosses announced that Time Inc. would be buying IPC Magazines, the biggest publisher of titles in the UK.

Suddenly we were reporting to editorial bosses in London, rather than New York, most of whom weren't imbued with the same editorial approach we were used to. This had been the only thing that made celebrity journalism palatable for me. Perhaps it was time to move on.

Ironically, it was another Magazine of the Year night that crystallised my thinking. We had produced at breakneck speed an outstanding issue of the magazine devoted to the September 11 terrorist attacks. We were on newsstands within 72 hours of the attacks, way ahead of any other title, including our stablemate, *Time*. The issue sold out and earned us another MPA nomination—for Cover of the Year at the 2002 awards.

We had gone with the same front *People* used in the United States on their September 11 issue. I had not seen the shot before we published it and I haven't seen it anywhere else since. Showing the second of the planes in silhouette flying towards the twin towers, it was just moments away from impact and only minutes after the first plane struck, sending smoke billowing into the sky above Manhattan. It was haunting, to say the least. Our cover line was simple but strong: 'The Day that Shook the World'.

We had two competitors in the best cover category, our stablemate *Time*, for its own September 11 issue, and *Harper's Bazaar* for a cover featuring a publicity shot of Nicole Kidman, dressed as the *Moulin Rouge* character Satine. We thought we were a shoo-in, with perhaps *Time* our only rival. But when the award was announced, the Magazine Publishers Association of Australia gave the prize to . . . *Harper's Bazaar*.

I made light of the decision to *Sydney Morning Herald* columnist Anthony Dennis, who had rung to seek my reaction the next day. Like me, Dennis was astounded that somehow the biggest news event of a generation could be bested by a publicity shot for a movie. I drew his attention to the 1976 Academy Awards when Sylvester Stallone's *Rocky* defeated *All the President's Men, Taxi Driver, Network* and *Bound for Glory* for the Best Picture nod.

But I was fuming. And reflecting. Had I spent more than 30 years in journalism to end my career in an industry segment that prized PR and publicity shots over genuine journalism? I was missing newspapers. It was time to get out and, somehow, find my way back to some serious stuff.

And that's when Rupert Murdoch re-entered my life.

21

The firm

The first approach from *The Australian* was an invitation to write for it, not to join it. That came later. It was August 2003 and the paper was approaching its fortieth birthday; the editor of its Media section, Martin Beesley, wondered whether I could write an anniversary assessment of the broadsheet. My first thought: what a hospital pass.

I could only imagine the sort of scrutiny such a piece might attract, both within News and outside the company. So I politely declined the invitation. Still, I was encouraged that there should be any sort of approach from News. I thought I had burned that bridge many years earlier when I had turned down *The Sunday Herald* editorship for the deputy editorship at *The Sunday Age*.

At News, people are often said to have had their card marked—'his card was marked a long time ago' or, 'I reckon we should mark her card with the black pen now'—meaning they are *persona non grata* within the organisation. I would get into trouble in mid-2005 for publishing a piece on someone who had clearly been put into this category.

I had left Time Inc. a few months earlier and was still deciding what I might do next, when there was a second approach from

The Australian. I was invited to dine with Mitchell and his editor, Michael Stutchbury, the former *Australian Financial Review* journalist whom I remembered from my days covering industrial affairs in Melbourne.

Queenslander Mitchell had also spent some time at *The Australian Financial Review* earlier in his career, but he was now a Murdoch man through and through. He had returned to *The Australian* in 2002 after an extended stint running Murdoch's Queensland daily, *The Courier-Mail*, in his hometown of Brisbane. Together, he and Stutchbury were aggressively targeting the Fairfax financial daily. They were also targeting *The Age* and this is where I came in. Or, rather, where they imagined I might.

Despite a circulation of 130 000-plus Monday to Friday and more than double that on Saturdays, *The Australian* was critically under-represented in Melbourne. On a good (week)day it struggled to sell 25 000 copies in Victoria and Mitchell was keen to crack the market.

In the earliest years after its launch in July 1964, the editor's office at the paper must have had a revolving door. Editors came and went at a furious and sometimes farcical pace, as Murdoch struggled to find the alchemy that would deliver success at the national broadsheet. It was said one editor lasted only one day, storming out after he was told he would have to sack dozens of staff.

The paper has never been profitable in any sustained way; the view within the company is that Murdoch has endured the enormous losses because *The Australian* gives him power in Canberra and some claims to seriousness in what would otherwise be an ocean of populism. Certainly Mitchell used to often complain about the difficulties of editing a serious broadsheet in a company of tabloids.

'They don't really get it,' he would say of Hartigan and Sydney managing director Peter Wiley, famous within the company for splashing with a *Daily Mirror* 'world exclusive' on a flying rabbit.

They had a much better understanding of tabloids, the lifeblood of the company, Mitchell would add.

The turnover of editors was one of the many inhibitors of early success at *The Australian*. Another was the production difficulties that flowed from Murdoch's decision to base the paper in Canberra. Stories abounded of the proprietor pleading with pilots at Canberra Airport to take off in pea-souper fog; often the plates used for printing the paper would have to be driven to Sydney with disastrous results for delivery deadlines. Ultimately, Murdoch surrendered, shifting its headquarters to Holt Street, Sydney, where he also produced *The Daily Telegraph* and *The Sunday Telegraph*.

Then there had been the infamous journalists' strike of 1975 when staff walked out in protest at biased coverage of that year's federal election. The fall-out resonated for years. It wasn't until Paul Kelly's appointment in 1991 that some stability came to the paper. By the time he vacated the chair five years later, *The Australian* was finally a respected broadsheet.

Mitchell had done a good job at *The Courier-Mail* during his seven years there, although there was one very serious mis-step. The paper had tried to portray esteemed historian Manning Clark as an agent of influence for the Soviets during the Cold War. It even suggested the prominent historian had been given the Order of Lenin. It was nonsense. But as if that weren't bad enough, Mitchell refused to let it go long after others had given up. My friendship with Clark's son Andrew, a former editor of both *The Sydney Morning Herald* and *The Sun-Herald*, gave me a particularly negative perspective on the mess.

The episode didn't derail Mitchell's progress through News Limited. As I would later learn, such mistakes rarely do—perhaps it's a rite of passage in the Murdoch empire—and in 2002 he was given the reins at the national daily. But it did give him a reputation as an editor who drove agendas. On the editorial floor of *The Australian* reporters would often complain that their copy had been changed by

Mitchell or Stutchbury to suit whatever cause they were embracing at a particular time.

The pair were proposing I return to Melbourne to become *The Australian's* Victorian editor and, as they put it, 'stick it up *The Age*'. While I liked the idea of returning to newspapers and quickly warmed to them—Mitchell, despite his steepled hair and ever-present crew-neck sweater under his suit, had a calm authority; Stutchbury had an almost puppy-like enthusiasm—I would have a hard time convincing my family we should go back. Besides, the job was really a dressed-up bureau chief's role. I would think about it, I told the pair.

Ultimately, I rejected the approach, delivering the news at another meeting with Mitchell and Stutchbury in Mitchell's office in November 2003. I didn't want to leave Sydney; that said, if any other opportunities came up, I would be keen to discuss them. It was at that moment Mitchell raised an exciting prospect.

'We might be looking for a new editor of our colour magazine,' said Mitchell. 'Harto thinks it's lost its way and needs a new direction. There aren't too many people out there who've edited papers *and* magazines like you have. Would you be interested?'

'Chris,' I said. 'I'll start tomorrow if you want me to.'

The Weekend Australian Magazine had been launched in 1988 by, of all people, Peter Blunden, as a response to Fairfax's *Good Weekend*. Blunden was fond of telling the story of how, while working in the chief of staff's office of *The Australian*, he was one day given a desk and a deadline and told to get the thing out. He had to beg, borrow and steal staff to make it happen but somehow he pulled it off. The magazine had always trailed *Good Weekend* in terms of readership and commercial success and the gap seemed to be widening. My brief was simple: try to boost both.

I started in February 2004 and I was genuinely excited to not only be back in newspapers, albeit in the Saturday supplement, as the Brits liked to call it, but also to be back at News Limited.

It had been almost 15 years since I had left them by quitting *The Herald* in Melbourne to help launch *The Sunday Age* in 1989. Back then Ken Cowley had been News Limited's Australian CEO. I had little doubt that if he had still been in the chair I wouldn't have been encouraged to rejoin the company. Word was he had few fond memories of 'the Beecher experiment', which is how the company remembered Eric's editorship of the Melbourne broadsheet from 1987 to 1989. Beecher's appointment was said to have been Cowley's idea and he didn't appreciate how it had turned out.

Mitchell confided to me soon after I started in the role that he had had to run my hiring past Murdoch, not because of my role in 'the Beecher experiment' but because of my 'controversial' editorship of *The Age*, particularly my run-ins with Kennett. Murdoch had no reservations apparently.

The most obvious change at News since I had last worked for them was the sheer scale of the business. It was truly a global media company with interests worldwide in newspapers, movies, television, magazines and book publishing. And, locally, John Hartigan was in the CEO's chair, having replaced Lachlan Murdoch in 2000 who, in turn, had replaced Cowley three years earlier after Cowley's extraordinary 17-year reign as Rupert Murdoch's number-one man in Australia came to an end.

Hartigan was the first person at my door on my first morning at *The Weekend Australian Magazine*, enthusiastically welcoming me back to the company. I was genuinely touched by the gesture. Over the next three years he would always be supportive and encouraging. Harto, as he is known throughout the company both in Australia and abroad, is very popular within News and respected for the job he has done in the decade since he replaced Lachlan in the CEO's role. We would eventually be pitted against each other through Blunden's treachery; Hartigan's standing—and our relationship— would be battered by the court case.

Hartigan once revealed to me that, when the younger Murdoch came to his Holt Street office in 2000 to ask him to join him for a mid-afternoon drink at a local pub, he was convinced he was going to be sacked. But instead of dismissing him, Lachlan revealed he was going off to run the *New York Post* and wanted Hartigan, then the company's group editorial director, to replace him as CEO. Hartigan told me: 'My first thought was, "I wish I'd paid more attention at school".'

My other abiding memory of my first day at *The Weekend Australian Magazine* was being told I had a second job, before I had even sat at my new desk. I had reported for duty at Mitchell's office, who after exchanging initial pleasantries showed me the dummy of a new monthly magazine called *Wish*. It was a high-gloss, big-format product, similar to *The Australian Financial Review*'s monthly magazine but it was shorter on substance, recalling the UK *Financial Times*' monthly supplement, *How To Spend It*.

'Lachlan's [he was still News Limited chairman at that stage] very keen to get this off the ground sometime this year, ideally around August,' said Mitchell, adding: 'So you'll have to get cracking on a new dummy sooner rather than later.'

Bloody hell, I hadn't sat behind my new desk and I already had an extra gig. (I would eventually launch *Wish*, but it would take 18 months, not six.) I would soon learn that a favourite technique of Mitchell's, indeed, News Limited's, is to throw a grenade in and see how executives react. Process is not necessarily a dirty word at News, but it's not that highly thought of either. This was in stark contrast to my memories of Fairfax—or, for that matter, Time Inc.—where the processes and planning could sometimes seem stultifying. Because News prides itself on being a company of journalists, it retains some of the 'seat of the pants' qualities that once drove the profession, particularly on daily newspapers. This can sometimes be a little unnerving, as it was on my first morning back, but it can also be liberating, even exhilarating.

News Limited's Australian headquarters in Holt Street, Surry Hills, is a wonderful place from which to produce newspapers. In the 1990s, Lachlan Murdoch had faced the same decision as HWT executives in Melbourne and Fairfax executives in Sydney: whether to stay or leave the company's traditional homes as printing plants moved out to the suburbs. The *Herald Sun* bid farewell to Flinders Street, *The Sydney Morning Herald* said goodbye to Broadway but Lachlan chose to stay at Holt Street, opting for a multimillion dollar refurbishment of the place rather than paying rent on some soulless office block. Thank God he did.

The main editorial floor of *The Australian* is huge, with departments spread far and wide. But, importantly, they are all contained on one floor, a definite advantage for editors. Not that Mitchell necessarily availed himself of it; he was renowned for wearing a path between his office and the backbench at night, but not much more besides.

The Weekend Australian Magazine occupied a large chunk of the north-east corner of the paper's editorial floor. Writers, sub-editors and designers, about 15 staff in total, worked in an open-plan area, while the editor and deputy editor had offices. It was a very comfortable environment, part of the newspaper, but sufficiently detached.

Soon after arriving, I instituted a redesign and would relaunch the magazine with great success. Our readership jumped by almost 100 000 in one survey, giving us more readers than the host newspaper. Hartigan and his fellow commercial executives loved this, but there were some on the editorial floor who struggled to understand how more people could read a component of a paper than the paper itself. It didn't confuse me at all: the paper was very blokey, quite earnest, and on its worst days, dull. Visually it was grey and drab. I couldn't imagine too many women plunging into it. So I added fashion to the magazine, even some health and beauty and changed the look and philosophy of our food pages to attract them. I also threw its pages open to anyone on *The Australian* who had a good idea for a magazine story. Having come from Time Inc., where editors are expected to turn dross into gold every day, I figured it would substantially increase the story pool. The approach was in contrast to, say, *Good Weekend*, which was written week in, week out, by mostly the same pool of writers. I wanted *The Weekend Australian Magazine* to be either the first thing people went to because they couldn't wait to read it, or the last thing they kept back to savour.

The huge readership boost meant we sold more ad pages, which, in turn, put the magazine into profit for the first time in its history. Peter Wylie, the crotchety but extremely likeable Sydney managing director, told me Rupert Murdoch could scarcely believe the magazine had actually started making money. If I wasn't careful, they would start thinking of me for other jobs, I thought to myself.

Other people thought so too; indeed, the speculation started very early in the piece. It went up a notch or two when, in March 2004, after barely a month back at News, I was invited by Lachlan Murdoch and Hartigan to attend a three-day conference of News executives from around the world at Cancun, Mexico.

As always with such get-togethers, the digs were lavish— the Ritz Carlton Hotel—the list of guest speakers impressive— Condoleezza Rice, then the National Security Advisor, was piped in from Washington and Stormin' Norman Schwarzkopf was on hand to regale us with war stories—and the pace frenetic—sessions ran all day from 8 a.m. through to 6 p.m. And then came the real challenge: surviving the nightly partying that invariably started at a restaurant, continued on at a nightclub and then wound down back at the hotel bar.

News prides itself on being a company that likes to party hard. As we bounced from bar to nightclub to bar at Cancun, I was reminded of Sam Chisholm's observation during his halcyon days at the Nine network: 'Losers have meetings, winners have parties.'

The defining moment of the conference came for me at the Saturday night dinner where Rupert Murdoch delivered a keynote address. It wasn't his speech that stayed in my mind—it was his introduction.

Roy 'Rocky' Miller is a legend at News Limited, having served the company for close on half a century, including eight years as editor of *The Sunday Telegraph* in Sydney. Miller was at Cancun as the managing director of Murdoch's *Gold Coast Bulletin*, a position he would hold until his retirement after a decade in the role. Miller typified the sort of executive Murdoch prefers: hard-driving, hard-partying, a doer rather than a thinker. He had all the requisite rough edges Murdoch seems to look for as well, including a preference for colourful language.

I had first become aware of Miller in 1987, soon after the Murdoch takeover of HWT. Steve Price swears he rang Miller one day when Rocky was working on *The Daily Mirror* in Sydney to update him on what *The Herald*'s chief political reporter, Kate Legge, would be filing from Russia, where she was following Prime Minister Bob Hawke on a visit. Given the *Mirror* was now our sister paper in Sydney, Legge's copy would go to them too.

'Hawkey's apparently going to visit some factory in Moscow today and then meet a couple of bigwigs from the government,' Price told Miller, adding: 'Oh, and she's going to do a feature on *perestroika*.'

To which Miller is said to have replied: 'Who's this bloke Perry Stroika?'

Which may or may not have made him a good choice to welcome Murdoch to the podium on this particular Saturday night in Cancun. Especially as he had had a few drinks in the afternoon to calm his nerves.

He began well enough. 'Good evening, ladies and gentlemen,' he said to the hundreds of guests, including British Opposition leader, Michael Howard, and his novelist wife, Sandra. 'My name is Roy Miller and I have the great honour tonight of introducing a very great man, Rupert Murdoch.'

He certainly had everyone's attention, particularly those who picked up on a certain uneven rhythm in his speech patterns. Then he got emotional.

'Just before you come up here, Rupert, I want to say one thing though: you're my fucking hero.'

Now, there were three distinct reactions in the ballroom at this point: the Australians guffawed, the Brits merely shook their heads and reminded each other that we were all descended from convicts and the earnest Americans couldn't believe it.

Miller went on, repeating his key phrase. 'No, no,' he said to an increasingly rowdy audience. 'You are my fucking hero, Rupert.'

As Murdoch rushed to the stage, grabbed the microphone and assured Miller he had 'said quite enough', you couldn't help but feel you were in the bosom of a particularly unique company. People like Miller weren't frowned upon for such behaviour; indeed, he seemed to fit the mould for all those who rose to great things. Sure, he would never take, much less top, an MBA class, but Miller delivered for Rupert in a variety of roles, ultimately growing his *Gold Coast Bulletin* into a cash cow. The Murdochs loved him for it.

Back in Sydney, I soon had a management challenge on my hands—one of the paper's key executives was in relationships with two of my writers and it was proving distracting, particularly as one of the relationships had produced two children and lasted 20 years. Some days our office resembled a French farce, as one woman left the building to avoid the other arriving. In the end, News dealt with it as only News can. *The Australian's* executive editor at the time, Deborah Jones, arrived in my office one afternoon to tell me our already slim headcount had been cut by one and no questions were to be asked. One of the two women had been given a redundancy cheque and was never seen again. The other relationship continued all the way to the altar.

It was another example of News Limited's blokey pragmatism, which kicks in when one of theirs needs to be protected and normal procedures and processes become too bloody difficult. It's almost biological. Murdoch sees it as an extension of company loyalty. He has talked of the need to both give and appreciate hard work and loyalty.

'I think when you're loyal to people and they're happy, you can get better work out of them,' Murdoch said in 2008. 'It makes for stability in a company, as well as happiness.'

Which is all very well, but I often found myself wondering when and how you qualified for such loyalty. Was it two years with the company, five years, 10 maybe? Or was the formula different— did you earn the company's loyalty by taking bullets for them? A demotion maybe, or a hardship posting accepted without complaint? Perhaps just a blind determination to put News ahead of everything else in life: marriage, family, stability. Was that what got you into the News family? Either way, there wasn't a great incentive for outsiders to join. Perhaps it was why News had so much difficulty assimilating talent from outside.

I knew what didn't qualify you to be part of the family. Or, at least, I learned the hard way. One of the elements I introduced into the forward section of *The Weekend Australian Magazine* was a bite-sized column by Melbourne journalist Douglas Aiton called 'Ten things you didn't know about ...' Each week the subject would change, but the general format didn't. In the 7 May 2005 edition of the magazine, Doug profiled television host Andrew Denton. The piece included, as fact five:

He has enjoyed watching *The Simpsons* beyond all other television shows. 'It is the *Gulliver's Travels* of our time and the great document about America. The fact that it's on Rupert Murdoch's payroll makes it even more extraordinary.' He believes Murdoch is the most influential international Australian 'by a country mile.'

223

At the time of publication I was diverted by my 'second job', devising *Wish* magazine for an October launch. But I made sure I was at my desk when the 7 May edition was closing. As proofs of pages poured in, the magazine's deputy editor, Graham Erbacher, a sure and steady pair of hands, drew my attention to Aiton's column.

'You know that Denton is *persona non grata* around here,' said Erbacher, almost in a whisper, as the edition took shape around us.

'No, I didn't. Why?'

'It all goes back to Super League,' said Erbacher.

This was a reference to the rival rugby league competition News Limited established in the mid-1990s. Called Super League, it competed against the traditional National Rugby League for one season before the two sides settled their differences in court. Because of his love for the South Sydney club, Denton famously led opposition to the News Limited offshoot.

In a 1999 episode of ABC television's *Australian Story*, Denton said of News executives: 'I wish I could take Lachlan Murdoch [and] . . . Ken Cowley by their smug little jowls and sit them down for a while and just explain something to them from a marketing sense. Tradition in sport is a very, very powerful thing.'

I didn't know the detail of this at the time and I would like to think I wouldn't have changed my decision to publish the Denton piece even if I had. In any event, I put the page through. I probably held my breath for a few days but there were no consequences the next week. Or the next. But they did come.

Towards the end of May, Chris Mitchell rang me from his office.

'Bruce, why did you put Andrew Denton in the magazine?' he asked, matter-of-factly.

'What, three weeks ago?' I replied.

'Yes, in that "Ten things" column,' said Mitchell.

'It was pretty innocuous stuff, Chris. He even said nice things about Rupert, didn't he? Why, what's up?'

'I've just had Lachlan on the phone from New York and he's not happy,' said Mitchell. 'In fact, he's very pissed off.'

The editor-in-chief then went on to flesh out the reasons for this: Super League and Denton's opposition to it.

'Sorry, mate, but I was a bit distracted by *Wish*,' I offered by way of explanation.

There is no finer political strategist at News than Mitchell and he could see a defence emerging here. He would simply tell Lachlan that I had been working away at one of his pet projects at the time and the column had fallen between the cracks. That should protect everyone.

'Before you go Chris, is there anyone else on the black list I should know about?'

'You'll know when it happens,' he said with a laugh.

The episode left me thinking News was like a landscape littered with landmines. I also realised that if there was a black list, there was probably also a list of protected species, those people who were particular friends of News and must never be touched.

I had first suspected this almost two decades earlier in the midst of a six-week editing stint on *The Herald* in Melbourne while Eric Beecher was travelling overseas. Our gossip columnist had gently chided *New Idea* boss and Channel Seven board member Dulcie Boling, for what he thought was her icy demeanour. Within a matter of hours I received a faxed rebuke from Rupert in New York. 'If you think this sort of garbage sells newspapers,' he wrote, 'you are sadly mistaken.' Fortunately he had addressed it to Beecher. I demonstrated early survival skills by replying: 'Eric's not in today, Mr Murdoch. I have dealt with the matter.'

It was becoming abundantly clear I would need all those skills and more to survive long term at News.

22

'An opportunity has come up . . .'

For John Hartigan, the urbane and seemingly ageless chairman and CEO of News Limited, 24 November 2006 must have been a difficult day. As king of the media jungle in Australia, Hartigan wasn't used to criticism. But on this Friday morning he had copped it with both barrels from, of all people, James Packer.

In a long cover story published that morning in *The Australian Financial Review*'s glossy *AFR Magazine*, the young Packer hopped into Hartigan with a relish that recalled some of his famous father's harangues. Written by Pamela Williams and Damon Kitney the piece said in part:

> One subject flicks the switch—a mention of News Ltd chairman and chief executive, John Hartigan. Ask Packer why he has fallen out with Hartigan and you smell smoke in the air. 'Who says I have?' Well, people say. 'Well, that's between Hartigan and I,' he snaps. Half an hour later, he returns to the issue. 'I think that the reality is that companies like Seek and CarSales are making life harder for newspaper companies, and John Hartigan probably had the choice to say to Rupert that

it is James's fault or he could have said to Rupert "I messed up". I think he has probably looked to blame me as opposed to looking in the mirror.'

Around Holt Street, the piece spread like news of an impending visit by the proprietor. Then everyone started reading the tea leaves: what was Packer up to? Was this some sort of square up? After all, News and PBL, the media group James had headed for almost a year since his father's death the previous December, were partners in Foxtel. Why would a partner behave like this?

I read the Williams' story with more angst than most. For several weeks one of *The Weekend Australian Magazine*'s most senior writers, Richard Guilliatt, had been toiling at a profile of Packer. It was to be the cover of our 9 December issue. Guilliatt had been unable to get an interview with Packer; Williams and Kitney had had spectacular success on this front. Would our piece have to be junked?

I decided to press on. While interviews with cover subjects are almost always preferred by editors, sometimes a write–around drawing on numerous sources can be more revealing. Guilliatt was confident he had nailed his subject and after reading his first draft I agreed. But what if we could get Hartigan to fire back at Packer? It was worth a try.

So I took the unusual step of sending Guilliatt's story to the CEO on the internal email system with a note suggesting to Hartigan that if he wanted to reply to Packer's diatribe, I would be happy to include his comments in our cover story, which we had just started editing. It would go to the printers in six days.

A little over an hour later, Hartigan's personal assistant rang, asking if I could pop up to see him in his fifth-floor office. As I got into the lift on the third floor, I ran through all the possibilities: he had decided to use us to hit back at Packer—a good result for the magazine and me; he was being polite and thought it best to keep his own counsel—a neutral result for the magazine and me; or, he thought the Guilliatt piece was no good and should be spiked— a terrible result for all.

In fact, it was none of these. After exchanging pleasantries, we chatted very briefly about Packer's comments. Hartigan seemed genuinely bewildered—and untroubled—by them. I told him I had sent through our own planned profile of Packer and an invitation to respond, if he was so inclined. Hartigan had seen the email, but hadn't had time to read the piece, he said. (He never took up the invitation.)

'I actually wanted to speak to you about something entirely unrelated,' Hartigan explained. In all my years of dealing with him, I don't think I had ever seen him do or say anything that suggested anything other than a preternatural calm. Everything about him seemed unhurried. This was particularly true of his speech patterns.

'An opportunity has come up,' Hartigan said, pausing for effect. In the second or two between his first sentence and his second, I immediately presumed I was about to be offered the position of editorial director of News Magazines, the bunch of titles the company had just purchased from the Federal Publishing Company. Chris Mitchell had indicated as much in a conversation several weeks earlier when we were returning from the News Awards ceremony, held that year in Melbourne.

That would have been an easy decision for me and a logical step for News. After all, I had spent the best part of a decade in magazines; News would have been able to put a trusted lieutenant atop a stable of titles and editors it neither knew nor understood and I would have taken it in an instant. But life isn't like that.

Hartigan went on: 'It [the opportunity] is interstate though and I realise it won't be an easy decision, given your family situation.' Another pause. And in that second or two, a couple of scenarios played out in my head. Perhaps he was speaking of the Adelaide *Advertiser*—or maybe *The Courier-Mail*. Adelaide or Brisbane? We had no connection to either of those cities; there was no way I could convince the family to move to either. At least it would be easy to say 'no'. Besides, both papers were in safe hands already. Then he hit me with a suggestion that was so off my radar I actually had to get him to repeat it.

'I'd like to offer you the position of editor of the *Herald Sun*,' Hartigan said.

'Pardon?' I replied.

'Editor of the *Herald Sun*.'

'But what about Blunden?' I stammered. It had long been believed they would have to carry him out of the HWT Tower, which prompted my next statement: 'I thought he'd have the job for life.'

Hartigan explained that Julian Clarke, who had headed up HWT since 1991, had decided to retire. Blunden would be groomed as his replacement throughout the new year, eventually stepping into the role on 1 December 2007.

'So you can take your time over this,' said Hartigan. 'There's absolutely no hurry.'

I knew instantly that I would need weeks, not days, if I was to convince my family. Hell, it would take days just for me to convince myself that I wanted the job. Sure, it was the biggest paper in Australia and it would be something of a triumphant return to newspapers and Melbourne if I accepted, but we were very happy in Sydney.

That night, Janne agreed it was a tremendous compliment to be offered the position, but thought it would be a disastrous move for the children. Susannah was on a scholarship at a small private girls' school and Scott was just completing a difficult first year at a selective private school with a tough entrance exam. Plus Janne had seen what daily newspaper editing had done to me 10 years earlier as editor of *The Age*. Why on earth would I want to put myself through it all again?

Intellectually, I could easily find reasons to reject the role, but emotionally I was drawn to it. In truth, I was missing newspapers and their ability to affect debate and bring about worthwhile change. I felt I needed a switch, but did it have to be as tumultuous as this?

Janne and the kids thought not. In the days immediately after Hartigan's offer, family discussions would invariably end up in argument and sometimes tears. More than once I wished he had never raised the bloody prospect. I was constantly reminded of a Gary Larson cartoon that features the devil, pitchfork in hand, standing outside two doors to hell. One is labelled, 'Damned if you do', the other, 'Damned if you don't'.

I next talked it over with Clarke, who was encouraging. I had no real interest in taking the job if I was merely expected to mimic Blunden's idea of what a newspaper should be.

Clarke indicated he wanted change, adding that while Blunden had done a good job over a long period, the *Herald Sun*'s circulation was in serious decline and it was time for new approaches. (In court, Clarke would deny saying this but any sales graph will confirm the paper had lost significant ground during 2006, Blunden's final year at the helm.) Clarke told me he thought the paper wasn't as intelligent as it could be, especially its opinion and editorial pages, adding: 'I think you could have particular impact there.'

By early December, the family was beginning to come around. But the more soundings I took, the more difficult the decision became. The most worrying advice came when I called a senior HWT executive to ask whether I should take the job.

'Well, I wouldn't,' the executive said. 'The place is a mess and there's very little talent amongst the senior editorial group.' Chris Mitchell put in his five cents' worth too. Blunden wouldn't be able to let go, he said. This was getting harder and harder.

There seemed to at least be a consensus that the *Herald Sun* could improve. People thought I could have a substantial impact on the paper, which, in their opinion, had fallen away drastically in 2006. I felt so too. Against that there was the almost universal assessment of Blunden: no matter what he or others said, he would not be able to let go of the *Herald Sun*.

I decided it was time to put it to him. On 8 December, two weeks after Hartigan had made his offer, Susannah and I flew to Melbourne. We were due to visit several schools that were options for her if we decided to make the move. I started the day by meeting Blunden in the office that would become mine just two months later.

From the outset, he was keen to take credit for my candidacy. 'You were my idea,' he said. 'Harto and I had lunch and he asked me to prepare a list of possible candidates. When I got back to the office, I sent him about three or four names. You were very much at the top and there was daylight between you and the second one.'

According to Blunden, Hartigan responded quickly and enthusiastically. 'He rang me within 60 seconds of getting the email and said, "That's a great idea, mate. It has to be Bruce Guthrie".'

I asked why had he decided to give up the editorship and move into management.

Because, he said, he had decided that if he turned it down to remain editor-in-chief, he might end up with a managing director he couldn't work with. And where would that leave him?

Besides, after 11 years in the job, he had had enough. 'I took my eye off the ball last year, I have to admit that,' said the veteran editor.

Hartigan, he went on to say, had promised to send him to an American management school in 2007 and he hoped to be there for an extended stint. I remember thinking this would be good for both of us. I've often said that if you got six newspaper editors in the one room before first edition deadline and gave them the same story and photo list, they would agree on probably 80 per cent of it and disagree, perhaps violently, on the remaining 20 per cent. Having your immediate predecessor one floor above you second-guessing each day's paper was a potential difficulty, to say the least. If we could pack him off to Harvard or Wharton for three months, that could only do us both a lot of good. As it turned out, News never delivered on this for Blunden, a failure he and I would both come to regret.

I had another conversation with Hartigan just before Christmas. I would understand if he wanted to bring matters to a head. But if he needed an answer then and there it would have to be 'no'. If he gave me more time the answer might be 'yes'. Professionally, I had decided it was the right job for me, a very significant peak in a 35-year career. But personally it was still a very tough decision that we might be able to resolve as a family, during a house-swap we were planning in Mexico.

'Then take the extra time,' he said. I was grateful for his patience, even though a small part of me would have preferred impatience and a withdrawal of the offer. It would have been so much easier if someone else made the decision for me. But life isn't like that either.

Finally, on 7 January 2007, I sat in the study of the hacienda we were staying at in the beautiful Mexican mountain village of San Miguel de Allende and rang Hartigan.

'I have two emails here ready to go,' I told Hartigan. 'One is quite short and says I've decided not to take the job. The other is quite long and says I'll take it on these conditions. Which one should I send?'

'Well,' said Hartigan. 'Why don't you send the long one first and hold on to the other one? You might not need to send that one at all.'

Within 48 hours of sending off my wish list, Hartigan had agreed to just about everything I had asked for. Indeed, News Limited was so quick to come back to me that I almost regretted not asking for a BMW or a light aircraft.

There was only one significant knockback. Mindful of the potential for Blunden to make mischief once he became managing

232

director, I asked that I report to Hartigan, not the managing director of the HWT. But Hartigan wouldn't budge, except to concede
a 'dotted line' to him, which I could use as required. It was a concession I should never have made.

Why did I take the job?

Writers would call it circularity, the technique you employ
where the start and finish of a piece share the same elements. I had
started my career at HWT in 1972 and now I had the chance to
end it there 35 years later. I would be completing a circle.

Also, in the end, we decided as a family that the obvious
downside to accepting wasn't a negative at all: the world our children would work and live in was going to be one of constant
change. Getting them used to it early on could only improve their
ability to cope. Besides, my mother—the children's only surviving
grandparent—was approaching 90. At the very least, a move back
to Melbourne would give us precious time with her.

News of my appointment was announced while we were
overseas. It seemed to have been received with great affection and
acclaim. When we returned to Sydney in late January, Janne and I
realised we had given ourselves a ridiculously short time to pack
up our house, organise the kids in schools, and start new lives in
Melbourne. We had barely a week to do it.

Somewhere amid the mayhem I managed a brief conversation with Hartigan about what sort of paper he wanted: more
'aspirational'—whatever that meant—and improved features sections. He agreed with Clarke that it should also become more
intelligent. And with that, I was off.

I officially started in the role on 19 February 2007. Our first few
weeks in Melbourne were especially trying as we struggled to convince our kids that we could make the move work. I don't think I will
ever forget the sight of my 12-year-old son nervously approaching
his new school in an ill-fitting uniform or my 15-year-old daughter
courageously staring down the looks of other Year 10 girls—there's

nothing quite as intimidating—as she entered her new school. I had asked a lot of them; News Limited had asked a lot of us.

Soon after arriving—nervously, hesitantly, just like my kids—on my first day at the *Herald Sun*, Blunden sought me out.

He wanted to give me his assessment of the editorial team I had inherited. Most of it was negative, his former senior editors either 'past it' or 'not up to it'. It was an ungracious appraisal, to say the least. Then he told me something that disturbed me and that, with hindsight, was a window into the very curious way he conducted his professional relationships.

'I've told you, Bruce, that I drove your candidacy and that's true,' he said matter-of-factly. 'But there's a couple of people here who are pissed off that they didn't get the job, so I've told them you were Sydney's idea.'

'Why wouldn't you just tell them the truth, Peter?' I asked. 'That would certainly make life easier for me.'

Said Blunden incredulously: 'But they'd never forgive me.'

Blunden would deny the exchange when it was put to him more than three years later under oath. But his double-dealing—telling one person one thing and another something else entirely—would emerge in court as the enduring theme of our relationship. And it would cost us both dearly in the end.

23

Coming to grips

If my first conversation with Peter Blunden was curious—my support for you will be our little secret—our first handshake was downright disturbing. I would quickly learn that it was the stuff of legend around Southbank Tower. It was more subtle than Mark Latham's infamous attempt to intimidate John Howard during the 2004 election campaign. But the intent was the same—to establish his authority over whomever he was meeting.

In a deft manoeuvre, Blunden would roll his right hand from the standard vertical position to a superior horizontal. When it happened on that first Monday morning, I didn't really see it for what it was. But just days later associate editor Shane Burke, a *Herald Sun* veteran who Blunden had unfairly maligned during his briefing about staff, asked me straight out: 'Has he given you the power handshake yet?'

Three years later at trial, my lawyer would mischievously ask Blunden: 'Your normal handshake is an unusual one, would you agree?' Blunden denied it unconvincingly, and only after one or two seconds' thought. At this point in the hearing I exchanged glances with a News Limited reporter in the press gallery and we both broke into smiles.

Elsewhere, my reception at the *Herald Sun* in my first days was warm, open and extremely generous. I recognised many people from my final days at *The Herald* almost two decades earlier. Perhaps this was an indication of the enduring appeal of working for Rupert Murdoch; then again, maybe it just underscored the limited opportunities on offer within the Australian newspaper industry. You clung to your job for dear life.

In contrast to Holt Street, the *Herald Sun* was spread across three floors at Southbank Tower, a pro forma office building on the southern bank of the Yarra River. The Business and Pictorial sections and reference library were housed on the tenth floor; Features, Online and artists on the eleventh floor; and News, Sport, Production and key columnists on twelve. My office was also on the twelfth floor, which meant I inevitably spent probably 75 per cent of my time dealing with News and Sport, the key drivers of the paper.

It was a far from ideal layout, forcing you to put a lot of trust in your department heads down below. Often I would rue the sale of the old HWT building in Flinders Street. We were operating in what could easily have been the headquarters of an insurance office.

I had arrived with certain things already clear in my head: the *Herald Sun* wasn't as intelligent as I remembered it and I needed to tackle that without making the paper boring; there was too much show business and gossip (in the week before my arrival they had devoted four of the first six pages to the death of *Playboy* model Anna Nicole Smith including World War II treatment on page one); and while News, Sport and Business were in good shape, I needed to get moving on the Features sections. From discussions with senior staff, it was also clear that the writing in the paper had slipped away.

Chris Mitchell had said to me in the days before I took the job that, although Blunden might have been a good day-to-day editor, he was not a change agent, adding, 'In many ways he simply edited Steve Harris' paper for 10 years.'

236

First impressions suggested Mitchell was right. The paper hadn't created enough stars in my time away. Eric Beecher had brought Terry McCrann, Mark Knight and Andrew Bolt to *The Herald* in the late 1980s and Harris had lured Mike Sheahan away from me at *The Sunday Age* in the early 1990s. Blunden could probably claim to have built Bolt's profile by giving him a column, but the actual recruiting of the four men had occurred long before he got there. It had all happened almost 20 years earlier, yet the quartet were still the building blocks of the paper. Where were the new stars?

We were well behind on the website too. I had launched *The Age* site in the mid-1990s and a decade later it was streeting ours. It was obvious to me that although it was well led by Roger Franklin, management had used the website as a dumping ground for its problem children, a little like how Mitchell sometimes used *The Australian's* magazine. It was also critically under-resourced.

I was also keen to empower people more. Blunden's emphatic manner meant staff felt excluded from decision making, so they simply withdrew. There was a former senior news executive of the paper who went back on the road because he had tired of Blunden's tantrums at news conferences. He explained his coping mechanism: each day before the afternoon news conference he'd write down, at the top of a fresh foolscap page, the names of his children. When the inevitable tirade came, usually over what Blunden perceived to be a lacklustre news list, he would simply focus on his children until the storm passed. In court I reflected on this more than once as Blunden, Clarke and Hartigan tried to paint me as a 'difficult' editor. Compared to my predecessor, I was Mahatma Gandhi.

Then there was the simple fact that I had been out of the day-to-day hurly-burly of newspapers for the best part of 10 years. And, I had never worked on a tabloid, much less edited one. Not that it bothered me overly much. *People* magazine and *Who Weekly* had certainly honed my tabloid instincts and I liked a big breaking news story as much as the next person.

In his piece on the changing of the guard at the *Herald Sun*, *The Age*'s media writer Matthew Ricketson made much of this, wondering whether I could master a tabloid. I thought it was simply a matter of shifting decision making from the head to the heart. In their purest form broadsheets or serious newspapers *think*; tabloids *feel*, driven by emotions, not all of them positive: greed, envy, anger, lust. I would simply have to shift emphasis. Tabloids were also about removing complexity from just about any story. The trick is to do it without talking down to your audience or insulting their intelligence.

My first big news test came in my second week on the job and, in the minds of many, I failed it. On 28 February 2007, Carl Williams, the gangland leader linked to dozens of killings that would eventually become the basis of books and television series, dramatically and unexpectedly pleaded guilty to three murders. The news broke just minutes before our daily 3 p.m. news conference got underway. I had gone into the conference believing we were in good shape—news that morning of the sudden death of Australian rock legend Billy Thorpe meant the page-one art was just about locked in—and all we needed was a page-one lead.

Now we had much more than that. I decided that while the Williams story should start on page one and then take out the first four pages of the 1 March paper, we should keep Thorpe as the picture on the front. My logic was simple: people interested in the Williams' guilty plea would buy the paper in huge numbers and people wanting to mark the passing of a rock legend would also buy it in huge numbers as a souvenir. We had a double whammy.

But other news executives weren't so sure. Deputy editor John Trevorrow made an impassioned plea to drop Thorpe back to a blurb and build the page around Williams. But I held the line, even though I was beginning to think he was right. There was a certain method to my madness. During my days at *People*, a veteran editor of the title, Landon Jones, had given me some advice just before I flew back to Australia to take up the editorship of *Who Weekly*.

'At your first opportunity cover a story in a way that your predecessor never would have, just to announce there's a new guy in town,' said Jones.

With that in mind, I stuck to my guns on Williams. Problem was, the 'old guy' was still in the building. Blunden didn't express any opinions directly to me but he let others know he was flabbergasted by my decision.

Soon he had another opportunity to second-guess. Our page-one lead the very next day was another court story, this time an unlikely battle between Carlton footballer Lance Whitnall and his brother Shane. They had been warring via text messages and somehow it wound up in the Melbourne Magistrates' Court. The page featured the brothers and their wives emerging separately from court above a headline that read, 'Oh Brother'. An overline ran the full width of the page directly under the masthead saying, 'Blues star in family SMS feud'. It was a perfect page one for football-mad Melbourne, preparing for a new AFL season.

Just after the news conference on the Friday afternoon, I spied Blunden talking to the paper's chief of staff, Damon Johnston. I thought it odd, given Blunden's new office was on the thirteenth floor. I also thought it inappropriate. After all, he had trod the editorial floor nearly every day for more than a decade. Surely he could make himself scarce in my first few weeks, so I could get a foothold. I asked Johnston what the fuss was about. He explained that Blunden was passing on some comments from a 'mate' of his—Blunden had 'mates' all over Melbourne—that we had got our page-one lead wrong that morning.

'Which mate?' I asked Johnston.

'Ricky Nixon,' he replied. Nixon was a prominent AFL player manager and his clients included Lance Whitnall. Blunden told Johnston that Nixon was unhappy with aspects of our coverage.

Blunden was still on the editorial floor, so I asked him into my office, away from public view. Very respectfully, I told him I thought his conversation with Johnston was unhelpful. If he had any intelligence on stories, negative or positive, could he in future share it directly with me. And, I'd appreciate it if he limited his appearances on the editorial floor during my first few weeks.

Blunden didn't take it well and went off in a huff. Reflecting on the exchange years later, I'm absolutely comfortable with what I asked of him. But I have no doubt it sowed the seeds of my demise.

Not that he took any of it on board. The next day, a Saturday, I received two phone calls from senior editors that suggested my predecessor was never going to let go of his old job, no matter what he told me or anyone else.

The first call came around 9.30 a.m. while I was watching my son play basketball. It was our website editor, Roger Franklin, who said he had just been woken by Blunden who had abused him over a missing story. Then, just hours later, Features editor, Matt Kitchin, rang to say Blunden had called him up to his office Friday afternoon—presumably just before or just after his conversation with Damon Johnston—to offer him Franklin's job. Now my head truly was spinning. Blunden might have the title of assistant managing director, but he was behaving like he was still editor-in-chief.

I needed to nip this in the bud straight away. I rang Julian Clarke at home on Saturday afternoon to tell him what had happened and enlist his help. His immediate response was instructive: 'He shouldn't be doing this; he shouldn't be doing it. I've told him.' He'd talk to Blunden, he assured me, but whatever was said didn't work. The clumsy interventions continued and when I brought them to Clarke's attention again I asked him to set up a three-way meeting where we could clear the air. That was more productive and soon we were meeting every week to deal with issues as they arose and to assist both of us in our new roles.

That sorted, I settled into the daily grind. Over coming weeks the news cycle was extraordinary, beginning with the Yogyakarta plane crash that killed 21 people, including five Australians, and left the Canberra-based *Sydney Morning Herald* reporter Cynthia Banham critically injured. Banham's battle for life resonated enormously with us as she was the partner of the *Herald Sun*'s chief political reporter, Michael Harvey. As fate would have it, Harvey had been in my office the morning of the plane crash, discussing with me an interview we were both going to conduct with Prime Minister John Howard later that day, which we abandoned when news came through of the terrible events in Indonesia.

Next came the dramatic fall from grace of West Coast Eagles star Ben Cousins. The story dominated page one for three days in mid-March, producing huge sales. It was only displaced from the front by an accident in Melbourne's Burnley Tunnel, in which three people died when a truck suddenly shifted lanes to avoid a stationary vehicle.

Editors are always at the mercy of the news cycle. The difference between a good sales audit and an ordinary one often comes down to a Ben Cousins story or, appallingly, a tragedy that galvanises readers to buy the paper, perhaps over two or three days. Such events seemed to be bobbing up everywhere.

There was a brief respite in May which coincided with a four-day conference in Monterey, California, called by Rupert Murdoch to examine the impact of online publishing on the newspaper business. It was an important gathering, not only because of the subject matter but also because it gave me a chance to get on better terms with Blunden and Murdoch. In the end, I had little success on either front.

That we were having the conference at all was something of a comment on the industry generally and News specifically. If the first body-blow against the Australian newspaper industry was Murdoch's takeover of HWT and the second body-blow Young

Warwick's disastrous takeover of Fairfax, the third and potentially fatal blow was the rise of the internet.

Unlike many, I don't blame the internet per se. I blame the industry's reaction to it. After all, most major newspapers had launched websites by the mid-1990s; certainly by the late 1990s. Here we were in Monterey supposedly discussing how best to take advantage of it. It was at least 10 years late. Once again, the digs were lavish and so was the guest list. Presenters included Facebook founder Mark Zuckerberg and eBay boss Meg Whitman. There was a lot of talk of first-mover advantage and disruptive thinking. Murdoch sat through every minute of the conference, using it to signal that although he had long been a doubter about the future of online publishing, he now had the fervour of the convert. (He had even more passion for *The Wall Street Journal* though—his efforts to buy the paper were gathering momentum at this time. By August, he owned it.)

If I was expecting some blinding insights into how to run the *Herald Sun* or its website, he didn't share them with me. We had only one brief exchange during the whole three days.

'Having fun down there?' he asked me between sessions.

'As a matter of fact, I am, Rupert,' I replied.

★ ★ ★

Back in Melbourne, the news team and I were suddenly confronted by two dramatic events—the Kerang rail disaster that claimed 11 lives and the capture of a fugitive who had been on the run for more than a year. Even more extraordinarily, the two events happened on the same day. I had fallen through the door at home at 10.15 p.m. only to receive a telephone call telling me the escapee had been caught. I promptly went back to the office.

Next came the infamous CBD shootings, in which good samaritan Brendan Keilar died at the hands of former Hell's Angel

Christopher Wayne Hudson. Solicitor Keilar and backpacker Paul de Ward had gone to the aid of Kaera Douglas as she was being bashed by Hudson. Dutch tourist de Ward survived terrible injuries.

By the end of June, our performance was being noted and praised. A profile of me in *The Australian* included this assessment of the paper by Guy Allen, publishing and communications lecturer at the University of Melbourne: 'I think Bruce has shifted it up a gear, he's kept a lot of the typical good tabloid features—it's strong on sport and entertainment—and when you look at the opening pages of the newspaper it has a lot of variety.'

Allen's comments were published on a Thursday, the same day as our weekly management meetings. On the day Allen's comments appeared, Blunden could barely bring himself to look at me. In fact, he barely looked at anyone. I was reminded of an observation Roger Franklin repeatedly made of the future managing director: 'There's only room for one light in the window when he's around, and it has to be his.' My instincts told me he resented my favourable press.

But the biggest story of my first six months in the role was yet to come—and with it, my first taste of what happens at News Limited when public interest clashes with corporate interest.

On 13 July news broke in the early hours of the morning that Nick Bracks, the 20-year-old son of Victorian Premier Steve Bracks, had crashed his car while driving with a blood alcohol content of 0.129. He was lucky to escape with only minor injuries. The car fared worse. We splashed with the story in our Saturday edition but the most memorable moment for me came at the Friday morning news conference when news executives were discussing the possible ramifications of the accident.

'I reckon Bracks will resign over this,' I told the gathering. I was speaking as the father of a teenage son with whom I was spending far too little time. An accident such as Nick's would surely be a wake-up call for a parent who might feel he had been absent from his son's life for too long.

Two weeks later, on Friday, 27 July, Bracks announced without warning that he was stepping down as premier. His deputy, John Thwaites, fell in behind him, announcing he'd be going too. Despite my foresight, like all other media we were completely wrong-footed. Our state political reporter, Ellen Whinnett, was on a plane about to take off for Sydney when the chief of staff reached her on her mobile. She hurriedly gathered up her carry-on luggage, exited the plane at great speed, and headed back to Spring Street to cover the story.

Over the next 12 hours we did a terrific job of covering the resignations, breaking it first online and then devoting the first 15 pages of the Saturday edition to tell the story of one of the most tumultuous days in Victorian political history. It was a monumental effort by all staff.

Around 9.30 that night, as the final pages of the Saturday edition were being sent to press, the phone rang in my office. To my surprise, it was John Hartigan.

After a brief discussion of the day's extraordinary political events, Hartigan asked me if I had had a chance to read 'Sackville's comments about Ian Philip'. Philip was, indeed still is, the chief general counsel of News Limited; it was his injudicious comments to me about settlement after my sacking that precipitated my writ against News. 'Sackville' was a reference to a judge of the Federal Court of Australia. I told Hartigan that, because of the Bracks and Thwaites resignations, I hadn't caught up on terribly much else that day. Certainly I wasn't aware of any comments made by Justice Sackville.

Hartigan took me aback when he said Sackville had gone 'completely over the top' in attacking Philip in the C7 judgement that had been delivered that day. He went on to say that he hoped I would bear in mind when publishing any report on the C7 case that 'Ian is a good fellow.' (C7 had been a pay-television sports channel owned and operated by media proprietor Kerry Stokes;

he unsuccessfully sued the Murdoch part-owned Fox Sports and 21 other defendants alleging anti-competitive practices.)

I was shocked, to say the least. Here I was dealing with a massive story and it appeared Hartigan was more interested in protecting the reputation of one of his executive mates. I told him I would read it immediately. When I found the story, I understood why Hartigan had been keen to marginalise it. It read in part:

> Justice Sackville was harshly critical of News Ltd's chief general counsel Ian Philip, saying he 'gave the impression of a man who quite willingly subordinated his sense of ethics and propriety to a single-minded determination to advance the commercial interests of his employer'.
>
> He will send a copy of his judgment to the Law Society of NSW, saying: 'For a solicitor still holding a practising certificate to engage in deliberately dishonest conduct calls out for further inquiry by the authority responsible for professional discipline.'
>
> The judge added: 'If News has taken no action against Mr Philip in respect of his admitted dishonesty, it would reflect very seriously indeed on News' standards of commercial morality.'

The story was slated to run on page 93 of the next day's paper, off the front of our business section. I left it there and the paragraphs about Philip intact. I had no doubt I had done the right thing journalistically, but had I transgressed some unwritten News Limited code by not editing out the Philip references? Here was another News landmine, unseen until you stepped on it.

At least I had finally heard from Hartigan. Although I had been in the job almost six months, he had been strangely silent. We had chatted in Monterey but there had not been any one-on-one meetings. Incredibly, there would be only one such meeting before the final conversation in which he sacked me. That took place 11 days after the phone call regarding Ian Philip and, like the call itself, would go on to become a controversial component of the court case.

Hartigan's office contacted me to say he would be in Melbourne on 7 August and would like to catch up for lunch. At the trial, both he and Blunden would try to suggest the sole reason for the CEO's visit was to put me on notice that I had to get on with the former editor. Like so much of their evidence at trial, my interpretation and recollection was very different.

Hartigan and I dined outside at Pure South restaurant at Southbank. We talked about a great many things, much of it unrelated to newspapers. It was only in the last 10 minutes of the lunch that Hartigan raised my relationship with Blunden. He told me Peter had complained to him that I wasn't talking to him enough.

Bloody hell, I thought. We were meeting every week for an hour in Julian Clarke's office and he could pop in any time he liked. How much more talking was I supposed to do? After all, I had a paper to get out. Besides, why did Blunden have to go behind my back with this stuff? Why didn't he raise it with me directly rather than tell tales to Hartigan? I hid my anger, and told Hartigan I was surprised to hear of Peter's complaint. I thought we were talking a great deal but, if he wanted more talk, I was happy to oblige. At that point Hartigan said something decidedly odd. It later came out in my evidence at trial in response to questioning by my senior counsel, Norman O'Bryan.

'I remember John said one thing to me which stuck in my memory,' I recalled during my evidence. '"Bruce, can I just give you one word of warning, never go up against Peter Blunden." Which I thought was a curious statement at the end of a convivial lunch.'

As I headed back to the office after the lunch—and Hartigan back to Sydney—I was left wondering what to make of his warning. In the end I decided he wasn't directing me to kowtow to

Blunden, as Peter would later claim in court, but telling me he was part of 'the family' and I wasn't. I suspected there was another element to his warning too: Blunden would do whatever it took to get me, if it came to that.

And it would come to that.

24

Change partners

If the modern Australian newspaper business was shaped by external forces such as takeovers and internet growth, there were plenty of internal forces at work too. The biggest of these was the growth in stakeholders—where once editors only had to worry about readers, in the modern era it's a constant juggling act, forever balancing the integrity of a paper's journalism with the ceaseless drive for increased revenues and profits.

A couple of generations ago, it was enough for an editor to cite reader interest to keep most pressures at bay. Then, as display advertising revenue became more and more important to a paper's commercial success, key advertisers began exerting considerable and, at times, undue pressure. Another stakeholder happened along as family companies like Fairfax moved to public ownership—now editors were being reminded in sometimes unsubtle ways about shareholder value.

Soon after I arrived at the *Herald Sun*, I realised that, in the 10 years I had been away from the inner sanctums of papers, yet another stakeholder had emerged: the corporate partner. In many ways, this was the most insidious of all. They were worth millions of dollars to companies like HWT in ad revenue, paper sales and, ultimately, profits.

Julian Clarke, the tall and toothy managing director of HWT who ran the place for 16 years until November 2007, liked a give-away as much as the next man and, as a fanatical fan of the Fox network show, took particular pride in his decision to offer *Simpsons* pins in the *Herald Sun* (the pins were a runaway success with read-ers). Clarke was an even bigger fan of corporate partnerships.

At first glance, these partnerships seem harmless enough. The paper and a partner, usually an event or a corporate entity, do a deal in which papers like the *Herald Sun* offer up editorial coverage and editorial tie-ins including, perhaps, a pre- or post-event liftout and, probably, page-one promotion. In return, the event guarantees an agreed level of advertising—say, $200 000. In addition, the paper and the partner agree on a certain number of copies to be distrib-uted free of charge throughout an event, perhaps 5000 a day, even more in some cases. This becomes a valuable way to pump up cir-culation—the rules of the Audit Bureau of Circulations provide for the inclusion of event copies, within limits.

Typically buried within the agreements, which usually run for pages and pages, is a clause supposed to make everyone comfortable with the arrangement. It usually says something like this: 'All edito-rial coverage shall be at the discretion of the editor.' If anyone dared suggest partners were buying positive coverage in a paper, manage-ment could point to the clause. The reality is that the hapless editor is under significant pressure to nurture the relationship, usually with editorial coverage at least neutral and, often, shamelessly support-ive. Worse, there's an unstated pressure to avoid stories that might embarrass partners or put these lucrative relationships at risk.

I had first encountered them during my editorship of *The Sunday Age* when our marketing manager approached me during the mid-1990s to ask if I would be prepared to match the *Herald*

Sun's pitch to the Australian Open tennis tournament. The paper was offering liftouts, special coverage—you name it—for the right to call itself the 'official paper' of the event. I declined—no paper should be the 'official' organ of anything.

The number of partnerships between the *Herald Sun* and Victorian businesses or events during my time as editor numbered more than 70. The commercial side of the business thought this a marvellous achievement but I thought it ate away at the editorial integrity of the paper. Even Blunden acknowledged privately that the partnerships were a headache for editors and he would have preferred they didn't exist. They simply threw up too many conflicts. But, as he would go on to say when he succeeded Clarke, there were so many of them they had become a fact of life. Without them the *Herald Sun*'s business model—and quite probably those of many other papers—would collapse.

Soon after I arrived at the paper, I tried to alleviate some of my concerns by laying down ground rules for how we covered these partners or partnerships. It was simple: the stories we were being asked to publish had to satisfy the normal criteria of truth, relevance and appeal to readers and so did the photographs. (If one more picture of a horse and leggy model had been put before me at picture conference in the lead-up to Victoria's spring racing carnival, I would have screamed.) Soon this filtered back to Clarke who interpreted it as some sort of attack on his partnership strategy. At Thursday management meetings, he would turn to me and speak as if our entire future turned on it: 'We've got to look after our partners, Bruce.'

I would usually sit mute, often wondering who would win the day if it came to the crunch, the editor or the partner. It didn't take long to find out.

On 28 August 2007, just three weeks after my only one-on-one meeting with Hartigan, Clarke expressed severe reservations about a story I was intending to publish about police investigations of possible drug trafficking at an AFL club. I had paid him the courtesy of alerting him to the story pre-publication. It was pretty obvious to me that Clarke was concerned the story, if published, would damage HWT's relationship with the AFL, one of our key commercial partners. He had become skittish just three days earlier when we had followed up a Seven network story alleging drug taking at an AFL club and then opposed an injunction won by the AFL against further reporting of the story. Now here I was preparing to come at it from a different angle.

The paper's partnership with the AFL was different from most in that HWT paid the partner, rather than the other way round. Each year the *Herald Sun* wrote them a very large cheque for the right to publish AFL promotional material in the paper. Most important here was the annual give-away of player swap cards, usually scheduled in the all-important second audit quarter (April to June). Without them, the paper's circulation would take a huge hit. No wonder Clarke was nervous; he wouldn't have been doing his job if he wasn't.

He finally sought the intervention of Hartigan, raising directly with the CEO his concerns about publication. To his credit, Hartigan was having none of it; he green-lighted the drug scandal story by our sports affairs reporter, Sam Edmund, on page one of the paper the next day.

Edmund had brought the story to me after the Seven network report about drug *use* at an AFL club. Months earlier he had been contacted by someone alleging drug *dealing* at the same club. He hadn't written anything then, urging the contact to take his concerns to police, which he had done. Edmund had thought little more about it until the Channel Seven story broke. It was like a large piece of a jigsaw falling into place; now he felt confident about writing his follow-up.

Around 11.30 on the morning of publication, Clarke was on the phone to me again. He had had a conversation with AFL boss

Andrew Demetriou who, according to Clarke, questioned the veracity of Edmund's report.

'What did we get wrong?' I asked my managing director.

'Andrew reckons your reporter was also the police informant,' he replied.

This wasn't my understanding and I told the managing director that. I asked Clarke who had told Demetriou our reporter was the informant.

His answer astounded me: 'According to Demetriou, it was Christine Nixon.'

What the hell was the police commissioner doing sharing details of a drug investigation with third parties outside the police force? Worse, if Clarke's recollections were right, my reporter had just been wrongfully fingered as an informant in a drugs investigation. That could expose him to all sorts of dangers.

As luck would have it, I was due to lunch with Nixon that day. I asked her if it was true she believed Edmund was the police informant. She replied that if he wasn't the informant he had at least 'fanned the flames' of the story. I refuted this vigorously, telling Nixon that Edmund had merely encouraged his contact on the story that, if he believed there was substance to the allegations, he should take them to police. He had done that several months before publication.

'What would you have said if he hadn't done that and simply rushed into print?' I asked the chief commissioner.

She could see instantly where I was going with this. 'I'd probably say that if the allegations had any merit, why didn't he bring them to police,' Nixon said.

'Exactly,' I replied. 'Yet he does that and still gets into strife.'

But if I thought this would lay the matter to rest, I was mistaken. Later that day I received emailed enquiries from representatives of the ABC *Media Watch* program and *The Age*, asking if it was true our reporter was the police informant on the story and that I had published in full knowledge of this. I was now extremely concerned that there was a whispering campaign designed to damage the reporter, me and, ultimately, the paper.

The next morning two talkback callers to radio station 3AW repeated the allegations and questioned my ethics in publishing the story. I was forced to call into the station's breakfast program and the Neil Mitchell program to categorically deny the accusations. Both programs put the denials to air.

It now seemed pretty clear Edmund and I were being subjected to an orchestrated, if heavy-handed, campaign of negative publicity designed to sully our reputations. So I rang the AFL's media officer, Brian Walsh, to ask if they were behind it. Walsh angrily rejected the suggestion and I accepted his assurances.

Corporate partnerships like that between the *Herald Sun* and the AFL are now a fact of life in newspapers. It's time for a little transparency. Papers should consider flagging stories involving their partners or, at least, publishing a full list of their deals. Readers could then better make their own judgements.

The skirmish over drugs at an AFL club was the only road bump in my relationship with Clarke, whom I respected a great deal. At least, I did until the trial began 30 months later. In his evidence and during cross-examination he did his best on behalf of News to paint me as a temperamental and difficult editor, devoid of news sense.

No doubt he felt indebted to News. Not only had the company given him a career, they had also employed his son, who often sat at his side during management meetings. Murdoch had farewelled Clarke in style too, with a black-tie function at the National Gallery of Victoria in mid-November 2007. Guests included Dame Elisabeth and hundreds of luminaries. Rupert and his sister Janet Calvert-Jones presented their favourite managing director with an original oil painting and a couple of tickets to Wimbledon. Tanya, his wife, was given a string of pearls. Blunden made a speech, so did Rupert. Clarke responded and it took him several minutes just to get through the 'distinguished guests' list. Not bad for a former clerk at a suburban newspaper chain.

Two weeks later Clarke rode off into the sunset. We had had a stellar year together—although in court he did his best to suggest otherwise—slowing the previous year's circulation slide almost to a halt, boosting readership and internet traffic and delivering a record profit. On 1 December 2008 Blunden formally took over as managing director. If 2007 had been an *annus mirabilis*, the new year would become my *annus horribilis*.

25

Storm clouds

The Clarke–Blunden handover wasn't the only significant change of leadership that happened at the end of 2007. In November Kevin Rudd unseated John Howard after more than 11 years in power to become Australia's new Prime Minister—and Rudd seemed to be working harder than my new managing director at building a relationship with me.

This was despite the paper supporting the return of the conservatives in its pre-poll editorial, a decision based more on the *Herald Sun*'s history of backing incumbents than any strong personal views. (Most of News Limited's papers backed Rudd.) That said, we were keen to have a Melbourne-based prime minister and the man best placed for that was Peter Costello. It was also obvious that the country was headed into difficult economic times and it would be good to have an experienced hand on the tiller. Our editorial advocated a Howard win, followed by a Costello handover a year down the track.

Rudd and I had dined together several times in the run-up to the poll. He was obviously a highly intelligent man who worked hard at being engaging—it didn't come entirely naturally—and he enjoyed almost rock-star status wherever we went. Our meals were regularly interrupted by autograph-hunters and diners wanting photographs with the rising politician. While the country was learning about his fluency in Mandarin, I was impressed one night to find him in deep conversation with some Swedish fellow diners.

Just weeks after he was deposed as prime minister by Julia Gillard, I bumped into Rudd at a restaurant at Queensland's Sunshine Beach. After introducing Janne to him it emerged that her father had been Swedish.

'Kevin speaks Swedish,' I said, addressing both of them, as our children looked on. 'In fact, one night I found him speaking it fluently to a table of Swedish diners in a restaurant and on another night, speaking fluent Mandarin to some Chinese people. Do you remember that?'

Said the former prime minister ruefully: 'Maybe that's why I lost the job.'

The comment immediately reminded me of an observation made by ad-man Ted Horton before the 2007 election. Rudd was a 'smarty', said Horton at a David Jones fashion event—he did their ads—and Australians didn't like 'smarties'. He wouldn't last, predicted Horton, who had helped to get Howard elected four times. Horton may have been right, but I was tempted to say to Rudd that News Limited had brought us both undone—*The Australian's* campaign against him had been relentless and unbalanced, I believed. But I held off.

With Rudd, I could never shake the cloying feeling that, more than most politicians, he shaped his words to suit his audience. This had best been summed up in a letter to the *Herald Sun's* 50–50 column on election eve. The writer said she didn't trust Rudd and would be voting for Howard because ultimately the Labor leader was a diplomat and 'he tells us what he thinks we want to hear'. I had brought Laurie Oakes and Steve Lewis to the paper to boost our political coverage and we had expanded the Canberra bureau too. But that brief assessment of Rudd was as good as any I read during my editorship of the *Herald Sun*.

I shared few meals with Howard, only dining with him once during his prime ministership, in May 2007, after we revealed in a page-one splash that Thérèse Rein, Rudd's wife, had underpaid some of her workers. That story prompted an invite to The Lodge on very short notice. It came in a late night phone call from Ben Mitchell, Howard's press secretary.

'The Prime Minister was wondering if you are free to dine with him at The Lodge tomorrow night,' said Ben.

'Why, did someone drop out at the last minute?' I replied.

Mitchell and I went way back. As a young journalism student he had actually applied for a copy boy's job while helping to landscape our backyard one blazing hot day in 1988. He had been so persistent I eventually gave him a position at *The Sunday Age* and here he was, almost 20 years later, inviting me to dine with the nation's leader.

Herald Sun writers Gerard McManus and John Ferguson joined me and when we arrived Howard was glued to the television, watching Kerry O'Brien on *The 7.30 Report* grill Rudd over our story. Because of this, there were few pleasantries exchanged; I was simply directed to sit in one of two matching armchairs in front of the telly. Howard was in the other. It didn't feel at all prime ministerial; it felt more like I had dropped in on an uncle in the suburbs who didn't want me to interrupt his favourite show. I expected dinner on our laps at any minute.

For all that, Howard was a first-rate host, swapping stories about George W. Bush—'He's much more impressive in person than he is on television'—the political cycle—'It's going to be very tough to win'—and his fondness for walking every morning.

'Do you walk wherever you are, or is it just when you are in Sydney, Prime Minister?' I asked over dinner.

'I have a route in every city,' said the Prime Minister. It was all I could do not to spray my soup over the assembled diners.

Once Rudd displaced Howard, the new Prime Minister worked assiduously at building our relationship. It had nothing to do with me, just my business card. Tony Abbott could have been editor of the *Herald Sun* and he would still have sought him out. Several times Rudd's minders rang without warning to say the Prime Minister was in town and would like to visit. What do you say to this, 'I'm sorry, but I'm too busy'? Of course not. So Rudd would drop in and swap stories about the political landscape. These meetings would sometimes last 90 minutes or more and at least once I missed afternoon news conference as a result.

Our dinners continued too, but now he had minders and federal police in tow. After one such gathering in early 2008 I wrote in my diary:

> [Rudd] ranged across a great many subjects including the forthcoming budget, performance of ministers, state relations, U.S. alliance, Hillary Clinton's chances at the next election if she got over Obama: 'The first thing she said to me was, "I regret nothing",' recalled Rudd, who'd just been to Washington, observing: 'I thought it was a bit early for a concession speech.' Admitted he enjoyed 'great political capital' at the moment and was keen to capitalise because 'it will rise and fall'. Asked me at dinner's end what sort of budget HS readers expected ... I presumed that was the point of the dinner, scheduled at his instigation. Said one curious thing: when I asked him how he was coping with the hours, he said he was throwing himself into the job because 'you never know when it might end'.

Given the events that unfolded in June 2010 it was eerily prescient. He was a smart man.

Meanwhile, my relationship with the new managing director was proving more of a challenge. This was despite us getting off to a great start, in terms of key indicators at least. Then again, maybe that was the problem.

In mid-February 2008, about the time of my first anniversary in the job, we received what Paul Keating might have called a beautiful set of numbers: circulation, readership and website traffic figures were pretty much all heading in the right direction, some massively up. Readership for the December quarter jumped an astonishing 144 000 year-on-year to an average of 1 536 000, a leap of more than 10 per cent; monthly internet traffic went up 44 per cent year-on-year from 353 000 visits to 510 000 visits; Saturday sales were up too, while circulation of the Monday to Friday paper came in at 530 000, signalling an end to the very significant decline that set in under Blunden between December 2005 (554 000) and December 2006 (535 000). We had plenty of reasons to celebrate but instead I was parrying the managing director's attacks.

Our first run-in came over journalistic ethics. Someone once joked that at News when you talked of ethics they thought you were referring to a county in the east of England. I should have learned my lesson at Aspen 20 years earlier but an issue arose in February 2008 that convinced me to speak up.

News owned the Melbourne Storm, the Victorian-based rugby league team that had taken out the 2007 NRL premiership. (The ownership would come back to bite News on the eve of the trial after massive salary-cap rorting was uncovered at the club.) Five months after their premiership win they were due to fly out to England to play off against Leeds for the right to call themselves world champions. Without my knowledge, it had been agreed between the club and HWT executives that one of our photographers would accompany the team on its UK tour and that the Storm would pay for her trip. This suggested to me a newspaper equivalent of 'cash for comment' so I emailed Blunden alerting him to my concerns, saying: 'I don't want to be Joan of Arc mate, but I think it's a problem if we start covering things because a third party is paying . . . let me sleep on it.'

Events quickly spiralled out of control; the managing director bombarded me with a string of intemperate emails, each one worse than the last. At one point he accused me of misrepresenting the circulation figures in an in-paper story. Huh? I'd raised an issue of integrity only to be accused of having no integrity. I eventually decided to call him and his voice was dripping with bile as he took me to task for not supporting the rugby league club.

'Peter, what on earth is wrong with you? Are you hating this job?' I asked, almost rhetorically. I had no doubt he was, especially as the economy was beginning to turn. Good companies don't put first-time managers in charge of half-billion-dollar businesses on the eve of a global financial crisis. He was clearly struggling.

In the interests of maintaining a working relationship, I backed down. The photographer would later go with the Storm on their UK tour (and, as it turned out, so would Blunden and his wife). And, as so often happened in my dealings with him, by the Monday after our phone conversation the managing director was contrite, calling me first thing to explain that there had been an illness in his family and the stress of coping with that meant he had overreacted and he regretted that. At trial, he denied making the call.

It was my first real look at the famous Blunden temper and throughout the episode I was reminded of the executive who had taken to staring at the names of his children to weather his tantrums. Clearly I would have to factor his short fuse in to my future dealings with him; the advice from other senior managers was to let him vent and then make your point. It was tiresome but that's what I did, usually to positive effect. What I wasn't to know was that Blunden didn't forget or forgive. I had moved on from the Storm row within 24 hours but he hadn't. I would learn at the trial that soon after he began agitating for my removal.

Most of an editor's battles are with external forces. And there are many of them; some just won't go away. Soon Police Commissioner Christine Nixon was back again. In March we initiated a groundbreaking poll of all police officers in the state, using new internet technology that gave individual police their own access code that worked only once—as soon as they completed the online poll, their unique code expired. This removed the possibility of people completing the poll multiple times and minimised the chances of the questions being completed by non-police.

Then we had gained access to the mailing addresses of all serving police officers by piggybacking on the monthly mail-out by the Police Association, which agreed to include a letter from me alerting members to the poll. (The union had absolutely no involvement in the poll itself.) In the end close to 3000 police completed the questionnaire—about 30 per cent of the force—and it painted a damning picture of morale within the ranks.

Police command, including Nixon and her deputy (later commissioner himself), Simon Overland, was not happy with us. An email was sent urging police not to cooperate. Overland made a couple of approaches to me to protest at the poll and to question our motivation. I tried to assure him there was no agenda other than to do a proper assessment of the state of the force. I'm not sure he accepted my assurances. In the end it was a case of publish and be damned.

The findings were published over three days, beginning on Wednesday, 9 April. We had originally intended to start the series on the Monday but I had acceded to a request from Nixon's office to delay publication until after a Police Association rally scheduled for that week. If Nixon appreciated the gesture, she didn't show it.

When the first story of our three-part series appeared under the headline 'Poll: Police Face Crisis', Nixon moved into high gear, attacking the paper and complaining upstairs to management, before hitting the airwaves, long and loud. She suggested we were in cahoots with the Police Association, with which she was at loggerheads, and then tried to paint herself as the victim of a reform process that a male-dominated force was resisting at every turn. It was an interesting card to play after almost eight years in the job.

The most worrying aspect of the series however was the internal reaction at HWT Tower. Around 10 a.m. on the Wednesday, news director Shane Burke, deputy editor Damon Johnston and I were in Johnston's office reflecting on the success of the poll. We were chuffed that everything had worked—the technology, the mail-out, the questions—producing a first-rate result that was dominating talkback radio. Suddenly Blunden appeared at the door.

My secretary had warned he was on his way down. I had deliberately stayed in Johnston's office, so they could see any hysterics for themselves. We didn't have to wait long.

'There better not be a fucking blue at Westgate this year, because we won't get a copper out there to help us,' said Blunden, his face flushing a familiar red and his hands flapping like mad and angry birds. At times like this they would rise to hover in a frenzy of fluttering beside his ears. He went on: 'Nixon's rung and she's not happy; in fact, she's furious.'

The Westgate printing plant, under the bridge of the same name on Melbourne's western fringe, was where the 600 000-plus copies of the *Herald Sun* and the Victorian copies of *The Australian*— all 28 000 of them Sunday to Thursday, more on Fridays—were printed each night. Blunden was clearly intimating that if the current negotiations over a new enterprise bargaining agreement went pear-shaped, resulting in pickets, there would be no police to ensure the paper got out. It's unclear whether Nixon had said this to him or whether it was just Blunden interpreting the tone of their conversation.

'We won't have any trouble getting police, Peter,' I said. 'In fact, there would be thousands willing to help now, I reckon. We might struggle to get a commissioner out there though.'

I was trying to make the point that we had given voice to thousands of police through our poll. Nixon's attitude, although understandable given the poll painted her as very unpopular, was of little moment. I was stunned that I had to explain this to a man who had edited the paper for more than a decade.

The whole episode was a further reminder of what happens at News and, increasingly, many other media organisations these days, when public interest butts up against corporate interests or relationships. I would later learn that Blunden and Nixon sat on the board of the same charity. If Blunden was building up an armoury against me, I had probably just given him another weapon.

Yet, despite our run-ins over the Melbourne Storm tour of England and our police poll, we were having considerable successes together. We posted a record profit for 2007–08 and the launch of the paper's new daily features section—'Herald Sun Extra'—went off extremely well too.

This was the lifestyle component of the paper I had first raised with Hartigan and Clarke before I had even started in the job. We had pulled it off after 16 months of reconfiguring pagination, press runs and the running order of the paper. The biggest decision here was to move the daily gossip column, 'Confidential', to the back of the daily liftout. I knew Blunden had reservations about it, but he had never expressed them to me, only to other managers. Certainly at the presentations we made to staff in the week before the launch he was upbeat and congratulatory.

Observers would have said we had bonded after some initial difficulties. They weren't to know—I didn't either—that just a month earlier at News budget meetings in Los Angeles in May he had apparently stormed away from John Hartigan 'in disgust' after Hartigan had turned down his request to dump me. That would only emerge at the trial.

Which, with hindsight, might explain Hartigan's curious response to 'Extra'. I knew that he was in HWT Tower on the day of the launch but he chose not to make contact. Instead, he rang me briefly the next day from Sydney asking how I thought it had gone. Pretty well, I thought. After the briefest of congratulations—strange given this was the biggest editorial innovation at the *Herald Sun* in more than a decade—he told me he thought we had one too many deks—lines—on our page one-headline that day and a few too many pictures on a sports spread. That was it.

The three-minute phone call on 11 June 2008 was the closest I ever came to a performance review while editing the *Herald Sun*. News Limited isn't big on such modern management approaches, probably because of Rupert Murdoch's professed disdain for MBAs and anything that suggests them. During my time at *The Australian* attempts had been made to institute an annual performance appraisal process but they had languished because of a complete lack of support and interest. (There had been such a system at *The Age* since the mid-1990s.)

In any event, I must have impressed Hartigan because three weeks later I received a hefty pay rise. It ushered in one of the most successful periods of my career, culminating in the PANPA Newspaper of the Year win at a glittering ceremony at Jupiters Casino on the Gold Coast in September.

I had actually arrived at the PANPA conference 24 hours earlier to take part in a debate on the importance of quality journalism to the future of newspapers. *Courier-Mail* editor-in-chief David Fagan, *Philadelphia Inquirer* publisher Brian Tierney and I took the negative—that quality journalism wasn't crucial to the future of journalism—and won. The next night I attended the gala dinner expecting to be an honourable loser to either Fagan or, perhaps, Alan Oakley from *The Sydney Morning Herald*. But when the winner was called, it was the *Herald Sun*. Pressed into making a speech, I thanked Blunden in glowing terms, recognising that he had built the paper up over a very long period (and won two PANPA awards of his own). By the time I had left the stage, he was texting me, saying my win meant more to him than his two. There was an awful lot of love in the air.

If it had been Hollywood, that's where the story would have ended: career editor returns to the industry and hometown he had left a decade earlier and against all odds claims said industry's most glittering prize. Roll credits.

But this wasn't Hollywood; how could I have possibly known the end was nigh?

26

The sting

The success the paper enjoyed in the second half of 2008 had prompted Janne and me not only to buy a new family home in Melbourne and sell in Sydney, but long discussions around the dinner table about a second contract at the *Herald Sun*. These turned on whether I should sign on for another two, three or even five years after my term expired in February 2010. It was surely my decision and my decision alone; it's almost embarrassing to reflect now on my corporate naivety.

That said, the level of professional double-dealing going on around me beggared the imagination. Quite apart from the pay rises, bonuses and gongs, my managing director was bombarding me with congratulatory notes on everything from our PANPA win and the purchase of our new home to the passing of the actor Paul Newman. On 29 September, just six weeks before my dismissal, he opened an email with: 'Paper looked great today. I liked the good run for Paul Newman, too. *The Sting* was a cracker.' Perhaps he was giving me a clue to his own behaviour.

Also, I had officially graduated to the status of a 'mate', one of the higher states of being at News. Blunden's emails, and my replies, particularly in the latter months of my editorship, were

peppered with the term, suggesting a good, harmonious relationship. If he really was just covering his tracks as he set me up for a
fall, he was doing a bloody good job of it. But occasionally I had
cause to doubt his sincerity.

In August I lunched with Melbourne broadcaster Neil
Mitchell, who had been my editor at *The Herald* in the mid-1980s.
After his own falling out with News Limited after their takeover
of HWT in 1986–87, he had left to pursue a career in radio. He
never looked back, soon commanding a large audience and regularly leading the ratings. Over sandwiches in the 3AW boardroom,
Neil told me he had recently lunched with Blunden only to have
him 'nitpick' the paper. Mitchell said: 'He clearly wants to be editor
of the *Herald Sun* again.'

I showed no emotion as he passed this on but inwardly I was
seething. After all, this was the sort of conduct by Blunden that
had derailed our relationship in the first place. Eighteen months on
and despite being promoted to the position of managing director,
he was still bad-mouthing the paper around town; worse, he was
doing it to a man with an audience in the hundreds of thousands.

Back in the office I wrestled with what to do about Blunden's
conduct. Quite apart from my personal views, I feared he was actually damaging the business with this sort of behaviour. I knew that
Mitchell and Blunden were part of a lunch club that also included
former treasurer Peter Costello, and the extremely well-connected
and successful media and football personality Eddie McGuire.
There was a fair chance that if the managing director was criticising the paper to one of his lunch companions, he was probably
doing it to all of them. Given their circles, the ripple effect could
be devastating.

Briefly I reflected on what had happened two decades earlier when similar conduct by the HWT managing director, John
D'arcy, had been brought to the attention of Murdoch. D'arcy had
been caught out criticising editor-in-chief Eric Beecher to third

parties and Murdoch had very swiftly dispensed with his services. I didn't expect the same fate to befall Blunden—he was part of the News family and D'arcy hadn't been—but surely his behaviour was worthy of censure.

John Hartigan had long ago said I could bring any problems to him at any time—he had called it the 'dotted line' between editor and CEO. I had never invoked this and, even though I was on absolutely solid ground here, was still reluctant to do so. But after a series of intemperate emails from Blunden in Beijing over several new staff appointments I had made—he and his wife were junketing at the Olympics, as guests of Australia Post—I decided to go to Hartigan with my concerns.

It was the only time I did so during my entire editorship and only the second time that year we talked one on one. It would also be the last time before my sacking. After listening to me patiently, Hartigan summed up Blunden's behaviour in one word: 'Bizarre.'

He advised me to sit down and talk with the managing director when he returned from the Games; he would get involved only if the talks didn't go well. I thought it curiously detached, given we were two of his most senior executives, but that seemed to be Hartigan's preferred way of running things.

The meeting with Blunden was due in a week and in the interim I created an *aide memoire* that I planned, in effect, to recite when the appropriate moment arrived. It detailed my concerns over Blunden's erratic behaviour, particularly his sniping at me behind my back and his apparent lack of support.

It sat in the draft tray of my email box until the appointed hour arrived. But when the meeting started, I had no need for it: Blunden turned on the charm. Gone was the angry and intemperate author of the Beijing emails and in his place was a conciliatory, even contrite, managing director. I knew it the moment he greeted me. He had forsaken the usual power grip—his palm over mine—for a generous and warm handshake. He even admitted the Mitchell indiscretion, promising to never do it again. I was so thrown by it all that I threw out the script. Our chat probably lasted 45 minutes and I left his office positively ebullient. When I got back to my desk I wrote a short email to Hartigan. It read: 'Meeting with Peter went well. No need for you to get involved. It's onwards and upwards from here.'

The meeting would feature prominently at the trial with News Limited lawyers, desperate to prove the relationship with Blunden had become unworkable, trying to make much of the email that was never sent—the *aide memoire*—but denying the existence of the one that was—my 'onwards and upwards' note to Hartigan. Miraculously, during the discovery process in the lead-up to the hearing, they had no trouble locating the unsent email, but never could find mine to Hartigan.

Blunden and I then clashed over, of all things, a DVD give-away. It happened at the weekly management meeting of 9 October 2008. He actually made mention of this in the post-sacking phone call, which was recounted in full in the statement of claim. In the transcript, Blunden says to me: 'We had a bit of a row ... at the management meeting. But that was over in 60 seconds. I would put that in the category of robust discussion. And that is good for business. And I encourage that.'

But by the time we got to trial, Blunden and Hartigan were putting it in an entirely different category. The managing director presented it as some sort of egregious failure on my part; Hartigan went as far as calling it 'the tipping point' that convinced him to sack me.

I had actually arrived at the meeting on 9 October 2008 tired and irritable. We had had another late night putting out the paper; the world's financial system was collapsing around us and we were devoting a lot of pages to it.

I was probably hoping to skate through the meeting unnoticed but, soon after arriving, Blunden, watched by a full complement of managers, rounded on me. Why had there been nothing in that morning's paper promoting the forthcoming *National Geographic* wildlife DVD series, he asked.

The *Nat Geo* series was an annual promotion that put on close to 300 000 extra sales during the fortnight we ran it in the paper. It was scheduled to kick off the following Monday with a free give-away of the first DVD. Readers could then buy the remaining 13 DVDs in the series at $2 each, provided they presented the day's token to their newsagent.

I had actually delegated the editorial marketing plan to my deputy, Damon Johnston, who had assured me everything was in readiness. The in-paper material would start the next day (Friday) and would then run across the weekend. This was in line with the previous year's highly successful approach under me.

'The public will know about it by Monday, Peter,' I told Blunden, whose body language spoke of pure aggression.

'I think we've wasted an opportunity,' he said. 'It should have been in there today.'

I was now getting aggressive too, angry that I was being called to account over an in-paper promotion when I had been up all hours trying to make sense of an imploding world economy. The promotion hadn't been our highest priority, I admitted.

'Who's supposed to be looking after it?' asked Blunden.

'Damon Johnston.'

'Well, Damon's clearly asleep.'

This was getting out of hand, so I told him so. 'Hang on a second, don't start insulting my senior executives who've been working their bums off producing world-class papers,' I said.

'Oh, when was that?' replied the managing director.

Now the gloves were off.

'Peter, how dare you say that—we're winning awards, producing great papers ... that's really an ordinary thing to say.'

At about this point in the exchange I asked him: 'Why didn't we talk about this last week if it was so important?' I was being mischievous and Blunden knew it.

Straight away, I thought he looked guilty. He knew and I knew why we hadn't talked about it the previous week; it was because he had decided to go on a joy-flight over Melbourne aboard the new Qantas A380 rather than chair the management meeting. I had been invited on the same flight but couldn't justify the time out of the office. Blunden didn't feel so constrained. While he dodged my question at the meeting, he would have less success at the trial.

Perhaps realising where the conversation was headed, Blunden requested we take the meeting 'off-line'. But I was having none of it.

'We're all here, let's clear the air,' I said.

Blunden's body language shifted at this point, from aggression to despair—he actually put his head in his hands and then offered up a sort of *mea culpa*.

'Look, I know everyone's working hard, but we really need this promo to work to get circulation up,' he said.

Which I promptly acknowledged: 'We're all working to that end. We think about little else. I'm sorry if there was an expectation that the promo would be in the papers today. It will certainly be in tomorrow but probably what this points to is the need to involve marketing more closely in these editorial promo matters. Why don't we do this? Why doesn't someone from marketing come to the editorial conference so this never happens again?'

'Great idea,' said Blunden.

'We'll start this from tomorrow,' I pledged to the management group, who were probably relieved hostilities had ceased.

Shortly after, as the meeting broke up, Blunden followed me out of the conference room. True to form, having lost his temper earlier, he was now contrite.

'I'm sorry about what happened in there, but I just want the figures to be as good as they can be for when Rupert arrives,' he explained.

'So do I, Peter, so do I.' Murdoch's visit was now just a couple of weeks away.

The in-paper pre-promotion of the DVD series started the next day, a full 72 hours ahead of when they would actually be available, and it was a great success. Yet, to hear Hartigan tell it in court, I was a goner from that moment on.

★ ★ ★

So, what really precipitated my sacking? I certainly didn't know when I left the HWT Tower for the last time in the early evening of 11 November 2008. After returning from my lunchtime meeting with Tony Macken—and my unpleasant telephone conversation with Ian Philip—I had attended the afternoon news conference, determined to call the paper in the usual way. It was emotionally charged but I was determined to get through it. At the end, I called the news section of the paper, nominating the leads and pictures on each page. Assistant editor Ken Burrowes said when we had finished allocating all stories and pictures: 'You nailed it.'

I went back to my office, which at that stage was largely cleared. A number of well-wishers called in. I walked the main editorial floor, shaking hands with staffers as I went, thanking them for their support over the previous 21 months. I called the staff together and addressed them at 6 p.m. I made a speech, telling the assembled group that I thought we had done some important journalism over my time there and admitting my treatment was a mystery to me. 'I'm not entirely sure what this has been about,' I told them. I left to a sustained ovation that only ended when I left the floor to head back to my office. It was extremely moving.

After clearing the next day's editorials and checking stories and layouts for page one and the back page, I left the building for the last time about 7 p.m. In the basement car park I encountered the new *Herald Sun* editor, Simon Pristel; in all my 21 months coming and going from the car park, I had never bumped into him there. Now he was telling me he had just come from a phone hook-up with senior Sydney management who wanted more budget cuts. Was this supposed to make me feel better, as if I was somehow being spared? There were many things I might have said to Pristel but I worried that if I started, I wouldn't stop. So, clutching a couple of framed front pages under my arms, I said simply: 'It's all yours now, mate.'

As I headed home, I reflected on my relationship with Blunden. True, I had had a handful of run-ins with him over the previous 12 months, some of them quite spirited, but we were posting good results and our relationship had been improving. The brief 'robust' exchange over the free DVDs was nothing in the context of newspapers, where rough-house discussions are the norm at the best of times. It had to be more than that. Was it the Nixon story two weeks later? Was it my call to Hartigan during the Olympics? Perhaps the messenger was being shot for raising Blunden's unprofessional behaviour.

For weeks afterwards I found myself reflecting on Blunden's curious reference in our final conversation to a 'third party' who had 'got involved' in my dismissal. He went on: 'That person said something to someone who said something to someone else and it went from there.'

It was either an attempt to shift the blame for my removal and he had invented the third person, or he was simply being indiscreet. Either way, he had form. The thing that suggested the latter was the nature of my dismissal. News Limited editors come and go, but they are rarely dismissed in such a brutal manner. This was designed to humiliate me. As one of my fellow editors wrote in an email on the morning after my removal: 'I feel for you and haven't quite seen anything like it at News Ltd.'

He was right. This wasn't just a change of editor; this was the corporate equivalent of summary execution, dripping with animus. And that wasn't Hartigan's way. No, this had to have come from someone above Hartigan. This had to have come from a Murdoch. Maybe the trial would get to the truth.

IV

Trials and tribulations

27

Fighting back

When news of our writ broke on 8 December 2008, it was strangely empowering to have the truth out there at last. Despite the modern world growing used to redundancies and career switches, there's a certain taint that goes with dismissal: for the first time since the sacking I felt my dignity returning.

Crikey carried two reports, the first picking the eyes out of the statement of claim, the other highlighting the contradictory conversations with Hartigan and Blunden on the day of my dismissal. Soon my mobile phone started ringing as newsrooms across the country caught up with what was happening. One News Limited employee later said there had been cheers as colleagues read the first online reports in their office.

The next morning *The Age* turned over most of page two to the story, describing the court documents as a rare window into the workings of News Limited. Reports also appeared in *The Australian Financial Review* and *The Australian* but the *Herald Sun* was silent. Funny that.

Just after our return to Melbourne from Byron Bay, we found a voicemail message on our answering machine that said simply: 'Welcome back. I didn't expect to see you on page one of *The Age*.'

I immediately raced out to buy a copy of the paper and, sure enough, there was a story—and pictures of Rupert Murdoch, Janet Calvert-Jones, Christine Nixon and myself—on page one, in column eight. Under a headline that read, 'Murdoch sister in Guthrie spotlight', it began: 'Conversations between Rupert Murdoch, chief executive of News Corporation, and his sister and Herald and Weekly Times Ltd (HWT) chairwoman, Janet Calvert-Jones, will be central to one of the highest profile unfair dismissal cases in Australian media history.'

The story suggested in its second paragraph that Calvert-Jones was the mysterious 'third person' referred to by Blunden in his telephone conversation with me on the night of my sacking. In the story's fifth paragraph was this: 'Insiders now believe the third party was Mrs Calvert-Jones, who was upset at the way the *Herald Sun* had covered the story of Victoria police chief commissioner Christine Nixon taking a free trip to Los Angeles.' It all stemmed from that front-page *Herald Sun* report of 23 October 2008 headlined 'Beverly Hills Cop'.

The most significant aspect of *The Age* story was a curiously evasive comment from the police commissioner when asked if she had complained to senior HWT management. The paper reported that through her media director, Nicole McKechnie, Nixon refused to deny she had said anything to Calvert-Jones about the article, quoting her as saying only: 'Chief commissioners have always had good relationships with senior executives from Melbourne media. However, any decision about who works for them is entirely a matter for them.'

Rightly or wrongly, many would have read the quote as confirmation of some sort of contact. Certainly it was a long way from a denial.

The reporting prompted an immediate and intriguing response from HWT Tower. In a four-paragraph statement issued on 15 December—the Monday after *The Age*'s story appeared—Blunden claimed 'recent reports bear no resemblance to the reasons behind Bruce Guthrie's removal as *Herald Sun* editor in chief', adding: 'If and when I'm asked to do so, I will provide a comprehensive and compelling case for our decision to terminate his employment.'

What had happened to the bloke who was 'sick to my stomach' over my dismissal? Clearly he was changing tack.

When the new year finally arrived, we moved into our new Melbourne home. It was a curiously solemn affair. Given we had bought it on the basis that I would be editor of the *Herald Sun* for, perhaps, another three to five years, and had been forced to sell in Sydney at an almost fire-sale price, there was none of the excitement you usually associate with such a move.

My state of mind wasn't helped either by an extraordinary lapse in News Limited papers in mid-March that brought into sharp relief the contrast between what I saw as my harsh treatment and the lax standards applied to others.

Mistakes happen in newspapers, indeed, any news medium, all the time; the miracle is not that they occur but that they don't occur more often. But they need to have repercussions. Good journalists hurt when they make a mistake—if they're not losing sleep over their errors, they should probably try another line of work. By extension, good news organisations need to demonstrate that they take mistakes seriously.

On 15 March, the *Sunday Herald Sun*, an improving paper under the editorship of my former deputy at the daily, Damon Johnston, splashed with semi-naked pictures it claimed were of the former federal parliamentarian Pauline Hanson. The posed pictures were purportedly taken decades earlier by a lover during a secret tryst.

I thought it curious news judgement by Johnston, given the previous day more than 80 000 people had gathered at the MCG for an all-day concert by bands including a re-formed Midnight Oil, fronted by Peter Garrett, to raise funds for the victims of Victoria's Black Saturday bushfires.

To me, that seemed the logical splash for Victoria's biggest sell-ing newspaper. After all, the bushfires had been the most significant local story for a generation—and, from all reports, a massive mover of papers.

Instead, the paper went with Hanson, in my view an increas-ingly ho-hum subject who was only in the news again because of her ill-fated attempt to win the seat of Beaudesert in that month's Queensland state election. Other News Limited Sundays also splashed with the Hanson story and pictures, which originated out of *The Sunday Telegraph* in Sydney.

But backing the wrong lead turned out to be the least of the *Sunday Herald Sun*'s worries. For, over ensuing days it emerged that it wasn't Hanson in the pictures, for which News allegedly paid $15 000. Even more alarming, as the controversy grew over such an egregious publishing error, it became obvious that the company's editors simply hadn't done the basic checks that would have exposed the hoax.

In interviews, the editor of *The Sunday Telegraph*, Neil Breen, accepted ultimate responsibility for the purchase of the photo-graphs. An extremely affable and amiable man, Breen had been given the reins of Australia's biggest selling paper in May 2006. It was his first editorship and he was under tremendous pressure as circulation had continued to decline in his three years at the helm.

In the normal scheme of things a senior editor would have agreed on the sum with the seller having already defrayed the costs around the group, asking for, say, $3000 from each of the Sundays after assuring them the photos were 'ridgy-didge'. And that would have been that.

Breen had first made his name as sports editor of the Brisbane *Courier-Mail* under editor-in-chief Chris Mitchell. When Mitchell moved to *The Australian*, he took Breen with him. Breeny, as he was known throughout Holt Street and beyond, was a favourite son at News. Hartigan was particularly fond of him, choosing him at the eleventh hour to head up News' coverage of the 2008 Beijing Olympics, much to the chagrin of those who had worked on the assignment for more than a year and didn't like having someone parachuted in over the top of them. Breen held strong opinions on many subjects and was never shy about expressing them in his broad Queensland drawl.

It appears he authorised the purchase of the pictures only on the Saturday morning before publication the next day. That was probably his first mistake. He was immediately putting himself under needless pressure. It suggests he was desperate for a story and took the leap, when waiting another week and painstakingly checking out the details of the photographs would have been much more prudent. Given there was an election campaign on in Queensland and Hanson was contesting it, the pictures were certainly topical. But where was the public interest in publishing decades-old, extremely private photographs? It's not clear whether that debate was even had.

The next mistake was never eyeballing the man who was peddling the pictures. As one *Sunday Telegraph* writer later told me: 'You only had to meet the bloke for 30 seconds to know things didn't add up.' Incredibly, that apparently didn't happen. Things got worse. Although Breen gave interviews saying his picture department had closely examined the shots to see if there had been any photoshopping, it later emerged on the ABC's *Media Watch* program that they had never actually received the original slides. It wasn't even clear they still existed. So much for forensic examination.

Finally, there were gaping holes in the story of Jack Johnson, the man who was peddling the pictures. For a start, the resort he claimed was the scene of the pictures didn't actually exist at the time of the alleged photo session. And he reportedly was telling people he had pictures of another very prominent Australian woman dressed only in her lingerie. It was clearly nonsense. It would be harder to imagine a more inept display.

In the end Breen, Johnston and others published grovelling apologies to Hanson. I felt for the two men, whom I had always liked and admired for their news skills, but this was the sort of error that could not be excused on any level. Knowing them both, I accept it was a genuine error; they would have published believing the pictures to be of Hanson. Still, it was a massive mistake.

Ultimately the Hanson saga was an example of what happens when editors under circulation and deadline pressure put aside sound judgement in order to chase sales. It was an extension of the old reporter's trick of never asking the last question, the one that might bring down the story that would otherwise get you on page one.

Despite the immensity of the error, no-one had paid with their job. What sort of message was Murdoch's company sending to readers? Come to think of it, what sort of message was the company sending to their journalists and their editors? No-one was more perplexed than me, sacked because of a personality clash.

Meanwhile, in late March, the wheels of justice finally turned. Supreme Court Judge David Beach was appointed to hear our matter, ordered a mediation session and scheduled a directions hearing for 31 July. This sudden flurry of activity prompted renewed interest from the media, with *The Age* carrying a report of News Limited's defence.

It appeared on page nine of the 1 April paper and revealed publicly for the first time that I had been paid more than $900 000 in December 2007 (net $521 431), which was the balance owing on my contract, including salary, holiday pay, long service leave built up over five years at News and a few other entitlements. (This was the war chest that allowed us to fund our court battle.) But it also said that I had been sacked with three months to run on my three-year contract.

I could almost hear the grumbling over breakfast tables that I had done all right for a bloke with only three months to go. In fact, I had almost 15 months to run, and was just nine months away from negotiating a new deal on the same or better conditions. There was a clause in my contract, inserted by News Limited, that said renegotiations would begin in August 2009. Given my performance in the role, I believed that would happen as a matter of course. The clause would become a major focus of the trial.

In the run-up to it, News changed their defence several times. The low point was when they lodged with my lawyers 'evidence' of disharmony in the newsroom under me—it consisted of three emails written by ageing Blunden loyalists several weeks after our writ was issued and, laughably, a handwritten new year's greeting from a fourth staff member that gave me a whack on the way through. By my calculation, that left about 285 staff who were presumably satisfied with life under me. Not surprisingly, News' lawyers abandoned the tactic by the time we got to court.

The mediation session in May was a curious episode that was almost doomed to fail from the outset. Held in a nondescript room at chambers in Queen Street, I didn't envy the Senior Counsel charged with bringing the two sides together; it was obvious from the get-go that we were a very long way apart. For a start, News didn't see fit to send any of its executives. Instead, my team of solicitors—Tony Macken, his son, Dominic, and Natalie Olive—had to deal with Ian Philip, the man whose dismissive comments to me straight after the sacking had pretty well precipitated the whole mess. He had flown down from Sydney that morning with a lawyer from the firm of Allens Arthur Robinson.

I had wanted to use the session to flag my determination to see the matter through to trial if necessary, but be open to settlement. I went in with a short, prepared speech in my pocket that talked of my family's sense of abandonment and my bewilderment at what had happened. If I got the chance I would remind Philip that the only explanation I was given for my dismissal was repudiated the same day, seven hours later, by the man to whom I reported.

Such mediations usually remain confidential but, given John Hartigan released a statement straight after the judgement had gone against him that the damages awarded to us were what News had offered at the session, I feel compelled to set the record straight. In fact, the judge's award amounted to hundreds of thousands of dollars more than News' offer that day.

Besides, it wasn't just about money. It never was. Hartigan would have known that if he or any other senior executive had bothered to show up. News made one offer at mediation and they weren't budging. It consisted of a sum of money and, extraordinarily, a confidential briefing session on why I was sacked if I accepted then and there. I rejected both.

Several hours later, both sides walked away—we were miles apart. Worse, News Limited wanted to attach conditions to any settlement that would have cloaked it in secrecy and prevented any future discussion. Several weeks later I offered to settle the matter for $950 000 plus costs—just one third of the claim before the court—believing it would kick-start the negotiating process anew. But they never budged.

Several months after the failed mediation, when a date for proceedings was set, *The Age* duly reported that the 'media trial of the century' would begin on 27 April 2010. Ultimately, the court case would cost News probably twice what they could have settled for and do incalculable damage to the reputation of their most senior executives.

As the year moved on, I tried my best to compartmentalise legal matters and find the positives in my situation. It wasn't always easy. I had very limited contact with my former colleagues from HWT and, when I did, it was usually a call from a public telephone box. Management had spooked them so much about dealing with me, they daren't make a call from home, office or mobile, in case they were identified. One colleague, who had taken redundancy since my departure, was ordered to refund his payout after Blunden learned he had communicated with me in less than positive terms about life at the paper under the new regime. He was forced to hire a lawyer and News eventually backed off.

We changed the way we went about our daily lives, refusing to discuss any legal matters on our home or mobile phones. Instead, we used a third dedicated line. Any significant discussions with our lawyers we had face to face. And we reined in our spending to cover the enormous costs of mounting the case.

But there were positives: I had started writing a book; I had made several well-received appearances on ABC Radio as a host; I was helping a group of Queensland investors establish a network of internet sites; and, most important of all, I had precious time with my mother.

We had visited specialists mid-year only to learn that there was nothing more that could be done for her after a lifetime of heart problems. Doctors had performed an aortic valve replacement on Ruby in 1989; it was something of a miracle that it had given her another 20 years of life and allowed her to see two of her grand-children grow to adolescence.

The realisation came to both of us after a visit to Epworth Hospital in September 2009. As I wheeled her back to my car, we passed the rehabilitation centre, formerly the nurses' home of the Salvation Army's Bethesda Hospital. My mother had trained there as a teenager, making the journey to Melbourne on the HMAS *Canberra* from Cairns, battling seasickness all the way. She had been just 17 and had farewelled her own mother at the docks in north Queensland. It would be the last time they would see each other; Ruby had lost her to illness soon after and she had received the news by phone at Bethesda. I had been born in the maternity ward directly opposite, 20 years later.

Although it was left unsaid between us, we both knew that she had only months, perhaps just weeks, left. I was grateful that my circumstances meant I could spend a great deal of time with her. My mother had been a nurse all her life and accepted that she would die. But she hated being sick.

While her body was slowly shutting down, her mind was as sharp as ever. We spoke only briefly about News' treatment of me. She thought it outrageous and encouraged me to fight them all the way to court, if it came to that. We would console ourselves by acknowledging that whatever the outcome of the case, my shift to Melbourne had brought us together again and given us these precious final days.

By November I was spending every day by her hospital bedside, holding her hands, occasionally rubbing balms or oils on them, combing her hair, feeding her. I would read while she slept. Sometimes I would cry. My mother was 91 and, by any measure, had had a full life. But it still felt unfair that I would lose her at this time. She fought and fought but, after three weeks in hospital, she eventually succumbed.

Can a 55-year-old man feel like an orphan? I would have thought not but, in the days and weeks after my mother's death, I felt terribly alone and at a low ebb. I was unemployed at what I did best, I was in mourning and I was facing a court battle with the biggest media company in the world, who seemed determined to make me suffer all the way. Could things get any worse?

A week after my mother's funeral, my son and I returned home from a visit to a local GP to find the study in disarray. My laptop computer was gone and papers were strewn over the floor. In the family room at the rear of our home I found broken glass scattered across the floor. The thief, wearing gloves, had smashed a window to gain entry. As we checked the rooms we quickly did a count: he had taken five laptops in all, including one or two that were unlikely to be worth much in any pawn shop or public bar. And that, save for a couple of watches and a couple of iPods, was it. Curiously, the burglar had left behind money and jewellery.

My brother Ross, a former policeman and private detective, had all sorts of theories on what may have motivated the crime. So did some of my legal team. Months later police arrested a man based on a blood sample taken from our house. He later pleaded guilty to a series of burglaries, including ours, and was sentenced to two years jail, with a non-parole period of 15 months. The goods were never recovered. Whether they knew it or not, someone had not only the unfinished manuscript of this book but also every piece of communication between my lawyers and me.

28

Guthrie v News Limited

On 31 March, just four weeks before the trial was due to begin, blogger Margaret Simons reported News Limited had been working for months to gather evidence 'with a view to destroying [Guthrie's] reputation'. Writing for *Crikey*, her piece concluded: 'If it goes ahead, there will be no better show in town in late April 2010 than Guthrie v News Limited.'

While Simons would be proven right when the trial finally did begin—News did seem more interested in destroying my standing than actually winning the case—I was distressed that a life-defining battle for my family and me was being presented as some sort of circus entertainment. After all, we were putting everything on the line—house, finances, my career—to take on the fight. It was a very curious feeling to be a media victim and I didn't like it one bit.

My concern was that News were trying to spook me and that Simons had been used for that purpose. Tony Macken was convinced it was an attempt to soften us up.

'You can expect something to happen pretty soon,' he said.

Sure enough, the next day News made an offer of settlement— except it was the same offer they had made almost a year earlier at mediation, prompting this observation by me to Tony: 'Maybe it's an April Fool's Day joke.'

We rejected the approach but, as part of the usual legal to and fro, expected a better one. But none was forthcoming, even when the National Rugby League announced just days before our hearing was due to begin that it would strip the News-owned Melbourne Storm of two premierships after it discovered massive salary-cap rorting at the club.

News' approach to the Storm problem bore more than a passing resemblance to its treatment of me. Certainly it highlighted the company's complete lack of regard for process, shooting first and only asking questions much, much later.

Throughout the 18 months since my dismissal I had anticipated or dreaded my day in court in almost equal measure. Now it was here—27 April 2010. I had spent the three-day Anzac Day weekend re-reading court documents in preparation for a week that promised to be brutal.

On the Sunday before the Tuesday hearing, Scott and I had headed off to the MCG for the Anzac Day clash between Essendon and Collingwood. At half-time in the match I had bumped into former *Age* media writer Matthew Ricketson, who earlier that day had been quoted at length in a *Sunday Age* story previewing the trial. In the piece Ricketson had expressed astonishment that News hadn't settled. He had underestimated Blunden's renowned pugnacity. I had no doubt the HWT boss had driven the case to court.

As some of the 90 000 fans at the game moved around us or queued for beers and pies, I told Ricketson that, despite all Blunden's bluster and blather in the lead-up to the hearing, he wasn't on their witness list. Ricketson, a professor in journalism at the University of Canberra, had an interesting take on my former managing director.

'He had more than 10 years editing the paper and would have gotten used to telling people what to do,' said Ricketson. 'He'd probably pick an argument with your QC.'

He was right. Editors have to be emphatic just to get their papers out. After more than a decade of telling people what to do on deadline, Blunden now had little time for alternative points of view. He would eventually appear but, ironically, he would be far from emphatic. To the contrary, throughout his evidence he would vacillate and hesitate, almost single-handedly derailing News' case.

In the early hours of Tuesday morning, Janne and I weighed up the possible outcomes. We had both had just a few hours of fitful sleep.

It was still my firm belief that the reporting of the Christine Nixon junket had played some part in my downfall. But was it the tipping point? Interestingly, in the days leading up to trial, the *Herald Sun* had gone after Nixon with an almost maniacal zeal. Day after day they called for her scalp after the revelation she had gone off to dinner at a pub at the height of the Black Saturday bush-fires. While there was certainly an argument to be made that the former chief commissioner, then chair of the Victorian Bushfire Reconstruction and Recovery Authority, should pay with her job, there was little justification for the paper's bloodlust. Their page one was looking more and more like a daily wanted poster. (Nixon eventually stepped down in July 2010.)

I wondered whether the paper had ramped up its indignation because of our impending court case and the expectation that we would make much of the conversations between Blunden and me over Nixon's Qantas junket. My suspicions were further fuelled by an anonymous tip that *Crikey* asked me to respond to just days before the trial. It suggested the attacks on Nixon were being delib-erately amplified to blunt any suggestions at trial that she was given preferential treatment in the lead-up to my sacking. I declined to buy into it. If it was true, News needn't have bothered. The issues surrounding matters about Nixon would be difficult to prove, so my legal team and I had decided to skip over it in my evidence, save for a mention in the timeline of my dismissal.

On the Tuesday we gathered at Norman O'Bryan's chambers at 10 a.m. and had a very brief discussion about what lay ahead. O'Bryan, 52, a Rhodes Scholar and son of a former eminent judge of the Victorian Supreme Court, offered no coaching. Long, lean and bespectacled, his only advice was: 'Keep your answers short and remain calm. Don't get rattled. Also, don't try to make the case— that's my job.' Point taken.

And with that, Janne, Susannah, Scott and I headed out into Queen Street, then left into Lonsdale Street, for the 200-metre walk to the Supreme Court, our legal team in tow. O'Bryan would be assisted by James McDougall, an expert in employment law. Paired up by the Mackens, it was only the second time he and O'Bryan had worked a case together but they would form a formidable duo. Solicitors Dominic Macken and Natalie Olive would sit with them at the bar table, providing whatever they needed to better take on 'the enemy', as O'Bryan liked to call the other side. Tony Macken, the principal of the firm, would sit with us throughout the trial, often feeding our hurriedly scrawled observations or questions to O'Bryan or McDougall.

Inside the court, the press gallery was packed. *The Age* had two reporters there, one writing the facts of the case, the other, an old *Sunday Age* colleague, Ian Munro, writing colour. Actually, *The Sunday Age* was well represented with two other former staffers—and long-term friends of mine—Lawrence Money and Kevin Norbury on hand to lend moral support. I was enormously grateful to them, even if Norbury nodded off through parts of my evidence.

Justice Stephen Kaye was presiding over the court that would in many ways decide my future. If we lost the case, my reputation and our finances would never recover. If we won, I might be able to rebuild both. I recalled using Kaye on a freedom-of-information

291

matter years before when he was a young barrister on the rise. The defendants knew of this but had no objection to his involvement. Now 57, he hadn't changed all that much in the intervening years.

Norrie Ross had drawn the short straw, reporting on the case for the *Herald Sun*. I rated Ross as a journalist but knew that, no matter what he wrote, his senior editors would bend his reports to their will. Over the next six days the paper would confirm my worst fears. In one particularly egregious attack, they headlined a report of the third day of the case 'He was a bad editor'. Not a quotation mark to be seen. The phrase was never uttered in court. The paper pulled other stunts too, their editors sinking to the level of gossip magazines by choosing for publication pictures that were unflattering, to say the least. This was News Limited at their absolute worst; I very quickly decided not to read their reports.

We started the trial in court three of the Supreme Court, one of the eight original courtrooms built towards the end of the nineteenth century. The room actually extended into the first floor of the building where a second public gallery was provided, often filled with schoolchildren. It had heavy wood panelling, extremely high ceilings and a huge carved canopy over the judge's bench. The acoustics—and the blue carpet—could have been better.

Justice Kaye presided from the highest point of the court. His associate sat directly below him, the tipstaff to her left, on constant alert for gum chewers or mobile phone abusers. The solicitors, two from each side, sat with their backs to the judge, but facing the senior counsel and their respective juniors. Janne and I, often accompanied by one or both of our children, sat at the rear of the court, with Tony Macken positioned just in front of us. The press gallery ran down the right-hand side of the court as we faced the judge, the public gallery to the left. This would be our world for six days.

O'Bryan, with tight, almost cherubic curls under his horsehair wig, put my evidence-in-chief. (Justice Kaye had actually requested the wigs be worn; in Victorian courts they are optional but only a very brave lawyer would go against the wishes of a judge.) Basically we argued that my dismissal 21 months into my three-year term was unlawful, hence I should have made it to 30 months, when a new contract was due to be negotiated. It said so in my existing one. Denying me this meant I had lost an opportunity that had genuine value; it would be up to the judge to decide the likelihood of renewal or, for that matter, redeployment elsewhere in News Limited. My solicitors had calculated that if I had been able to successfully negotiate a new three-year term either at the *Herald Sun* or elsewhere in News, with a termination and redundancy clause at the end of it, I had stood to earn around $3 million. We knew that News would say there had never been any chance of a contract extension and would rate the lost opportunity at zero. We would argue that it had some value, but was it 10 per cent of $3 million, 20 per cent, 30? As O'Bryan told Justice Kaye: 'We accept it wasn't 100 per cent, but it sure as hell wasn't zero either.'

We had also proposed 'another way home', as O'Bryan put it. If Justice Kaye wanted to avoid getting caught up in the messy business of calculating a lost opportunity claim—always speculative—he could simply find that News should have made a termination payment as well as a redundancy payment. They had offered 20 weeks, which, we held, was not only less than the contract suggested but mean as well. We thought 18 months was about right.

As to the sacking, O'Bryan's argument was simple. My contract only provided for dismissal for serious misconduct. None was alleged, much less proven, so the sacking was unlawful. News' argument that they could sack me for any reason provided they paid out my three-year term—which they did—was nonsense in our view. If that was the case, why have a misconduct provision at all? In a sense then, all the evidence that would be led over and above that was embroidery.

When O'Bryan finished his outline, it was my turn. I was nervous and throaty because of a cold. But I had the key events clear in my head and O'Bryan took me to them one by one. First he walked me through the negotiation process, then the move to Melbourne and my first days as editor-in-chief. So far, so good. Then we attempted to get into evidence a brief summary of events at the Monterey Online conference that Blunden and I had attended in May 2007. We hoped to demonstrate that I was overseeing not one but two platforms during my editorship—the paper and the website. But News' Queen's Counsel, Will Houghton, was very quickly on his feet, questioning its relevance. He gave the impression of being a man out of sorts, probably not surprising given he and the HWT had lost a defamation case just that morning.

Ironically, the last time I had been in the Supreme Court, the 59-year-old Houghton had been in *my* corner. He had been representing me in an action brought by the Commonwealth Director of Public Prosecutions against HWT, reporter Keith Moor and me over an inadvertent breach of a suppression order in 2007. It had ended well for Moor and me—the charges were dropped—but resulted in a fine for the company. The thrice-married, father-of-six Houghton was Blunden's go-to advocate and shared some of his aggression. A board member of the North Melbourne Football Club, he would be a formidable adversary.

Houghton was on his feet again as we tried to bring up John Hartigan's call to me on 27 July 2007 over Federal Court Justice Ron Sackville's criticisms of Ian Philip in the C7 case. Justice Kaye ruled in his favour after Houghton assured the court his side would not be calling any evidence about the matter and that it was not a factor in my dismissal.

O'Bryan returned to our timeline, with me recounting my lunch with Hartigan at Pure South restaurant on Melbourne's Southbank on 7 August 2007. This was an important element of our case: it represented the only one-on-one meeting between Hartigan and me apart from the hiring and firing discussions.

When I remarked that I thought Hartigan's caution to me at the restaurant—'Bruce, can I just give you one word of warning, never go up against Peter Blunden'—was a curious statement at the end of a convivial lunch, Houghton was on his feet once more, seeking the judge's intervention. Justice Kaye gently chided me with: 'Your thoughts aren't relevant Mr Guthrie; it's what is said that's relevant.'

Lawyers and judges assume you know this stuff but, even though I had had more experience of courts than most thanks to various reporting stints and one or two contempt actions, it was largely uncharted territory for me.

Then O'Bryan highlighted the only other contact: a handful of brief telephone conversations. Eventually, O'Bryan would accuse Hartigan of being derelict in his duty as CEO.

I had briefed O'Bryan that there had been only two phone conversations between Hartigan and me in all of 2008—one at my instigation, the other at Hartigan's. Now we zeroed in on his call, made the day after the launch of the *Herald Sun*'s new daily features section, Extra.

There was another reason for introducing this: it marked the start of an extraordinarily successful five-month period that included pay rises, bonuses and both industry and company awards. O'Bryan took me through them before turning to my run-in with Blunden during the Beijing Olympics over staff appointments and his indiscreet comments to Neil Mitchell.

Next we tendered a whole series of emails sent and received throughout September and October 2008 that suggested a positive and productive working relationship between Blunden and me. Many of them were notes of congratulation from the managing director, praising stories, even entire editions of the paper. Houghton was again on his feet—when he did this he usually had to adjust his gown, which, like the glasses perched on the end of his nose, seemed forever in danger of falling to the floor—and this didn't surprise us one bit. Arguing the emails weren't relevant, he was keen to have them excluded because they appeared to negate a key plank of the News case—that the working relationship between the managing director and me had irretrievably broken down. These emails suggested the exact opposite. Justice Kaye allowed them in.

Soon we were into the Calvert-Jones and dismissal conversations. I managed to recount matter-of-factly the two conversations with Blunden over our reporting of the chief commissioner's junket—the first behind the closed doors of my office, the second at Sydney Airport—but struggled a little with my recapping of the Hartigan meeting at which he sacked me. Eighteen months on, it still affected me in the retelling.

Then, around 2.45 p.m., it was Houghton's turn to grill me. The ABC's Michael Rowland would later call it 'a searing cross-examination'. That was certainly overstating things but it was less than pleasant, primarily because of a couple of low blows early on.

Under court rules, both sides are expected to provide outlines of evidence to enable the other party to better prepare for trial. Ours were very detailed and expansive; theirs were so broadbrush as to be almost worthless to us. Certainly we had no warning of Houghton's early salvos.

The first related to a meeting I had had with star columnist Andrew Bolt soon after I had started at the *Herald Sun*. Andrew and I had known each other a very long time and, although neither of us would probably describe the other as a friend, I was absolutely confident there was respect on both sides. Certainly I admired his ability to produce three extended and informed columns a week that, in turn, provoked an extraordinary level of debate both in print and online. Around April 2007, we met to discuss the fallout over a column he had written about law firm Slater & Gordon. There was a frank and open exchange of views not only about the row his S&G column had started, but also my page-one treatment of the guilty plea by accused Australian terrorist David Hicks. I had headlined it

'I want to go home', and Bolt believed that excused Hicks' guilt. I explained that, like any good tabloid editor, I was simply trying to find the emotional centre of the story. In any event, after a conversation that lasted more than an hour, we parted on good terms. Now Houghton was accusing me of disrespecting Bolt.

'His complaint, was it not, is that you had dismissed his matter in a light-hearted way?' asked Houghton.

'No, that wasn't his complaint,' I said, while thinking, *Where the hell is this going?* After recapping the row with Slater & Gordon, I concluded: 'I said, "Andrew, this is turning into a bit of a tennis match, why don't we leave it here?" and he took exception to that.'

Houghton would go on to suggest I had been pulled into line by Clarke over my alleged light-hearted treatment of Bolt but I didn't have a clue what he was talking about. Was this really the best they could throw at me?

Next Houghton questioned me about a tense meeting with *Herald Sun* advertising director Fiona Mellor in September 2007. At least, that's how I remembered it. If you believed Houghton, it was akin to the shower scene from *Psycho*.

'You attacked Ms Mellor, yelling at her at the top of your voice,' Houghton said. It was a statement demanding an emphatic denial, and he got one. But if I was perplexed by the first couple of matters Houghton raised, we were soon on to one that threw me completely. Perhaps that was the point of it.

As the clock ticked down to the end of the court day, Houghton handed up a bunch of emails over some discounted airfares Janne and I had obtained on a family visit to South Africa in 2008.

This was pure Blunden bastardry. The printout of the emails between the South African Tourism Authority and me bore his name. At some point they had been retrieved from my hard drive at work—we were never given access to it—and sent to his desktop before being handed to News' lawyers. O'Bryan objected to the emails being introduced as they'd never been made available to us during discovery. Houghton countered that they weren't required to be as they only went to my credit, not the facts of the case. They purported to show me seeking cheap airfares in return for favourable publicity about the trip. The airfares, although slightly discounted, cost more than $16 000 for four of us—and no stories were ever written about the holiday. Houghton tried to suggest I had taken the high ground on the *Herald Sun*'s proposed coverage of the Melbourne Storm tour of the UK and the low ground on my own trip. His attempts bordered on belligerence.

'Can I make the point that my wife is a professional travel journalist?' I asked Houghton.

'No, no, don't make any points, Mr Guthrie,' he spat back.

Justice Kaye took a different view, jumping in with: 'I'll allow you to do so.'

It was a small but marvellous moment; Houghton had been put in his place and acknowledged this with the time-honoured: 'If your Honour pleases.'

I went on: 'My wife is a professional travel journalist ... when she travels she writes stories from her travels. That's all this is saying.'

It was a minor victory for me at the end of an exhausting day. That night and the next morning, television, radio and the *Herald Sun* made much of our 'cheap' airfares. I was angry about this but strangely comforted too: News Limited was playing to the press gallery while we were only interested in an audience of one—the judge. Something else occurred to me too: the News case appeared to consist entirely of ephemera, a grab-bag of trivia, half-truths and worse. It had clearly been thrown together after the event. At least, it was clear to me.

The next morning, as we headed out of the house for the drive into court—to the tune of what would become our theme song for the trial, Tom Petty's 'Won't Back Down'—I resisted the urge to rush things. 'I know we desperately want this to be over,'

I said to Janne. 'But I reckon we should try to savour it. This is going to be one of the biggest weeks of our lives.'

That morning *The Age* had carried a sidebar piece to its main news story on page five of the paper. Headlined '"Key player" missing from court showdown', it dubbed Peter Blunden the 'invisible man'. Reporter Ian Munro had learned the HWT managing director was not on News' witness list. At least, he wasn't supposed to be.

But as Will Houghton resumed his cross-examination, it became clear to me that Blunden was going to make a 'surprise' appearance. It was also clear to me he was going to give very different accounts of the key events in our working relationship. What had changed his mind? Either it was Munro's piece or, much more likely, my testimony the previous day about the Calvert-Jones and dismissal conversations. I suspect the other side had waited to see if I had taped them. I hadn't. Given no third parties were present, Blunden now had deniability. He and his lawyers immediately flagged their intentions, asking a series of questions about the conversation with Blunden in my office regarding our reporting of the Nixon junket. Suddenly Houghton cut to the chase.

'I want to put to you Mr Guthrie that that conversation never took place.'

'Well, I reject that,' I replied. Of course I did. Why on earth would I make such stuff up? Why would I risk everything I stood for, not to mention owned, on lies?

But Houghton wasn't finished. Now he was suggesting I had made up the second conversation with Blunden about Calvert-Jones too. This was the one that had taken place at Sydney Airport on 31 October, en route to a meeting of editors and managing directors at Holt Street.

'I want to suggest to you that that conversation never happened,' said Houghton.

'I reject that.'

I had no doubt now that Blunden would be appearing—Houghton couldn't ask such provocative questions without an alternative version of events on record—and that he was going to deny all. And not just about this either. Obviously he would offer up a different version of the dismissal conversation and plenty more besides.

Over the next hour something else dawned on me too. News was going to try to suggest it wasn't the 'Beverly Hills Cop' reporting that cost me my job but another event in October—the pre-promotion of the annual *National Geographic* DVD series.

Were they serious? For good measure they threw in the placement of a Princess Mary story and then, bizarrely, a suggestion that I didn't grasp the importance of football to the fortunes of the *Herald Sun*. I didn't know whether I was more offended as an editor or as a fan, given I had grown up with the game, usually attended at least one AFL match every weekend and watched several more on television.

As I stepped down from the witness box, my hunch about Blunden was proven right. He was going to appear and a brief outline of evidence had already been prepared. We chose not to seek an adjournment, even though we knew we would probably have been entitled to one.

The trial was going to be a knock-down, drag-'em-out contest.

29

Here comes the enemy

Rupert Murdoch's number-one man in Australia, John Hartigan, didn't walk into court on day two of the trial, he swaggered in, mobile phone in hand. 'He's a self-important bastard,' someone observed. 'Let's see how he shapes up in cross-examination.'

Not well, as it would turn out. For whatever reason—pressures of work perhaps or maybe the Melbourne Storm debacle—Hartigan struggled with detail during more than five hours in the witness box over two days. This wasn't entirely surprising. While the case was the biggest thing in my life, it was probably just another diary entry for Hartigan. And, if the worst happened, he would be spending Rupert Murdoch's money, not his own.

Still, at the end of it all, I would reflect on the words of a corporate crisis manager who remarked on hearing Hartigan would appear: 'Smart companies never, ever, put their CEOs in the witness box.'

Hartigan had particular problems with dates, even though I had supplied most of them in an extensive outline of evidence we had provided several weeks previously. Obviously he hadn't done his homework and his lack of clarity was evident long before my SC, Norman O'Bryan, got to him.

But at least one thing was clear: based on Hartigan's evidence, Peter Blunden had bombarded the CEO with criticism of me throughout my editorship. Worse, he had never confided any of it to me; worse still, he never told Hartigan he wasn't telling me. It was double-dealing on a grand scale. The full extent of it emerged slowly but profoundly throughout Hartigan's evidence and unsettled me as I sat listening at the rear of the court and realised I had never had a chance of surviving this stuff. At one point I whispered to Janne: 'What did I do to deserve these people?'

In the lead-up to the trial, I had reflected on my own failings as an editor. My critics would say I managed down better than I managed up. I would argue that a large chunk of this goes with the job; strong editors need to occasionally stand up to the commercial side of the business in the interests of readers and journalism. Sadly, during my 20 years as an editor, managing 'up' had become more and more important, to the point that many editors were now managers, driven to please boards and CEOs first, readers second.

I had also realised too late that, politically, I had too few points of contact on the wall. Climbers understand that the more tethers you have on the mountain, the better your chances of survival if one comes adrift. My only point of contact at the *Herald Sun* had been my managing director; I had put all my faith in him, he had betrayed me and I had paid dearly for it. As Hartigan responded, first to Will Houghton, and then to Norman O'Bryan, I realised the fundamental error I had made: I had never developed the other points of contact—Hartigan, Calvert-Jones perhaps, Murdoch himself maybe—who might have saved me when I began teetering. Frankly, I had been too busy doing the job of editing.

For his part, Hartigan demonstrated a detachment that didn't reflect well on him. At several points in his evidence, I found myself wondering why he hadn't simply gotten Blunden and me in a room and laid down the law. I will always wonder about it. It was such an egregious failure of management that, for me at least, it called into question Hartigan's version of events. He was a better executive than that, surely. When O'Bryan finally put this failure to him, he came up short. Too short.

At the beginning of his evidence, Hartigan went to great lengths to suggest I had been a very demanding person to deal with, asking for the world and stretching negotiations for weeks. 'It was a long and very difficult process,' he said early on, when questioned by Houghton.

I had put in my list of requirements to do the job—I would hardly call them demands—on 7 January 2006, while overseas, and Hartigan had accepted just about everything within 72 hours. His attempts to suggest otherwise would eventually lead to an embarrassing back-flip within minutes of O'Bryan starting his cross-examination.

At the outset though, Hartigan was in the safe hands of Houghton, who guided his client through his evidence: I had apparently misjudged the potential sales impact of a one-off give-away of a computer game called *Spore*; I had inadequately blurbed an AFL final and fumbled the promotion of a special series we did on the game's 150th anniversary; I had put a story about Princess Mary of Denmark on page 18 rather than page three or five of the paper one Saturday morning with, apparently, disastrous effects on circulation.

Then there was the 'Collingwood factor'. Hartigan told the court that 'if you put a specific football team, namely Collingwood, on the front page it will sell anything up to 30 000 over and above the week before sale.' Even the judge, an ardent Hawthorn supporter and, from all reports, an amateur player of some ferocity and skill, seemed unconvinced by that one. If it were that easy, why would any editor hesitate to put Collingwood on the front page?

Hartigan wasn't only interested in deriding my skills; he was also keen to deride my achievements, especially those during my last months in the job. I thought this was particularly mean-spirited. After all, they had taken my job from me, wasn't that enough? Did they really have to take my accomplishments too? Apparently so: Hartigan claimed the much celebrated—and promoted—Newspaper of the Year win was a 'printers' prize'; my pay rise was little more than an automatic CPI adjustment; my bonus was a reflection of company performance, not my own; my inclusion in the empire's worldwide incentive scheme went with the position— funny, he had never mentioned it when I got the job.

Hartigan tried to make much of the pre-promotion of the *National Geographic* DVD give-aways in October 2008. This was the promotion that had been preceded by a 'robust discussion' at the Thursday management meeting immediately before it. In Hartigan's words, this stumble was the 'tipping point' in my editorship, the moment when he decided to get rid of me.

It was all pretty thin stuff, hardly justification for summarily removing an editor and setting in train all that had followed. If Hartigan had ever bothered to ask, it could have been dealt with over one lunch: the *Spore* promotion was a dud from the get-go; it had been my idea to do a magazine series on the 150th anniversary of football's first game and AFL boss Andrew Demetriou had publicly praised it; I wasn't anywhere near the news desk on the night of the Princess Mary dinner because I was handing out the paper's Teacher of the Year Awards at a dinner at the MCG; any disagreement over the timing of the DVD pre-promotion would have been removed if the managing director had attended the relevant weekly management meeting instead of taking a Qantas joy-flight over Melbourne. Were these really the grounds for a career-ending sacking?

In court, as reporters from the major dailies scribbled in their notebooks, my mind wandered to bigger questions about the future of newspapers. There was broad consensus that with the growth of the internet, the industry was confronting a Gutenberg moment, a shift as seismic as his invention of the printing press, that would forever change how we consumed media. Yet here was the Australian boss of News' global business suggesting I had lost my job because of a mistimed DVD promotion.

Blunden was into Hartigan's ear about me on a constant basis almost as soon as he took over as managing director in December 2007, as this exchange between Houghton and Hartigan made clear.

Houghton: 'How often or how frequently did you receive reports from Mr Blunden after November 2007?'

Hartigan: 'I would estimate initially on a fortnightly basis, but ultimately it got down to a weekly basis and sometimes more than once a week.'

It was a wonder Blunden had time to deal with anything else at Southbank, given the hours he apparently spent on the phone to Hartigan trying to do me in. The CEO went on: 'Ultimately at one meeting in Los Angeles when we were there for the purpose of our budgets, [Blunden] walked away from me in disgust.'

So there had been hissy fits by the managing director because Hartigan wouldn't sack me. At Los Angeles budget meetings, no less. Rupert Murdoch always presided at these gatherings; it wasn't a stretch to believe Blunden had been in Murdoch's ear as well. It was a miracle I lasted 21 months.

But the most curious part of Hartigan's testimony was to come. Houghton asked him whom he had informed of my sacking before he actually carried it out. Peter Blunden and Rupert Murdoch, replied Hartigan, before confirming the details of my transcript of the dismissal conversation. (The next day, under cross-examination, he added another two names to the list: human resources director Keith Brodie and News chief operating officer, Peter McCourt.) He even confirmed the use of the term 'shit sandwich' and opened the door to our lost opportunity claim by telling the court: 'I indicated to [Bruce] that I didn't want him to leave the company.'

'Prior to your meeting on that day with Mr Guthrie, had you had any conversation with Mrs Calvert-Jones, then chairman of the

Herald and Weekly Times, about the pending or possible dismissal of Mr Guthrie as editor-in-chief?' Houghton asked.

To which Hartigan replied: 'I'd had one discussion with Mrs Calvert-Jones about Mr Guthrie and it was to inform her upon his acceptance of the editorship of the newspaper, that he would be taking over from Peter Blunden as editor-in-chief.'

'That was, what, back in early 2007?' asked Houghton.

'Exactly,' said Hartigan.

I found it astonishing that Hartigan hadn't given Calvert-Jones a heads-up about what was going to happen on 10 November 2008, even though she was chair of the company and he was going to use her office to do it. Moreover, based on his testimony, he had never discussed my editorship with her, even though her managing direc-tor was forever trying to get me sacked.

Soon it was O'Bryan's turn to take on Hartigan. I had never seen him cross-examine but his reputation had preceded him. Within minutes he was forensically taking apart the News CEO's story. Having tried to suggest the contract negotiations were pro-tracted and difficult, Hartigan was immediately befuddled when confronted by the company's announcement of my appointment— just 11 days after my letter from overseas. Hartigan did his best to avoid admitting his error.

'Every appointment of an editor has comments from myself and this doesn't so I would suggest that someone has broken the story prior to it being announced,' said Hartigan of News' 18 January press release, which O'Bryan had just presented to him. Hartigan wasn't to know it but he had just made things much, much worse. O'Bryan moved in for the kill.

'Mr Hartigan, you are personally quoted in this release,' he said, matter-of-factly. 'Do you see your name there and the quotation marks around your quote?'

Hartigan had to concede that his memory of the negotiations was flawed. It was a significant victory for us on two levels: one, it called into question other aspects of Hartigan's evidence and, also, the swagger was gone, never to return while he was in the witness box.

As the minutes ticked down to the 4.15 p.m. adjournment, O'Bryan raised Hartigan's call to me after the C7 judgement and Justice Ron Sackville's criticisms of Ian Philip. It was a particularly interesting exchange, given Philip watched it all from the public gallery. He seemed relaxed, almost detached; I watched with a mix of anger and disbelief as Hartigan's memory of the call failed him.

'Do you deny making the call at all?' asked O'Bryan.

'I don't recall the call,' said Hartigan. 'I'm not saying I'm deny-ing the call.'

O'Bryan was having none of it. 'Mr Hartigan, on 27 July, when you rang Mr Guthrie, you rang him to look after the interests of News Limited in connection with the *Herald Sun*'s publication of this story, didn't you?'

Houghton was again on his feet. Hartigan and, by extension News Limited, are particularly sensitive about suggestions they put corporate interest ahead of public interest, even though it happens a great deal. Hartigan, having been given breathing space by Houghton's objection, reacted accordingly.

'One [I] don't recall the telephone conversation,' said Hartigan emphatically. 'And two, my job as the senior editorial person in this country is to have things published, not to have them not published.'

It was a good concise response, but any ground made up was quickly lost again when Hartigan responded to O'Bryan's next question. 'Do you recall reading any of the News Limited papers on the morning of 28 July to see how they had covered the Ian Philip story?' asked O'Bryan.

'No, I don't sir,' replied Hartigan, adding: 'And I would argue strenuously that I didn't. But, again, I don't have direct reflection on that day.'

Back in O'Bryan's chambers we discussed Hartigan's uneven performance in the box. Justice Kaye had the habit of staring at the witness during testimony. Janne had told me he had done this during my evidence and he was certainly doing it during Hartigan's. I could only assume he was looking for 'tells', the signs that tip a card player to a fellow player's real intentions. What would he make of Hartigan's performance?

As day three got underway, O'Bryan turned his attention to Hartigan's suggestion the previous day that Blunden had reacted with disgust at the Los Angeles budget meetings when his request to have me sacked had been turned down. This exchange led to the infamous 'drinking' question that, in turn, led to Hartigan withdrawing from the court.

'Have you observed that [Blunden] becomes more expressive . . . after he's had a few drinks Mr Hartigan?' asked O'Bryan.

'That I'm not aware of sir,' replied Hartigan.

By now, Hartigan had two minders in court—Philip and News corporate affairs director, Greg Baxter, both watching from the ground-floor public gallery. Both appeared to sit up a little straighter during this exchange. O'Bryan went on: 'He [Blunden] has had some problems in his life as a result of drinking, hasn't he?'

I had actually been surprised that it took until the second question to get Houghton to his feet, but now he was up and spoiling for a fight, tut-tutting like a disappointed schoolteacher. 'No, no, no,' he uttered with disdain to the judge.

'You don't have to answer Mr Hartigan,' said Justice Kaye, before inviting him to take a break outside the court. The press gallery was now well and truly awake and scribbling.

I had had no idea O'Bryan was going to pursue this line of questioning but I was certainly untroubled by it. Houghton might well have thought it a low blow but O'Bryan could have mentioned Blunden's well-publicised conviction for drink-driving in 2003, and he didn't. Besides, in Hartigan's absence, the SC crystallised one of my key misgivings about the CEO's conduct during my time as editor-in-chief of the paper.

'He [Hartigan] adopted a bizarre and we would submit, unprofessional approach in dealing with the issues that had arisen between Messrs Blunden and Guthrie,' O'Bryan said to Justice Kaye, as he began building his justification for asking the question, adding: 'He did practically nothing about it in his dealings with Mr Guthrie, at all. He met with him face to face only once before he sacked him and he had a couple of telephone calls and that's about it. By contrast he talked to Blunden repeatedly on his case, twice a week at a high point throughout this period.'

Justice Kaye was largely unconvinced though that this allowed any questions about Blunden's drinking habits. But O'Bryan persisted—if Blunden had been drinking when he made his criticisms of me to Hartigan, surely the CEO would have had to have taken that into account.

Throughout their exchanges, Hartigan waited outside the court, which was a pity, because I felt he needed to hear this stuff. He was finally being held to account for his failure to get my side of the story, and yet he wasn't hearing any of it.

When Hartigan returned, the 'drinking' question passed in a moment—according to the CEO, Blunden had been unaffected by alcohol when he had walked off in disgust after failing to convince Hartigan to sack me.

The whole exchange was but a warm-up for what I regarded as one of the key questions for Hartigan, one that I had wondered about since the day of my sacking. O'Bryan finally put it in the last minutes of his cross-examination.

'Did it ever occur to you during the course of these events in 2008 that it would be a good idea for you to get together with both Mr Guthrie and Mr Blunden at the one place, at the one time and have it out with them together, all three of you?'

'No sir,' replied Hartigan, adding Julian Clarke had already tried that and failed.

'Isn't that all the more reason why at least by August 2008, if not earlier, you would intervene yourself and get the three of you together in the one room at the one time?'

To which Hartigan replied: 'I don't see that as the performance of my job.'

No doubt his minders would later tell him it was a perfectly acceptable explanation for a CEO whose inaction had led his company to an embarrassing week in court. But for me the words hung heavy in the court, a damning indictment of a manager who simply didn't do his job properly. Minutes later, with the cross-examination concluded, I bumped into Hartigan in the public foyer of the court. We exchanged the briefest of greetings but I swear he had the look of a man filled with regret. Then again, perhaps I was just searching for signs of it.

Later, during the luncheon break, I encountered News' PR spinner Greg Baxter in the men's toilet. 'We've got a job for you at Melbourne Storm if you like,' said a chuckling Baxter, mid-pee. Philip was using the urinal next to him.

After lunch it was Julian Clarke's turn in the box. He was largely irrelevant to the case, having retired at the end of 2007 before the key events unfolded. His primary function seemed to be to echo Hartigan's emphatic claim that I would never have had my contract at the *Herald Sun* renewed. By saying this, News hoped to take the lost opportunity claim off the table.

Even though Clarke was of little importance to the case, I was probably more disappointed by his evidence, brief as it was, than that of Hartigan and Blunden. They behaved exactly as I expected; he surprised me with his exaggerations, something Justice Kaye would later remark on in his judgement.

Over the two hours of his evidence, it became clear that there was a kind of song sheet the News executives were singing from.

Recurring sentiments, even phrases, were everywhere. Not only that, no-one had notes of anything, strange for a company of journalists. Not one meeting was diarised—which spoke volumes for the processes at News. Clarke was at his least impressive when he was exaggerating the Andrew Bolt and Fiona Mellor incidents and when confronted with the Blunden emails of September and October 2008, which were fulsome in their praise of the paper and peppered with the use of the word 'mate'. Did these change his opinion that our relationship was beyond salvaging, asked O'Bryan. 'Nuh', 'nuh', and 'no', said Clarke in short order.

Now the main event was looming. Blunden was due in the box and Janne and I could only hope it would be a day he and News would regret for a very long time.

30

Checkmaaate!

When I had decided to pursue court action after my dismissal, one of the key drivers was a search for the truth of what had happened in the lead-up to my sacking by News. But, as proceedings entered the second half of what would be a six-day trial, I felt further from it. This had led to some anxious conversations at home. What was the point of all this, I had said to Janne more than once, if the truth doesn't come out?

I suspected Blunden would give very different accounts from mine of the key events leading up to my dismissal—about my performance, about our relationship, the Calvert-Jones–Christine Nixon exchanges, the dismissal conversation, pretty much everything—and we had to be ready for that.

After two days of listening to evidence from Hartigan and Clarke, I was forced to concede that Blunden had been playing both sides of the street in his dealings with me—saying one thing to his editor and an entirely different thing to his superiors—from the very start.

Janne and I had worked on our laptops at our kitchen table till late Thursday night sourcing material that O'Bryan could use in his cross-examination of Blunden. This included everything from details of the Qantas A380 joy-flight the managing director had taken through to a newsagent blog praising the DVD promotion that was supposed to have cost me my job.

O'Bryan used it all to good effect the next morning. Indeed, within five minutes of his beginning his cross-examination, News' star witness was looking extremely shaky.

The HWT boss had entered the box looking suitably grave. Ian Philip was in court to monitor events and once again the press gallery was packed. Houghton took Blunden through his evidence-in-chief and it was quickly clear that he was singing from the same song sheet as his fellow executives, Hartigan and Clarke. As I sat listening to him trotting out the Princess Mary story, my failings as a footy fan and my shortcomings as a pre-promoter of DVDs, I began anticipating how he would handle the major components of his evidence: the conversations about Janet Calvert-Jones and Christine Nixon, the post-dismissal phone conversation and email, and a story published a week later in *The Australian*.

It had been written by one of the paper's South Australian-based reporters, Verity Edwards; I had discovered the story online almost by chance on the weekend before the trial began. I remembered reading it in print the week after my sacking. Headlined, 'Dynamic Gardner takes charge at HWT', it said Blunden had denied my dismissal had 'anything to do with his relationship with Mr Guthrie', and quoted him saying 'everybody who knows the place knows Bruce and I get on well' and 'the concept that Bruce and I might have had a personality clash is untrue'. Given Hartigan's evidence the previous day of Blunden's constant carping against me, this was astonishing stuff. How would Blunden talk his way out of this one; indeed, how would he talk his way out of any of it?

Throughout his evidence to Houghton, Blunden stood almost to attention in the witness box, arms straight at his side and his body immobile. Only his head moved, usually in short, almost violent bobs before he would start answering questions. Under stress, he had a slight tic in his cheek. I noted, perhaps unkindly, that his girth had grown considerably since I had last seen him, although the impeccably tailored dark suit did a good job of camouflaging it.

The Calvert-Jones questions came late in his evidence-in-chief. And he did not surprise: he denied everything, claiming the closed-door conversation ('Janet's not happy') and the Sydney Airport conversation ('I'm not sure we got it right on Christine Nixon') never happened. He even added another flourish, saying he thought it 'a good front page ... I supported the story'. It was news to me. While I had anticipated this moment throughout, it still disappointed.

Next, Houghton introduced the dismissal-night conversation. As Blunden presented his version of the phone call, I found myself wondering how I apparently got the Hartigan conversation entirely right but the Blunden conversation substantially wrong. Answer: I hadn't. I had written extensive and detailed file notes on both conversations immediately after them. Along the way I had learned something: in moments of high drama and heightened awareness, a person's recall can be fabulous.

Blunden tiptoed his way through my transcript, acknowledging some phrases, changing others and dispensing with a few altogether. Then Houghton presented him with the 11 November email in which he denied any personal tensions were responsible for my removal. He went into a tortuous explanation of the difference between personal and professional issues. Finally, Houghton presented him with the Verity Edwards story. Blunden opted for denial again, but this time he did it directly to the judge.

'Did you say those words?' asked Justice Kaye.

'No, I didn't,' replied Blunden.

At the rear of the court, I quickly tallied up the score card. Of the five most sensitive and damning matters he was to confront, Blunden had denied three outright (the two Calvert-Jones conversations and *The Australian* quotes), contested another vigorously (the immediate post-dismissal phone call) and reinterpreted the fifth (the Tuesday email). He had created a minefield for himself; O'Bryan could barely wait to get to his feet.

He began with the 'integrity' issue. In one of his earliest answers to a Houghton question about the flawed circulation graphic, Blunden had made a short speech: 'I could not convince the editor-in-chief of the *Herald Sun* that integrity was a core part of our business.'

It was an outrageous thing to say, particularly given the evidence that would follow. O'Bryan was straight on to it, forcing Blunden to admit that he had done nothing to resolve this apparently heinous breach of the paper's code of conduct, save for mentioning it in an intemperate email. It set up the next attack on Blunden—over his comments to *The Australian* a week after my sacking.

It took O'Bryan only a matter of moments to tie Blunden in knots. The HWT managing director stuttered, hesitated and mumbled his way through his answers. Along the way he made the extraordinary claim that he had only read the story for the first time 48 hours earlier even though it had been published in November 2008; given it was the first major interview with my successor and that it quoted Blunden at length, this seemed incomprehensible. But Blunden persisted, angering O'Bryan.

'You are giving truthful evidence to His Honour are you that you did not have any idea of the existence of this article published on 17 November 2008, referring to you, attributing comments to you and quoting you, until 28 April 2010, two days ago?' asked O'Bryan, adding for emphasis: 'Is that an honest answer you give His Honour?'

'It is,' replied Blunden.

'Mr Blunden?' O'Bryan asked incredulously. At times like these he would crane his neck, turn his face full on to the witness box and adopt a look that fairly dripped with scepticism.

'It is,' repeated Blunden.

As the Senior Counsel forensically pulled apart *The Australian* story, I felt Blunden's standing within the court went the same way. Soon my SC was almost mocking him.

'Having regard to the professional standards you consider the News Limited group newspapers should adhere to, you must have been deeply shocked on 28 April when, as you say, for the very first time you read these things attributed to you, including in quotation marks when they are so wrong on your evidence, is that correct?'

'Yes, I was very surprised to see it,' replied Blunden.

'What have you done about that?'

'Nothing.'

Soon Justice Kaye was questioning Blunden again, asking: 'Tell me, in the days after Mr Guthrie's termination, did you read what was being said about it in other newspapers?'

'Oh sporadically,' said Blunden, before stuttering through the rest of his answer. 'I, I didn't see every story. I didn't look, I didn't look at the stories on it, Your Honour.'

Justice Kaye continued: 'You weren't looking for stories on it?'

Blunden: 'Um, I saw, I saw some stories, but not a lot. I didn't see this particular article, which, which I'm not even sure exactly where it, where it appears. I, it's in the media section. I didn't see it.'

The tic in Blunden's cheek was working overtime now—and so were his mind and mouth. While responding to questions about his 11 November email to me—'no way that any personal tension, real or perceived, is responsible for this'—he let slip that 'the final decision' on my fate was made in 'late, late October'. This meant it coincided with Rupert Murdoch's visit to Australia and, based on the first sentence of Blunden's answer to O'Bryan's question, almost certainly his visit to Melbourne on 27 October 2008. It was the day Murdoch had praised my page one and later chaired the lunch where Janet Calvert-Jones had been unusually cool towards me. Hartigan had been in the HWT Tower that day too and had mentioned in his evidence that he had told Murdoch of his decision to sack me; it seemed reasonable to conclude that Rupert had been part of the decision-making process. Perhaps his sister was too, which was also interesting given Hartigan had told the court he had only ever spoken to her once about me as editor and that was when he had informed her of my appointment in early 2007.

Now Blunden appeared to have given the game away, prompting O'Bryan to ask: 'What event or communication enables you to date it at late October, 2008?'

It was a very simple straightforward question that required only a simple straightforward answer. The most obvious would have been: 'Because Rupert was in town', but instead Blunden began with 'John was in Melbourne late, late that month' and continued on with largely incomprehensible babble that lasted 482 words and spread across three pages of transcript.

There was one more extraordinary piece of evidence to play out before lunch. I remember it as one of the defining moments of the case—and appalling for what it said about the company's corporate values and management practices. With Blunden clearly struggling in the witness box, O'Bryan turned his attention to the managing director's history of double-dealing—telling me one thing, right down to congratulatory emails addressed 'mate', and Hartigan another. Blunden was forced to admit he had never told me he was constantly criticising me to the CEO.

Asked O'Bryan: 'Do you think it might have been the decent thing to do, Mr Blunden, to have let Mr Guthrie know that you were talking to Mr Hartigan all these times during 2008, criticising him?'

It wouldn't have been proper, Blunden replied. There was a momentary hesitancy in his voice, almost as if he realised how appalling it sounded.

Soon the ever-alert Justice Kaye jumped in again. 'Did you not consider it might have assisted if you told Mr Guthrie, "This is getting so serious that I'm talking to Mr Hartigan about this and about the fact that I do not think you are any longer the appropriate man to be editor of the *Herald Sun*"?'

Blunden responded: 'I told Mr Guthrie in no uncertain terms that I don't believe he was the right person for the job.'

I can say categorically that we never had any conversation along those lines.

In court, Justice Kaye persisted: 'Did you tell Mr Guthrie that you were communicating that to Mr Hartigan, the situation had become so serious?'

Blunden: 'No, no, I didn't Your Honour because I believed it was a conversation between John and I.'

At the lunch break there was absolute consensus that O'Bryan had just about dismembered Blunden. We weren't to know but Blunden and Philip had adjourned to a patisserie in William Street, a short walk from the court. An *Age* photographer had followed them and snapped the pair through the restaurant's front window. It would become the most telling image of the trial—Blunden looking haunted, Philip perplexed. *The Age* would ultimately dub it the $565 000 lunch, after Justice Kaye said in his judgement that when Blunden returned to the court for an afternoon session some of his evidence sounded rehearsed, as if he was making a prepared speech.

He was almost certainly referring to an exchange between O'Bryan and the HWT managing director immediately after the lunch break. O'Bryan was questioning Blunden about an email he had sent to me in 2007 promising 'honest and regular requests and feedback'.

'But you weren't intending to be honest or regular with [Mr Guthrie] in connection with your communications with Mr Hartigan, were you?' asked O'Bryan.

To which Blunden replied: 'It was improper for me to tell Bruce about my dealings with Mr Hartigan, because had Mr Hartigan continued to form the view that it was not yet ready for a change, our position would have been unworkable, completely. If Mr Hartigan decided not to terminate the contract after my discussions, I wasn't, then I couldn't, have gone back to the office and worked with Mr Guthrie and said by the way I'm here, trying to do it. I was working to my superior, giving him feedback on the best interest of our overall business.'

It was clearly an attempt to rationalise his lack of candour over his persistent entreaties to Hartigan to off-load me. Worse, it sounded like he had been coached, although there was nothing slick about his evidence regarding his communications with Neil Mitchell.

'You had a lunch with Neil Mitchell in August 2008, is that correct?' asked O'Bryan.

'I have a lunch—a monthly lunch with Mr Mitchell,' replied Blunden.

'It follows doesn't it,' asked an exasperated O'Bryan, 'that the answer to my question is yes, you had a lunch with him in August 2008, is that right?'

'I would have to look in my diary, but once a month I do,' replied Blunden. 'I'd say yes, I would have a lunch with him in August, yes. Once a month I have a group of people—we meet once a month for lunch.'

O'Bryan soon moved to the infamous joy-flight aboard the new Qantas A380 on 2 October 2008. The managing director gave another long-winded answer, prompting O'Bryan to ask provocatively why he was 'so defensive' about missing the management meeting scheduled that day.

'What are you nervous about?' he asked Blunden.

'Nothing at all,' came the reply.

'Let me put it to you, Mr Blunden, that having gone on your flight on the A380, you missed the opportunity of addressing the lead-up for the *National Geographic* promotion because of your decision about where your priorities lay; do you agree with that?'

'No, I do not,' said Blunden.

Two things happened at this point: Tony Macken leaned back in his chair and whispered, concerned, to me, 'This man's not well'—and Justice Kaye offered Blunden a glass of water and a break, adding: 'Are you all right?' It was clear to most people in court that Blunden was struggling under the relentless pressure of O'Bryan's cross-examination. Soon the decency issue was on the table again.

In late September 2008, two weeks after we had won Newspaper of the Year and six weeks before I was dismissed, Blunden had sent a very chatty and cheery email that concluded with the line 'Great news about the house'. It was a reference to our decision to buy a home in Melbourne and sell in Sydney to consolidate the move we had made on behalf of News Limited. Obviously, if I had even suspected I was going to be sacked, we would never have done it. Blunden could have easily warned us, but chose not to. Instead, he sent the congratulatory note, prompting this from O'Bryan: 'Even when you knew that he was about to outlay, or his family was about to outlay a very substantial amount of money on a home in Melbourne and sell their home in Sydney, did it not occur to you morally that that would be a proper thing to do?'

Replied Blunden: 'I had the interests of the paper and the business at heart and if there was another issue like that, it had to be tackled separately.'

O'Bryan let it hang in the air for a few seconds, so the full scale of Blunden's bastardry could sink in around the court. He had withheld information that could have saved us from a financial crisis, but chose not to. Janne and I exchanged rueful glances—if we lost this case we would be facing an even deeper one.

Now it was time for O'Bryan to put three key conversations to Blunden: the two concerning Janet Calvert-Jones' alleged misgivings about our treatment of Christine Nixon and the phone conversation with me the night of my sacking.

O'Bryan forcefully put to him that both conversations about Nixon had happened exactly as I had said they did. Then he added a twist that surprised not only the defendant, but also me, his client.

'Can I put it to you that the reason why you said these things to Mr Guthrie, whether they were true or not, is because you wanted to give Mr Guthrie some other explanation for his termination [rather than] the true reason for it?' said O'Bryan.

While Blunden sought clarification, I considered this surprise scenario. If O'Bryan was right, Blunden may have invented the Calvert-Jones conversations to cover his tracks.

O'Bryan went on: 'You wanted to be able to give Mr Guthrie an explanation for his sacking that deflected attention away from your role in it, didn't you?'

'No, I did not,' said Blunden.

I had no idea where this alternative scenario had come from— certainly O'Bryan had never discussed it with me—but it was far from implausible. I would now have to add it to my growing list of possible explanations.

It was just after 4 p.m. when O'Bryan finally finished his questioning of Blunden. It had been an illuminating day; the managing director's lack of self-awareness was astonishing throughout. Only once did he show any flicker of conscience but even then it was unconvincing.

'Do you regret writing this email to Mr Guthrie, saying the things that you said to him on Tuesday, 11 November, Armistice Day 2008? Do you regret any of that?' asked O'Bryan at one point.

'No,' said Blunden, before adding, almost begrudgingly: 'If there was one part that I would regret [it] is not pinning enough blame on me driving the agenda.'

'I beg your pardon?' said O'Bryan, with an upward inflection that conveyed his surprise.

'I'd say the only part that I would say is when I've said, "When the company decides. It was always the company's decision", it wasn't. I probably should have been more open with him in saying it was actually—I was involved in the process.'

It was the closest Blunden came to admitting his complicity. But it was a long, long way from contrition.

When Justice Kaye finally excused Blunden from the witness box he all but scampered out of the court, Philip at his side.

They left in such a hurry they were probably already halfway back to the HWT Tower when the judge asked everyone to be seated and made a short statement from the bench. It was extraordinary, by any measure. Long-time observers said they had never heard anything quite like it.

'I have now heard four witnesses,' Justice Kaye began. 'There are clearly some very strongly contested issues of fact, many of which I will need to resolve, some or many of which will involve findings by me as to veracity and credibility. I think the curial process is the best way to do it but it's not perfect.

'All I can do is assess the credibility and veracity of the four men who have given their evidence in this case from where I sit here, subjected to cross-examination, and those findings are not always perfect but findings to that effect can have a reach well beyond the confines of the particular case.

'All I can do is—no doubt counsel understand that already— encourage them to convey that to their clients. I am not expressing any views about anyone's credibility in saying this but it is clearly obvious I'm going to have to make some findings and encourage the parties to try to resolve them over the weekend. Otherwise, as I am required to do, I will proceed to make the appropriate findings after, no doubt, giving the matter very anxious consideration. But I do think this is a case which, whilst it has gone a long way, it still does deserve careful consideration and an attempt to compromise.'

Janne and I looked at each other wide-eyed. Tony Macken's face was full of wonder. As Justice Kaye left the bench, Macken whispered: 'I've never heard a judge make such a statement in all my life in the law.'

I looked to the press gallery and only *Crikey*'s Andrew Crook and Stephen Mayne were on hand to hear what Justice Kaye had said. Mayne wandered over to me. 'He's just put Blunden on notice that, if it goes to judgement, he's going down,' said Mayne, who had been in court for the past two days. 'You'll cop half a million, won't you?' he asked with a smile.

Janne and I tried to hide our joy as we headed out onto Lonsdale Street, but it was difficult. Instinctively I gave a thumbs up to the media pack and immediately regretted it. The last thing we needed at that point was triumphalism from me. We fairly skipped down Lonsdale and into Queen before heading up to a conference room at Melbourne Chambers. We all agreed: the judge was surely sending News a message.

Then we headed from O'Bryan's chambers to Macken's offices and the mood was joyous. As we entered the foyer of their building, Janne pulled me away from the main group. Watched by our lawyers and our daughter Susannah, who had been in court for almost every minute of the week's proceedings, we embraced. 'We've done it,' she whispered into my ear. 'I think we've won.'

31

Harsh judgements

No-one can say News Limited wasn't warned. In addition to his entreaty to parties at the conclusion of the fourth day of the trial that they work towards settlement, Justice Kaye had another go at the end of the sixth and final day, saying: 'I only repeat to the parties the very wise words I imparted to them last Friday.'

Despite the clear messages the judge was sending, News never budged. My legal team had made themselves available over the weekend separating the fourth and fifth days of the trial, anticipating an approach from the other side. It never came. I later learned Blunden had been telling anyone who cared to listen at television's Logie awards, held in Melbourne at Crown Casino on the Sunday night, that he believed News had right on their side and would win the case. Clearly Justice Kaye's words had been wasted.

This was despite it being obvious to most observers that Blunden certainly and Hartigan probably were going to suffer if the matter went to judgement. So why wouldn't they settle? They may have genuinely believed the judge's words were directed at us or they may simply have been in denial. But more likely it's because News believed they could act inside the court as they routinely do outside it—with arrogance, aggression, hubris.

Besides, they dominated the court of public opinion and could manipulate it pretty much any way they wanted. I had learned this to my cost over the first four days of the trial: the Murdoch press selectively presented what actually happened in court. If the judge did make adverse findings against senior News executives, their papers could simply ignore them, leaving such trifling matters to the Fairfax press or the ABC.

Certainly no News Limited readers were made aware of Justice Kaye's comments on the Friday evening. By then the representatives of the mainstream media had left for the day, meaning they had missed one of the most dramatic moments of the entire case. In another journalistic era it would have been an unforgivable sin, drawing punishment by an enraged news editor or chief of staff.

Only blogger Stephen Mayne reported it in real time (*The Sunday Age* reported it two days later), posting his account within hours of the court rising at 4.15 p.m. on Friday. It was a very real comment on the changing nature of mainstream media. Mayne wrote:

> Herald & Weekly Times managing director Peter Blunden spent all of Friday in the box and at the end of it Justice Stephen Kaye sent his legal team a very strong message to settle, warning that there was [sic] substantial contested facts and he would be making judgments on people's credit which could have implications well beyond the court.

Mayne predicted 'the parties will heed the judge's advice and reach a confidential settlement over the weekend', adding: 'News will pick up Guthrie's legals and give him a useful six figure sum to make the whole messy saga go away.'

But against all expectations, they did not do that. Instead, the trial ground on for another two days—Hartigan was safely back in Sydney and Blunden in his thirteenth-floor office at HWT Tower when Janne and I resumed our seats at the rear of the court on the morning of Monday, 3 May.

For much of the last two days, we sat through complex legal argument but there were fiery moments towards the end of Houghton's summing up on Monday afternoon. It provoked out-rage in me and anger in O'Bryan, who immediately decided to flip his approach to his own summation.

After several hours of calm and largely dignified summary, Houghton suddenly turned to what he called the 'grand conspiracy theory'—the conversations with Blunden over alleged complaints by Janet Calvert-Jones after the Christine Nixon junket report. Once again I was bemused that the defendant was returning to the subject; we had barely mentioned it. Houghton was extremely energised by it, calling on the judge to find that Blunden's denials were honest and that I had made it all up. (In the end, Justice Kaye did exactly the opposite.)

'Your Honour ought make a finding in our respectful submis-sion that Mr Guthrie was untruthful in his evidence to this court about those two conversations,' said Houghton.

I had been tempted to rush to O'Bryan's side and instruct him to deal with Houghton's claims of lies forcefully and immediately. I needn't have worried. He was straight on to it as he took the floor. 'Your Honour, since my learned friend has closed with the virtues of Mr Blunden I might open with some of his vices,' said O'Bryan, much to my delight.

He directed the judge to Blunden's email to me on 11 November 2008, the day after my dismissal. It was the email that had drawn a begrudging admission of guilt from Blunden in court five days earlier.

He had begun it with the words, 'I sincerely regret that it ends this way' and rejected suggestions of difficulties between us. 'There is no way any personal tension (real or perceived) is respon-sible for this,' Blunden had written, before rejecting Andrew Rule's story the same day in *The Age* as 'rubbish'. He went on: 'When the company decides to move in another direction, it simply happens.' Given he had just succeeded in a year-long campaign behind my back to have me sacked, it was appallingly duplicitous.

On the way up to court on the Monday morning, O'Bryan had promised me: 'I'm going to let Blunden have it today— Hartigan too.' Now, angered by Houghton's closing remarks, he decided to give Blunden both barrels.

'Perhaps the most important document in the case, Your Honour, is the document at p. 208 [of the court book] in which Mr Blunden obviously, blatantly, clearly and deliberately lied three times within three sentences to Bruce Guthrie on the day after his termination,' said O'Bryan, adding: 'Peter Blunden had, of course, been lying to Bruce Guthrie at this point for at least nine months.'

O'Bryan was kinder towards News CEO Hartigan, but not much. 'I'm not here, Your Honour, to say that Mr Hartigan is a liar,' he began, before taking another swipe at Blunden. 'I regret to say I am here to say Mr Blunden is a liar and I will give Your Honour copious reasons for reaching that conclusion.'

He went on instead to accuse Hartigan of exaggeration, mis-remembering, even offering absurd evidence. But perhaps his most damning assessment went to his abilities as a CEO. It was Hartigan's duty to deal with the deteriorating relationship between Blunden and me, but he did nothing, said my senior counsel.

'These were not minuscule issues,' said O'Bryan, adding: 'For Mr Hartigan to suggest that ... it was not his responsibility and duty as the chief executive officer and chairman of this company to do something about this rapidly deteriorating situation demonstrates, in our submission, that he has no idea what his job was in this company.' It all amounted to a 'dereliction of duty', said O'Bryan. Ouch.

Not surprisingly, the stoush between the two counsel generated plenty of heat and plenty of headlines. But no-one was more pleased than I was when the case finally wound up at 4.15 on the afternoon of Tuesday, 4 May. I held out little hope that News would heed Justice Kaye's second warning from the bench to settle. Clearly, our fate was now in his hands.

As we left the court to be greeted by a solitary cameraman—apparently the media pack was exhausted by it all, too—I asked O'Bryan how he thought it had gone. 'Oh, we'll win the breach of contract case, Bruce, no doubt,' he said without a moment's hesitation. 'It's just a matter of what we win.'

We were less sure about the lost opportunity claim. The sheer weight of numbers—three witnesses against one—meant the judge had been bombarded by evidence that there was absolutely no prospect of me being renewed as editor-in-chief of the *Herald Sun*.

The trial brought into very sharp focus the extraordinary burden that a judge inevitably has to bear. I had once heard a very senior member of the bench refer to the loneliness and stress of the role, particularly on the night before a judgement. It would fall to Stephen Kaye to, in effect, decide between my account and those of three very senior members of one of the country's biggest companies. Would he be intimidated by their standing?

We had prepared ourselves for a wait of weeks, if not months, before judgement would be handed down. In the end, Justice Kaye delivered in just 10 days. Janne and I were driving in country Victoria, trying to escape, for a couple of days, the constant questioning and speculation arising from the hearing, when Tony Macken rang on a Thursday morning to tell us the judgement had been scheduled for the next day: Friday, 14 May. We immediately turned the car around to head back to Melbourne—and got a very rare speeding ticket along the way.

Justice Kaye had scheduled his findings for noon, an odd hour forced on him by the funeral of Peter Galbally, QC. Janne and I struggled to sleep and were both up around 3 a.m., drinking tea and imagining outcomes. We avoided the most unpleasant one: defeat. Even though I left them unsaid, the potential ramifications were coming into sharp focus for me; I realised that if I was to lose the claim my career, already under great pressure, would be over.

Around 4 a.m. we returned to bed and managed a few hours sleep. We stuck to our trial routine for luck—Tom Petty on the car radio, parking at Queen Vic market and a slow stroll to Norman O'Bryan's chambers. As we did, we struggled to categorise our feelings. Janne hit on the best analogy—it was a little like childbirth: we were hoping, praying and expecting all to go well, but there was always the potential for disaster and terrible distress.

There had been much discussion the previous day as to whether we should even go to court. Tony Macken cautioned that if we lost, we wouldn't want to be there and, if we won, we could be there in a matter of minutes if we waited for a text message at chambers. But I was having none of it. Eventually it was agreed we would take our seats—and our medicine—just as we had done during the trial.

We gathered at O'Bryan's chambers around 11.30 a.m. and there was a noticeable tension in the air. Our entire legal team was waiting for us—O'Bryan, McDougall, Tony and Dominic Macken and Natalie Olive. Very little was said.

At 11.45 a.m. we took the final stroll north on Queen Street and west on Lonsdale. The media pack was back, bigger than ever, stretched right across the footpath.

Then it was into court three again, where the whole process had begun. There was barely a spare seat in sight—Tony Macken counted 18 people in the press gallery, while the public gallery upstairs was well populated too. Every second person seemed to be a lawyer—and an HWT lawyer at that. We were outnumbered about three to one. Then it dawned on me that they were not there for our matter but the next, a defamation action. It meant there were plenty of familiar faces on hand and I found myself in the curious position of swapping nods and greetings with people who were working for the other side, albeit on another matter.

In the spirit of Eisenhower, I had in my pocket two versions of what I might say on the court steps: one for victory, one for defeat. I was very nervous but tried desperately not to show it.

Then, right on midday, came the familiar double knock on the judge's door and, with that, Justice Kaye entered and strode to the bench. Whether it was the funeral he had just attended or the fact that judgement was at hand, his face was set in stone. I was momentarily terrified we were going to lose. But, after telling the court he would publish his reasons for the judgement, he delivered the key finding matter-of-factly: 'I find that the defendant breached the plaintiff's contract of employment by terminating his appointment as editor-in-chief of the *Herald Sun* newspaper on 10 November 2008.'

With that, a wave of relief flowed over me; Tony Macken, who was sitting immediately in front, turned around and mouthed the word 'congratulations'. I was so elated and so relieved that it hardly mattered that Justice Kaye immediately went on to reject our lost opportunity claim; in any event, I was buoyed again by his acknowledgement that I had suffered 'loss and damage' as a result of the breach. How much loss and damage? The judge had done his sums and come up with a figure of $580 808. With interest it would come to more than $665 000, in line with my pre-judgement, if not my pre-trial, expectations. It was two-and-a-half times what News had offered on 10 November 2008 and more than $200 000 up on what they had put on the table at mediation and restated just six weeks earlier.

Within seconds of the judge delivering his headline findings, Norman O'Bryan was on his feet arguing for costs and interest to be awarded against News. Houghton appeared to accept this immediately. There would need to be negotiations but it was a great outcome for us. But the best was yet to come. As various journalists pressed me for a comment, O'Bryan, McDougall and the Macken team pored over the judgement with us. Within seconds it was clear that News' witnesses had taken a terrible battering. On the question of credit, the judge had come down on our side very strongly.

'Mr Guthrie was by and large an impressive witness,' wrote Justice Kaye, praising my memory and direct answers. 'I did not detect any attempt by him to evade difficult questions in cross-examination or to prevaricate.' While he chided me for the flawed circulation graphic and what he perceived as a tendency to under-estimate the seriousness of my run-ins with Blunden, he partly excused both too: Blunden's high dudgeon in court over the circu-lation story wasn't matched by his actions at the time and I didn't properly perceive the significance of some of my rows with the managing director because he was constantly sending mixed mes-sages. Ultimately, Justice Kaye concluded, I was a 'credible witness'.

Blunden was shredded. The judge spent 16 pages of a 92-page judgement recounting, assessing and, in many places, denouncing his evidence. Taken together, Justice Kaye's criticisms were damn-ing, beginning with: 'There are a number of matters in relation to the evidence of Mr Blunden, which emerged in cross-examination, and which significantly affected my assessment of the credibility and reliability of Mr Blunden as a witness.'

He condemned Blunden's tendency to portray his own con-duct in a favourable light and to downplay the significant role he had played in my demise. He accused him of exaggerating flaws he perceived I had as editor and the central incidents in his evidence, beginning with the role he played in my initial selection, right up to my dismissal and the communications between us immediately after. He pointed to inconsistencies within answers to questions about the row over the Melbourne Storm tour of England and the meeting with Neil Mitchell.

Importantly, he expressed reservations about Blunden's evi-dence regarding the wretched *National Geographic* DVDs. 'In my view this aspect of the case has some significance,' said the judge, not least because Hartigan considered it 'the last straw' in deciding to remove me as editor. Yet, as the judge noted, Blunden struggled to articulate where I had fallen short in my handling of it. Most significantly of all, the judge preferred my version of what had happened at the 9 October management meeting. Taken together, I felt this meant that if Hartigan really did sack me over the DVDs, he had done so on a false premise. I was delighted Justice Kaye had identified the shortcomings in Blunden's evidence on this but, at the same time, I was distressed that this could have happened at such a high executive level in one of Australia's biggest companies.

Perhaps most significant of all, Justice Kaye preferred my evidence on the post-dismissal conversation phone call from Blunden. 'Even without the aid of the [11 November] email, I would have accepted Mr Guthrie's version of that conversation,' he said, before adding this damning assessment of my former managing director:

> [He] was concerned to disclaim any role in the dismissal of Guthrie, and rather, to hint that there were other people involved in the decision, and not him ... that version is supported by Blunden's complete lack of candour with Guthrie, both before and after the dismissal, about Blunden's central role in obtaining the dismissal of Guthrie as editor of the *Herald Sun*.

Importantly, he pulled back on making any finding as to whether there was any significant breakdown in the relationship between Blunden and me. While he accepted Blunden believed there had been, he was satisfied I didn't, in part because Blunden kept sending me emails 'which gave the impression of a relatively cordial relationship between the two men'.

Finally, the judge backed me on the Calvert-Jones conversations after our 'Beverly Hills Cop' front page. Or, at least, he accepted that Blunden had said Calvert-Jones was unhappy about the coverage; there was no evidence that she actually did. It was a double blow against Blunden. 'On balance, based on my general assessment of the credibility and reliability of the two witnesses, I prefer the account of Guthrie,' said Justice Kaye. 'However, I do not consider that the episode was relevant to the issues in the case.'

So did Blunden make up the Calvert-Jones conversations? Certainly my SC believed he did. Only Blunden and Calvert-Jones know. If O'Bryan's instincts were right, that left a very simple scenario: Hartigan had eventually caved in to Blunden's incessant demands to sack me, with or without Rupert Murdoch's input.

While Hartigan didn't suffer the same damage as Blunden, he certainly took a battering. Justice Kaye rejected his evidence on the contract negotiations, preferred my version of the Pure South lunch, called his evidence on football's 150th anniversary 'plainly wrong', said he showed an 'evident lack of care' in his evidence on my treatment of the AFL 2008 finals, preferred my evidence on the number and nature of contacts between us and, perhaps most damning of all, accused Hartigan of putting together his reasons for dismissing me 'after the fact'.

As I slowly digested these attacks on Blunden and Hartigan by the judge, two thoughts jumped into my head: Blunden would have been better advised spending the evening of Sunday, 2 May, with his lawyers mapping out a settlement than at the Logies; and whoever advised the CEO of News Limited that it would be a good idea to appear in court had sent him on a professional suicide mission.

Julian Clarke got a couple of whacks too, first for his inclination to look for matters 'with which he might criticize' me and, secondly, for 'an element of exaggeration and unconscious embellishment by him about his perception of Mr Guthrie'.

After hugging Janne and fielding with great laughter a question from my daughter—'What just happened, Dad? Did we win?'—we headed for the court steps where the media pack waited in great numbers.

As a passer-by nudged Susannah, pointed at me and asked, 'What did he do?' I began my prepared speech. While I was pleased with the outcome, the matter should never have gone to court; that said, I was glad I was able to set the record straight about my time as editor. News was a good company in many ways, with some great people, but they got this one horribly wrong; they had played the man, not the ball. And finally: 'They forgot the first rule of journalism. They didn't get the other side of the story . . . someone should have got my side of the story.'

And with that we headed off to chambers, followed, for the first hundred metres or so, by assorted cameramen, photographers and sound recordists. As Janne, Susannah and I grinned for the cameras, I told the pack, 'I'm really going to miss you guys.' It was my first untruth of the entire proceedings, and I got caught out on it, with one cameraman responding: 'No, you won't.'

32

Paper cuts

O ne of the most profound ironies of Justice Kaye's judgement was its timing. On the day he delivered it, the Australian Bureau of Audited Circulations published new sales figures and the newspaper industry was forced to acknowledge further falls, interpreted widely as more evidence of an industry in decline.

The *Australian Financial Review* reported that only one of the 25 capital-city and national weekday, Saturday and Sunday newspapers gained sales during the three months that ended 31 March 2010 and that was *The Sunday Age*, the paper I had helped to launch 20 years earlier and where I had spent six of the happiest years of my career, three as editor. The other 24 major papers posted sales falls.

The *Herald Sun* wasn't immune from any of this, acknowledging way back in the paper that the daily had slipped 1.74 per cent over the previous 12 months to 509 000 copies. (It's unknown whether the managing director complained about the editor deliberately burying the bad news.) This suggested the Tuesday paper was almost certainly selling under 500 000 on most days—excluding, of course, those with a prominent Collingwood or Princess Mary story—and the Thursday paper wouldn't be far behind.

Readership of the paper was performing even worse, with the daily shedding almost 100 000 year-on-year from 1 411 000 to 1 314 000. If part of the rationale for changing editors was to improve the paper's fortunes, it had had the opposite effect.

No doubt the management team of the *Herald Sun* would be working overtime to ensure its figures stayed above the all-important 500 000 mark. They would be reviewing partnership arrangements, chasing new ones, plotting even bigger give-aways—cold, hard cash might be next—pumping as many papers as they could into major events and driving their newspapers through school and university programs, cut-rate ways of boosting sales by tens of thousands of copies. Take them all out and the *Herald Sun* would be selling anywhere from 50 000 to 100 000 fewer copies a day.

These high-cost components are designed to stave off the inevitable decline of print circulations and readership and the consequent negative impact these falls have on advertising sales. They might as well try to hold back the tide.

During almost four decades in newspapers, I never ceased to be astounded by printing technology. Quite apart from the romance of picking up an edition fresh and, yes, hot off the press, I would be amazed that these massive machines actually ever got the job done. To me they seemed like enormous, whirring meccano sets that could come crashing to a halt at any time. It was as if small advances in technology had been added again and again to the point that the presses seemed to function in spite of themselves.

Somewhere along the way, these extraordinarily complicated devices became, to me at least, metaphors for the industry that relied on them at the end of each publishing day. Over 40 years, newspapers had piled on so many disparate elements to keep circulations buoyant that it was now hard to tell what was actually driving them. Was it journalism or was it marketing?

If you believed the evidence of some of News' most senior executives, I had lost my job because I had failed as the 'chief marketer' of the paper. As for the journalism, I had faced my biggest internal fights when seeking to publish stories that encroached upon important corporate relationships. A generation ago my reporting on the junketing of the Victorian governor, Sir Brian Murray, had helped to get *him* sacked; now, if my suspicions were right, our reporting on the junketing of the Victorian police commissioner, Christine Nixon, had helped to get *me* sacked. (And my determination as editor of *The Age* to hold to account the Victorian premier, Jeff Kennett, hadn't done wonders for my career either.)

If I needed any further evidence of how toothless some newspaper journalism had become, I needed only to look at *The Australian's* reporting of Justice Kaye's judgement. The national broadsheet failed to mention the judge's damning findings against Hartigan and Blunden. If, say, executives at the same level in BHP Billiton or Fairfax had been similarly denounced by a Supreme Court judge, their credit and honesty called into serious question, it would have almost certainly led *The Australian's* business section and, quite possibly, the paper itself. But it didn't rate a mention in Rupert's flagship. The eight-paragraph story the paper carried on page seven did manage to squeeze in the company's denunciation of the judgement and their completely false claim that the damages were in line with their settlement offer a year before. It wasn't journalism: it was corporate spin. The *Herald Sun's* story on page 12 was similarly slanted against me.

The company's reporting of the judgement—selectively, even barely honest and lacking transparency—was in keeping with its management style or, at least, my experience of it. Interestingly, two months after it was handed down, the former chairman of the Melbourne Storm rugby league club, Rob Moodie, sacked by News Limited along with his fellow independent directors after they mounted a court challenge alleging lack of due process—there's that word again—in the club's treatment, likened News and its tactics to those of big tobacco. Added Moodie: 'I have been shocked by their approach to ethics.' He should have called me; I could have warned him about what lay ahead.

I had been an editor/manager for roughly half my print career and had long ago learned that the single most important thing a new appointee must obtain from his employer is 'the mandate'; the second is an absolute guarantee of open and honest communication throughout the appointment. I had obtained a mandate for change at the *Herald Sun*—to make it more intelligent and more 'aspirational'—but, trouble was, those that gave it to me never upheld it or passed it along. As for open and honest communication at News, I struggled to get that in a courtroom, much less the corridors of the company.

I'm not sure when my career as a newspaper editor ended. Was it 10 November 2008, the day I was summarily dismissed, or was it 14 May 2010, the day a judge found I shouldn't have been? It was probably somewhere in between.

For some time I was bitter about that but then I realised I had had the best of the industry's very best years. I had entered it when new titles were being launched and I left, albeit with a boot up the bum, as mastheads were disappearing around the globe. It was hard to be bitter about having worked at such a high level in the industry for so long.

What went wrong with newspapers? We had been boiled in a beaker, of course, just like that frog at the Melbourne Yacht Squadron all those years ago. We had been so profitable for so long that none of us, least of all people like Rupert Murdoch, could ever seriously entertain it ending. We simply didn't want it to. Not only that, because direct competition was so limited in this country, there was very little pressure to innovate. When we did, finally, it was too late. Instead of taking some of the massive profits the industry generated throughout the 1980s and 1990s and 'changing the paradigm', we allowed others to get 'first-mover advantage'. Then there was all the time wasted on internecine turf wars, boardroom spats, takeovers.

If the effect of all this is to break down the corporate behemoths that sprang up when newspapers suddenly became massively profitable, then perhaps that's no bad thing. If we worry less about artificially propping up circulations that are largely a marketing and promotional construct anyway—that was the irony of Blunden's hysterical beat-up over a 'flawed' sales graphic—then perhaps we can return to what the famed former editor of *The Washington Post*, Ben Bradlee, used to call 'holy shit' journalism.

I, for one, do not believe that journalism is about to collapse simply because the delivery system changes from dead trees to digital. The internet didn't kill newspapers; it was the lazy, undisciplined and uncertain way papers responded to the threat that did it.

In the days immediately after my dismissal, when my heart was at its heaviest, I took a call from veteran Canberra reporter and commentator Laurie Oakes. Even though I didn't know Oakes all that well, he had been a journalist hero of mine since the 1970s, when as a young Canberra reporter for *The Sun News-Pictorial* he had broken the federal Budget and dozens of other scoops. I had been particularly proud of helping to attract him to the *Herald Sun* as a columnist after the demise of *The Bulletin*.

'What on earth happened to you, Bruce?' asked Oakes on the Saturday after my sacking. 'I thought the paper was flying.'

He wasn't to know it but his assessment lifted my spirits. I struggled for an answer though; I still would today. But I managed this: 'Laurie, I got the job right, but the politics wrong.'

I realised as I said it that it was probably true of so many jobs, of so many chapters in my life. Certainly my two most important editorships—*The Age* and the *Herald Sun*—ended much too soon and for the wrong reasons. Whenever I reflect on that now I'm reminded of Jordan Baker's observation to Nick Carraway in *The Great Gatsby* after the fateful—and fatal—crash. 'I met another bad driver, didn't I?' Baker says to Carraway. 'I mean it was careless of

339

me to make such a wrong guess.' Ultimately, we all live with the danger of running into a bad driver now and then.

On that Saturday after my dismissal, Oakes acknowledged the truth of my observation about the role politics can play in a career, before observing: 'Better to get the job right and the politics wrong, rather than the other way round. I've known a lot of people who get it back to front.' And, though he left it unsaid, survive in the process.

He was right. Better to do the job well, and leave the politics to others. As credos go, it wasn't a bad one.

In the hours immediately after winning the court case, a small group of family and friends celebrated our victory at a Queen Street trattoria. Was it all worth it, someone asked.

Of course it was, if only for this: now, instead of reflecting on John Hartigan's words all those years ago—'We've decided to make a change'—I can reflect on those of Stephen Kaye—'I find that the defendant breached the plaintiff's contract.'

In the great tradition of news and what defines it, the man had bitten the dog.

Index